BOOKS BY ALBERT CAMUS

NOTEBOOKS 1942–1951   1965
 (*Carnets, janvier 1942–mars 1951*)

NOTEBOOKS 1935–1942   1963
 (*Carnets, mai 1935–février 1942*)

RESISTANCE, REBELLION, AND DEATH   1961

THE POSSESSED   (*Les Possédés*)   1960

CALIGULA AND THREE OTHER PLAYS   (*Caligula, Le
 Malentendu, L'État de siège, Les Justes*)   1958

EXILE AND THE KINGDOM   (*L'Exil et le Royaume*)
 1958

THE FALL   (*La Chute*)   1957

THE MYTH OF SISYPHUS   (*Le Mythe de Sisyphe*)
 AND OTHER ESSAYS   1955

THE REBEL   (*L'Homme révolté*)   1954

THE PLAGUE   (*La Peste*)   1948

THE STRANGER   (*L'Étranger*)   1946

These are BORZOI BOOKS
published in New York by ALFRED A. KNOPF

CALIGULA & THREE OTHER PLAYS

CALIGULA

THE MISUNDERSTANDING *(Le Malentendu)*

STATE OF SIEGE *(L'État de siège)*

THE JUST ASSASSINS *(Les Justes)*

*With a preface written specially for this edition,
and translated by* JUSTIN O'BRIEN

CALIGULA

& THREE

OTHER

PLAYS

ALBERT CAMUS

Translated from the French by

STUART GILBERT

New York 1970

ALFRED A. KNOPF

L. C. Catalog card number: 58-11227
© *Alfred A. Knopf, Inc., 1958*

This is a BORZOI BOOK, *published by* ALFRED A. KNOPF, INC.
Copyright 1958 by Alfred A. Knopf, Inc.

PUBLISHED SEPTEMBER 15, 1958
REPRINTED TWICE
FIFTH PRINTING, APRIL, 1970

The four plays included in this volume were originally published in France as follows: LE MALENTENDU SUIVI DE CALIGULA, *copyright by Librairie Gallimard 1944;* L'ÉTAT DE SIÈGE, *copyright by Librairie Gallimard 1948;* LES JUSTES, *copyright by Librairie Gallimard 1950.*

CALIGULA *and* THE MISUNDERSTANDING *were originally published in English in 1948 in Great Britain by Hamish Hamilton, Ltd. and in the United States by New Directions under the title of* CALIGULA AND CROSS-PURPOSE.

AUTHOR'S PREFACE (*December 1957*)

T HE PLAYS making up this collection were written between 1938 and 1950. The first, *Caligula*, was composed in 1938 after a reading of Suetonius' *Twelve Cæsars*. I intended the play for the little theater I had organized in Algiers, and my artless intention was to play the part of Caligula myself. Inexperienced actors often show such guilelessness. Besides, I was only twenty-five, the age when one doubts everything except oneself. The war forced me to modesty, and *Caligula* was first played in 1945 at the Théâtre-Hébertot in Paris.

Hence *Caligula* is an actor's and director's play. But of course it takes its inspiration from the concerns that were mine at that moment. French criticism, although it greeted the play very cordially, often astonished me by speaking of it as a philosophical play. Is there any truth in this?

Caligula, a relatively attractive prince up to then, becomes aware, on the death of Drusilla, his sister and mistress, that this world is not satisfactory. Thenceforth, obsessed with the impossible and poisoned with scorn and horror, he tries, through murder and the systematic perversion of all values, to practice a liberty that he will eventually discover not to be the right one. He challenges friendship and love, common human solidarity, good and evil. He takes those about him at their word and forces them to be logical; he levels everything around him by the strength of his rejection and the destructive fury to which his passion for life leads him.

But, if his truth is to rebel against fate, his error lies in negating what binds him to mankind. One cannot destroy everything without destroying oneself. This is why Caligula depopulates the world around him and, faithful to his logic, does what is necessary to arm against him those who will eventually kill him. *Caligula* is the story of a superior suicide. It is the story of the most human and most tragic of errors. Unfaithful to mankind through fidelity to himself, Caligula accepts death because he has understood that no one can save himself all alone and that one cannot be free at the expense of others.

Consequently it is a tragedy of the intelligence. Whence the natural conclusion that the drama was intellectual. Personally, I think I am well aware of this work's shortcomings. But I look in vain for philosophy in these four acts. Or, if it exists, it stands on the level of this assertion by the hero: "Men die; and they are not happy." A very modest ideology, as you see, which I have the impression of sharing with Everyman. No, my ambition lay elsewhere. For the dramatist the passion for the impossible is just as valid a subject for study as avarice or adultery. Showing it in all its frenzy, illustrating the havoc it wreaks, bringing out its failure—such was my intention. And the work must be judged thereon.

One word more. Some found my play provocative who nevertheless consider it natural for Œdipus to kill his father and marry his mother and who accept the adulterous triangle if it is placed, to be sure, in the best society. Yet I have little regard for an art that deliberately aims to shock because it is unable to convince. And if I happened, by ill luck, to be scandalous, this would result solely from that immoderate devo-

tion to truth which an artist cannot renounce without
giving up his art itself.

THE MISUNDERSTANDING was written in 1943 in
occupied France. I was then living, quite reluctantly,
in the mountains of central France. That historical
and geographical situation would be enough to explain
the sort of claustrophobia from which I suffered then
and which is reflected in that play. It is true that its
atmosphere is suffocating. But we were all short of
breath at that time. Nonetheless, the play's gloominess
bothers me as much as it bothered the public. To encourage the reader to approach the play, I shall suggest: (1) granting that the play's morality is not altogether negative, and (2) looking upon *The Misunderstanding* as an attempt to create a modern tragedy.

A son who expects to be recognized without having
to declare his name and who is killed by his mother
and his sister as the result of the misunderstanding—
this is the subject of the play. Doubtless, it is a very
dismal image of human fate. But it can be reconciled
with a relative optimism as to man. For, after all, it
amounts to saying that everything would have been
different if the son had said: "It is I; here is my name."
It amounts to saying that in an unjust or indifferent
world man can save himself, and save others, by practicing the most basic sincerity and pronouncing the
most appropriate word.

The language shocked too. I knew this. But if I had
dressed my characters in peplums, everyone might
have applauded. Putting the language of tragedy into
the mouths of contemporary characters was, however,
my intention. Nothing, indeed, is more difficult, since
a language must be found that is natural enough to be
spoken by contemporaries and yet sufficiently unusual to suggest the tragic tone. In an effort to approach that ideal I tried to give aloofness to the char-

acters and ambiguity to the dialogues. Thus a member of the audience was to feel simultaneously at home and out of his element. A member of the audience, and the reader. But I am not sure of having achieved the proper dosage.

As for the character of the old manservant, he does not necessarily symbolize fate. When the widow calls upon God at the end, he is the one who replies. But this is perhaps one more misunderstanding. If he answers "No" when she asks him to help her, this is because, in fact, he has no intention of helping her and because at a certain level of suffering or injustice no one can do anything for anyone. Pain is solitary.

Furthermore, I don't really feel that such explanations are very useful. I still am of the opinion that *The Misunderstanding* is a work of easy access if only one accepts the language and is willing to grant that the author has deeply committed himself in it. The theater is not a game—that is my conviction.

WHEN *State of Siege* first opened in Paris, there was no dissenting voice among the critics. Truly, few plays have ever enjoyed such a unanimous slashing. This is the more deplorable since I have never given up thinking that *State of Siege*, with all its shortcomings, is, of all my writings, the one that most resembles me. Still, the reader is quite free to decide that, however faithful it may be, he doesn't like that image. But in order to give greater force and freedom to that judgment, I must first challenge certain presumptions. For instance, it is better to know that:

(1) *State of Siege* is in no sense an adaptation of my novel *The Plague*. To be sure, I gave that symbolic name to one of my characters. But since he is a dictator, that appellation is correct.

(2) *State of Siege* is not a play of classical conception. It might better be compared with what were

called *"moralités"* in the French Middle Ages and in
Spain *"autos sacramentales"*—a sort of allegorical
drama which staged subjects known to the whole audience in advance. I focused my play on what seems to
me the only living religion in the century of tyrants
and slaves—I mean liberty. Hence it is utterly useless
to accuse my characters of being symbolical. I plead
guilty. My avowed aim was to divest the stage of
psychological speculations in muffled voices so that it
might ring with the loud shouts that today enslave or
liberate masses of men. From this point of view alone,
I am still convinced that my attempt deserves attention. By the way, this play about liberty is as badly
looked upon by dictatorships of the Right as by dictatorships of the Left. Played constantly for years in
Germany, it has never been produced either in Spain
or behind the Iron Curtain.* Much might still be said
about the hidden or obvious intentions of this play.
But I wish merely to enlighten my readers' judgment,
not to influence it.

THE JUST ASSASSINS had more luck. It was well
received. Sometimes, however, praise, like blame, arises
from a misunderstanding. Hence I should like to make
clear that:

(1) The events recounted in *The Just Assassins* are
historical, even the surprising interview between the
Grand Duchess and her husband's murderer. One must
therefore judge merely the extent to which I managed
to give plausibility to what was true.

(2) The form of the play must not mislead the
reader. I tried to achieve dramatic tension through
classical means—that is, the opposition of characters
who were equal in strength and reason. But it would
be wrong to conclude that everything balances out and

* It has been played in Yugoslavia. At present a Polish
theater is planning to put it on.

that, in regard to the problem raised here, I recommend doing nothing. My admiration for my heroes, Kaliayev and Dora, is complete. I merely wanted to show that action itself had limits. There is no good and just action but what recognizes those limits and, if it must go beyond them, at least accepts death. Our world of today seems loathsome to us for the very reason that it is made by men who grant themselves the right to go beyond those limits, and first of all to kill others without dying themselves. Thus it is that today justice serves as an alibi, throughout the world, for the assassins of all justice.

ONE WORD MORE to tell the reader what he will not find in this book. Although I have the most passionate attachment for the theater, I have the misfortune of liking only one kind of play, whether comic or tragic. After a rather long experience as director, actor, and dramatist, it seems to me that there is no true theater without language and style, nor any dramatic work which does not, like our classical drama and the Greek tragedians, involve human fate in all its simplicity and grandeur. Without claiming to equal them, these are at least the models to set oneself. Psychology, ingenious plot-devices, and spicy situations, though they may amuse me as a member of the audience, leave me indifferent as an author. I am willing to admit that such a conception is debatable. But it seems to me only fair to present myself, in this regard, as I am. Forewarned, the reader may, if he wishes, abstain from reading further. As for those who are not discouraged by such a bias, I am more likely to awaken in them that strange friendship which, over and above frontiers, joins reader and writer and, when it is devoid of misunderstanding, is the writer's royal reward.

(*Translated by* JUSTIN O'BRIEN)

CONTENTS

CONTENTS

CALIGULA

A PLAY IN FOUR ACTS

To my friends of the THÉÂTRE DE L'ÉQUIPE

CHARACTERS IN THE PLAY

CALIGULA

CÆSONIA

HELICON

SCIPIO

CHEREA

THE OLD PATRICIAN

METELLUS

LEPIDUS

INTENDANT

MEREIA

MUCIUS

MUCIUS' WIFE

PATRICIANS, KNIGHTS,

POETS, GUARDS, SERVANTS

CALIGULA *was presented for the first time at the* THÉÂTRE-HÉBERTOT, *Paris, in 1945.*

ACT I

A number of patricians, one a very old man, are gathered in a state room of the imperial palace. They are showing signs of nervousness.

FIRST PATRICIAN: Still no news.

THE OLD PATRICIAN: None last night, none this morning.

SECOND PATRICIAN: Three days without news. Strange indeed!

THE OLD PATRICIAN: Our messengers go out, our messengers return. And always they shake their heads and say: "Nothing."

SECOND PATRICIAN: They've combed the whole countryside. What more can be done?

FIRST PATRICIAN: We can only wait. It's no use meeting trouble halfway. Perhaps he'll return as abruptly as he left us.

THE OLD PATRICIAN: When I saw him leaving the palace, I noticed a queer look in his eyes.

FIRST PATRICIAN: Yes, so did I. In fact I asked him what was amiss.

SECOND PATRICIAN: Did he answer?

FIRST PATRICIAN: One word: "Nothing."

[*A short silence.* HELICON *enters. He is munching onions.*]

SECOND PATRICIAN [*in the same nervous tone*]: It's all very perturbing.

FIRST PATRICIAN: Oh, come now! All young fellows are like that.

THE OLD PATRICIAN: You're right there. They take things hard. But time smooths everything out.

SECOND PATRICIAN: Do you really think so?

THE OLD PATRICIAN: Of course. For one girl dead, a dozen living ones.

HELICON: Ah? So you think that there's a girl behind it?

FIRST PATRICIAN: What else should there be? Anyhow—thank goodness!—grief never lasts forever. Is any one of us here capable of mourning a loss for more than a year on end?

SECOND PATRICIAN: Not I, anyhow.

FIRST PATRICIAN: No one can do that.

THE OLD PATRICIAN: Life would be intolerable if one could.

FIRST PATRICIAN: Quite so. Take my case. I lost my wife last year. I shed many tears, and then I forgot. Even now I feel a pang of grief at times. But, happily, it doesn't amount to much.

THE OLD PATRICIAN: Yes, Nature's a great healer.

[CHEREA *enters.*]

FIRST PATRICIAN: Well . . . ?

CHEREA: Still nothing.

HELICON: Come, gentlemen! There's no need for consternation.

FIRST PATRICIAN: I agree.

HELICON: Worrying won't mend matters—and it's lunchtime.

THE OLD PATRICIAN: That's so. We mustn't drop the prey for the shadow.

CHEREA: I don't like the look of things. But all was going too smoothly. As an emperor, he was perfection's self.

SECOND PATRICIAN: Yes, exactly the emperor we wanted; conscientious and inexperienced.

FIRST PATRICIAN: But what's come over you? There's no reason for all these lamentations. We've no ground for assuming he will change. Let's say he loved Drusilla. Only natural; she was his sister. Or say his love for her was something more than brotherly; shocking enough, I grant you. But it's really going too far, setting all Rome in a turmoil because the girl has died.

CHEREA: Maybe. But, as I said, I don't like the look of things; this escapade alarms me.

THE OLD PATRICIAN: Yes, there's never smoke without fire.

FIRST PATRICIAN: In any case, the interests of the State should prevent his making a public tragedy of . . . of, let's say, a regrettable attachment. No doubt such things happen; but the less said the better.

HELICON: How can you be sure Drusilla is the cause of all this trouble?

SECOND PATRICIAN: Who else should it be?

HELICON: Nobody at all, quite likely. When there's a host of explanations to choose from, why pick on the stupidest, most obvious one?

[*Young* SCIPIO *enters.* CHEREA *goes toward him.*]

CHEREA: Well?

SCIPIO: Still nothing. Except that some peasants think they saw him last night not far from Rome, rushing through the storm.

[CHEREA *comes back to the patricians,* SCIPIO *following him.*]

CHEREA: That makes three days, Scipio, doesn't it?

SCIPIO: Yes . . . I was there, following him as I usually do. He went up to Drusilla's body. He stroked it with two fingers, and seemed lost in thought for a long while. Then he swung round and walked out, calmly enough. . . . And ever since we've been hunting for him—in vain.

CHEREA [*shaking his head*]: That young man was too fond of literature.

SECOND PATRICIAN: Oh, at his age, you know . . .

CHEREA: At his age, perhaps; but not in his position. An artistic emperor is an anomaly. I grant you we've had one or two; misfits happen in the best of empires. But the others had the good taste to remember they were public servants.

FIRST PATRICIAN: It made things run more smoothly.

THE OLD PATRICIAN: One man, one job—that's how it should be.

SCIPIO: What can we do, Cherea?

CHEREA: Nothing.

SECOND PATRICIAN: We can only wait. If he doesn't return, a successor will have to be found. Between ourselves—there's no shortage of candidates.

FIRST PATRICIAN: No, but there's a shortage of the right sort.

CHEREA: Suppose he comes back in an ugly mood?

FIRST PATRICIAN: Oh, he's a mere boy; we'll make him see reason.

CHEREA: And what if he declines to see it?

FIRST PATRICIAN [*laughing*]: In that case, my friend, don't forget I once wrote a manual of revolutions. You'll find all the rules there.

CHEREA: I'll look it up—if things come to that. But I'd rather be left to my books.

SCIPIO: If you'll excuse me. . . .

[*Goes out.*]

CHEREA: He's offended.

THE OLD PATRICIAN: Scipio is young, and young people always hang together.

HELICON: Scipio doesn't count, anyhow.

[*Enter a member of the imperial bodyguard.*]

THE GUARDSMAN: Caligula has been seen in the palace gardens.

[*All leave the room. The stage is empty for some moments. Then* CALIGULA *enters stealthily from the left. His legs are caked with mud, his garments dirty; his hair is wet, his look distraught. He brings his hand to his mouth several times. Then he approaches a mirror, stopping abruptly when he catches sight of his reflected self. After muttering some unintelligible words, he sits down on the right, letting his arms hang limp between his knees.* HELICON *enters, left. On seeing* CALIGULA, *he stops at the far end of the stage and contemplates him in silence.* CALIGULA *turns and sees him. A short silence.*]

HELICON [*across the stage*]: Good morning, Caius.

CALIGULA [*in quite an ordinary tone*]: Good morning, Helicon.

[*A short silence.*]

HELICON: You're looking tired.

CALIGULA: I've walked a lot.

HELICON: Yes, you've been away for quite a while. [*Another short silence.*]

CALIGULA: It was hard to find.

HELICON: What was hard to find?

CALIGULA: What I was after.

HELICON: Meaning?

CALIGULA [*in the same matter-of-fact tone*]: The moon.

HELICON: What?

CALIGULA: Yes, I wanted the moon.

HELICON: Ah. . . . [*Another silence.* HELICON *approaches* CALIGULA.] And why did you want it?

CALIGULA: Well . . . it's one of the things I haven't got.

HELICON: I see. And now—have you fixed it up to your satisfaction?

CALIGULA: No. I couldn't get it.

HELICON: Too bad!

CALIGULA: Yes, and that's why I'm tired. [*Pauses. Then*] Helicon!

HELICON: Yes, Caius?

CALIGULA: No doubt, you think I'm crazy.

HELICON: As you know well, I never think.

CALIGULA: Ah, yes. . . . Now, listen! I'm not mad; in fact I've never felt so lucid. What happened to me is quite simple; I suddenly felt a desire for the impossible. That's all. [*Pauses.*] Things as they are, in my opinion, are far from satisfactory.

HELICON: Many people share your opinion.

CALIGULA: That is so. But in the past I didn't realize it. *Now* I know. [*Still in the same matter-of-fact tone*] Really, this world of ours, the scheme of things as they call it, is quite intolerable. That's why I want the moon, or happiness, or eternal life—something, in fact, that may sound crazy, but which isn't of this world.

HELICON: That's sound enough in theory. Only, in practice one can't carry it through to its conclusion.

CALIGULA [*rising to his feet, but still with perfect calmness*]: You're wrong there. It's just because no one *dares* to follow up his ideas to the end that nothing is achieved. All that's needed, I should say, is to be logical right through, at all costs. [*He studies* HELICON's *face.*] I can see, too, what you're thinking. What a fuss over a woman's death! But that's not it. True enough, I seem to remember that a woman died some days ago; a woman whom I loved. But love, what is it? A side issue. And I swear to you her death is not the point; it's no more than the symbol of a truth that makes the moon essential to me. A childishly simple, obvious, almost silly truth, but one that's hard to come by and heavy to endure.

HELICON: May I know what it is, this truth that you've discovered?

CALIGULA [*his eyes averted, in a toneless voice*]: Men die; and they are not happy.

HELICON [*after a short pause*]: Anyhow, Caligula,

it's a truth with which one comes to terms, without much trouble. Only look at the people over there. This truth of yours doesn't prevent them from enjoying their meal.

CALIGULA [*wth sudden violence*]:   All it proves is that I'm surrounded by lies and self-deception. But I've had enough of that; I wish men to live by the light of truth. And I've the power to make them do so. For I know what they need and haven't got. They're without understanding and they need a teacher; someone who knows what he's talking about.

HELICON: Don't take offense, Caius, if I give you a word of advice. . . . But that can wait. First, you should have some rest.

CALIGULA [*sitting down. His voice is gentle again*]: That's not possible, Helicon. I shall never rest again.

HELICON: But—why?

CALIGULA: If I sleep, who'll give me the moon?

HELICON [*after a short silence*]:   That's true.

CALIGULA [*rising to his feet again, with an effort*]: Listen, Helicon . . . I hear footsteps, voices. Say nothing—and forget you've seen me.

HELICON: I understand.

CALIGULA [*looking back, as he moves toward the door*]:   And please help me, from now on.

HELICON: I've no reason not to do so, Caius. But I know very few things, and few things interest me. In what way can I help you?

CALIGULA: In the way of . . . the impossible.

HELICON: I'll do my best.

[CALIGULA *goes out.* SCIPIO *and* CÆSONIA *enter hurriedly.*]

SCIPIO: No one! Haven't you seen him?

HELICON: No.

CÆSONIA: Tell me, Helicon. Are you quite sure he didn't say anything to you before he went away?

HELICON: I'm not a sharer of his secrets, I'm his public. A mere onlooker. It's more prudent.

CÆSONIA: Please don't talk like that.

HELICON: My dear Cæsonia, Caius is an idealist as we all know. He follows his bent, and no one can foresee where it will take him. . . . But, if you'll excuse me, I'll go to lunch.

[*Exit* HELICON.]

CÆSONIA [*sinking wearily onto a divan*]: One of the palace guards saw him go by. But all Rome sees Caligula everywhere. And Caligula, of course, sees nothing but his own idea.

SCIPIO: What idea?

CÆSONIA: How can I tell, Scipio?

SCIPIO: Are you thinking of Drusilla?

CÆSONIA: Perhaps. One thing is sure; he loved her. And it's a cruel thing to have someone die today whom only yesterday you were holding in your arms.

SCIPIO [*timidly*]: And you . . . ?

CÆSONIA: Oh, I'm the old, trusted mistress. That's my role.

SCIPIO: Cæsonia, we must save him.

CÆSONIA: So you, too, love him?

SCIPIO: Yes. He's been very good to me. He encouraged me; I shall never forget some of the things he said. He told me life isn't easy, but it has consolations: religion, art, and the love one inspires in others. He often told me that the only mistake one makes in life is to cause others suffering. He tried to be a just man.

CÆSONIA [*rising*]: He's only a child. [*She goes to the glass and scans herself.*] The only god I've ever had is my body, and now I shall pray this god of mine to give Caius back to me.

[CALIGULA *enters. On seeing* CÆSONIA *and* SCIPIO *he*

hesitates, and takes a backward step. At the same moment several men enter from the opposite side of the room: patricians and the INTENDANT *of the palace. They stop short when they see* CALIGULA. CÆSONIA *turns. She and* SCIPIO *hurry toward* CALIGULA, *who checks them with a gesture.*]

INTENDANT [*in a rather quavering voice*]: We . . . we've been looking for you, Cæsar, high and low.

CALIGULA [*in a changed, harsh tone*]: So I see.

INTENDANT: We . . . I mean . . .

CALIGULA [*roughly*]: What do you want?

INTENDANT: We were feeling anxious, Cæsar.

CALIGULA [*going toward him*]: What business had you to feel anxious?

INTENDANT: Well . . . er . . . [*He has an inspiration.*] Well, as you know, there are points to be settled in connection with the Treasury.

CALIGULA [*bursting into laughter*]: Ah, yes. The Treasury! That's so. The Treasury's of prime importance.

INTENDANT: Yes, indeed.

CALIGULA [*still laughing, to* CÆSONIA]: Don't you agree, my dear? The Treasury is all-important.

CÆSONIA: No, Caligula. It's a secondary matter.

CALIGULA: That only shows your ignorance. We are extremely interested in our Treasury. Everything's important: our fiscal system, public morals, foreign policy, army equipment, and agrarian laws. Everything's of cardinal importance, I assure you. And everything's on an equal footing: the grandeur of Rome and your attacks of arthritis. . . . Well, well, I'm going to apply my mind to all that. And, to begin with . . . Now listen well, Intendant.

INTENDANT: We are listening, sir.

[*The patricians come forward.*]

CALIGULA: You're our loyal subjects, are you not?

INTENDANT [*in a reproachful tone*]: Oh, Cæsar . . . !

CALIGULA: Well, I've something to propose to you. We're going to make a complete change in our economic system. In two moves. Drastic and abrupt. I'll explain, Intendant . . . when the patricians have left. [*The patricians go out.* CALIGULA *seats himself beside* CÆSONIA, *with his arm around her waist.*] Now mark my words. The first move's this. Every patrician, everyone in the Empire who has any capital—small or large, it's all the same thing—is ordered to disinherit his children and make a new will leaving his money to the State.

INTENDANT: But Cæsar . . .

CALIGULA: I've not yet given you leave to speak. As the need arises, we shall have these people die; a list will be drawn up by us fixing the order of their deaths. When the fancy takes us, we may modify that order. And, of course, we shall step into their money.

CÆSONIA [*freeing herself*]: But—what's come over you?

CALIGULA [*imperturbably*]: Obviously the order of their going has no importance. Or, rather, all these executions have an equal importance—from which it follows that none has any. Really all those fellows are on a par, one's as guilty as another. [*To the* INTENDANT, *peremptorily*] You are to promulgate this edict without a moment's delay and see it's carried out forthwith. The wills are to be signed by residents in Rome this evening; within a month at the latest by persons in the provinces. Send out your messengers.

INTENDANT: Cæsar, I wonder if you realize . . .

CALIGULA: Do I realize . . . ? Now, listen well, you fool! If the Treasury has paramount importance, human life has none. That should be obvious to you. People who think like you are bound to admit the logic of my edict, and since money is the only thing that counts, should set no value on their lives or anyone else's. I have resolved to be logical, and I have the power to enforce my will. Presently you'll see what logic's going to cost you? I shall eliminate contradictions and contradicters. If necessary, I'll begin with you.

INTENDANT: Cæsar, my good will can be relied on, that I swear.

CALIGULA: And mine, too; that I guarantee. Just see how ready I am to adopt your point of view, and give the Treasury the first place in my program. Really you should be grateful to me; I'm playing into your hand, and with your own cards. [*He pauses, before continuing in a flat, unemotional tone*] In any case there is a touch of genius in the simplicity of my plan—which clinches the matter. I give you three seconds in which to remove yourself. One . . .

[*The* INTENDANT *hurries out.*]

CÆSONIA: I can't believe it's you! But it was just a joke, wasn't it?—all you said to him.

CALIGULA: Not quite that, Cæsonia. Let's say, a lesson in statesmanship.

SCIPIO: But, Caius, it's . . . it's impossible!

CALIGULA: That's the whole point.

SCIPIO: I don't follow.

CALIGULA: I repeat—that is my point. I'm exploiting the impossible. Or, more accurately, it's a question of making the impossible possible.

SCIPIO: But that game may lead to—to anything! It's a lunatic's pastime.

CALIGULA: No, Scipio. An emperor's vocation. [*He lets himself sink back wearily among the cushions.*] Ah, my dears, at last I've come to see the uses of supremacy. It gives impossibilities a run. From this day on, so long as life is mine, my freedom has no frontier.

CÆSONIA [*sadly*]: I doubt if this discovery of yours will make us any happier.

CALIGULA: So do I. But, I suppose, we'll have to live it through.

[CHEREA *enters.*]

CHEREA: I have just heard of your return. I trust your health is all it should be.

CALIGULA: My health is duly grateful. [*A pause. Then, abruptly*] Leave us, Cherea. I don't want to see you.

CHEREA: Really, Caius, I'm amazed . . .

CALIGULA: There's nothing to be amazed at. I don't like literary men, and I can't bear lies.

CHEREA: If we lie, it's often without knowing it. I plead Not Guilty.

CALIGULA: Lies are never guiltless. And yours attribute importance to people and to things. That's what I cannot forgive you.

CHEREA: And yet—since this world is the only one we have, why not plead its cause?

CALIGULA: Your pleading comes too late, the verdict's given. . . . This world has no importance; once a man realizes that, he wins his freedom. [*He has risen to his feet.*] And that is why I hate you, you and your kind; because you are not free. You see in me the one free man in the whole Roman Empire. You should be glad to have at last among you an emperor who points the way to freedom. Leave me, Cherea; and you, too, Scipio, go—for what is friendship? Go, both of you, and spread the news in Rome that freedom has been given her at last, and with the gift begins a great probation.

[*They go out.* CALIGULA *has turned away, hiding his eyes.*]

CÆSONIA: Crying?

CALIGULA: Yes, Cæsonia.

CÆSONIA: But, after all, what's changed in your life?
You may have loved Drusilla, but you loved many
others—myself included—at the same time. Surely
that wasn't enough to set you roaming the countryside for three days and nights and bring you back
with this . . . this cruel look on your face?

CALIGULA [*swinging round on her*]: What nonsense is this? Why drag in Drusilla? Do you imagine
love's the only thing that can make a man shed
tears?

CÆSONIA: I'm sorry, Caius. Only I was trying to
understand.

CALIGULA: Men weep because . . . the world's all
wrong. [*She comes toward him.*] No, Cæsonia.
[*She draws back.*] But stay beside me.

CÆSONIA: I'll do whatever you wish. [*Sits down.*]
At my age one knows that life's a sad business. But
why deliberately set out to make it worse?

CALIGULA: No, it's no good; you can't understand.
But what matter? Perhaps I'll find a way out. Only,
I feel a curious stirring within me, as if undreamed
of things were forcing their way up into the light—
and I'm helpless against them. [*He moves closer to
her.*] Oh, Cæsonia, I knew that men felt anguish,
but I didn't know what that word anguish meant.
Like everyone else I fancied it was a sickness of
the mind—no more. But no, it's my body that's in
pain. Pain everywhere, in my chest, in my legs and
arms. Even my skin is raw, my head is buzzing, I
feel like vomiting. But worst of all is this queer
taste in my mouth. Not blood, or death, or fever,
but a mixture of all three. I've only to stir my
tongue, and the world goes black, and everyone
looks . . . horrible. How hard, how cruel it is, this
process of becoming a man!

CÆSONIA: What you need, my dear, is a good, long sleep. Let yourself relax and, above all stop thinking. I'll stay by you while you sleep. And when you wake, you'll find the world's got back its savor. Then you must use your power to good effect—for loving better what you still find lovable. For the possible, too, deserves to be given a chance.

CALIGULA: Ah but for that I'd need to sleep, to let myself go—and that's impossible.

CÆSONIA: So one always thinks when one is over-tired. A time comes when one's hand is firm again.

CALIGULA: But one must know where to place it. And what's the use to me of a firm hand, what use is the amazing power that's mine, if I can't have the sun set in the east, if I can't reduce the sum of suffering and make an end of death? No, Cæsonia, it's all one whether I sleep or keep awake, if I've no power to tamper with the scheme of things.

CÆSONIA: But that's madness, sheer madness. It's wanting to be a god on earth.

CALIGULA: So you, too, think I'm mad. And yet— what is a god that I should wish to be his equal? No, it's something higher, far above the gods, that I'm aiming at, longing for with all my heart and soul. I am taking over a kingdom where the impossible is king.

CÆSONIA: You can't prevent the sky from being the sky, or a fresh young face from aging, or a man's heart from growing cold.

CALIGULA [*with rising excitement*]: I want . . . I want to drown the sky in the sea, to infuse ugliness with beauty, to wring a laugh from pain.

CÆSONIA [*facing him with an imploring gesture*]: There's good and bad, high and low, justice and injustice. And I swear to you these will never change.

CALIGULA [*in the same tone*]: And I'm resolved

to change them . . . I shall make this age of ours a
kingly gift—the gift of equality. And when all is
leveled out, when the impossible has come to earth
and the moon is in my hands—then, perhaps, I shall
be transfigured and the world renewed; then men
will die no more and at last be happy.

CÆSONIA [*with a little cry*]:   And love? Surely you
won't go back on love!

CALIGULA [*in a wild burst of anger*]:   Love, Cæsonia!
[*He grips her shoulders and shakes her.*] I've
learned the truth about love; it's nothing, nothing!
That fellow was quite right—you heard what he
said, didn't you?—it's only the Treasury that counts.
The fountainhead of all. Ah, now at last I'm going
to live, really *live*. And living, my dear, is the opposite of loving. I know what I'm talking about—and I
invite you to the most gorgeous of shows, a sight
for gods to gloat on, a whole world called to judgment. But for that I must have a crowd—spectators,
victims, criminals, hundreds and thousands of them.
[*He rushes to the gong and begins hammering on it,
faster and faster.*] Let the accused come forward.
I want my criminals, and they all are criminals.
[*Still striking the gong.*] Bring in the condemned
men. I must have my public. Judges, witnesses, accused—all sentenced to death without a hearing.
Yes, Cæsonia, I'll show them something they have
never seen before, the one free man in the Roman
Empire. [*To the clangor of the gong the palace has
been gradually filling with noises; the clash of arms,
voices, footsteps slow or hurried, coming nearer,
growing louder. Some soldiers enter, and leave
hastily.*] And you, Cæsonia, shall obey me. You
must stand by me to the end. It will be marvelous,
you'll see. Swear to stand by me, Cæsonia.

CÆSONIA [*wildly, between two gong strokes*]:   I
needn't swear. You know I love you.

CALIGULA [*in the same tone*]: You'll do all I tell you.

CÆSONIA: All, all, Caligula—but do, please, stop. . . .

CALIGULA [*still striking the gong*]: You will be cruel.

CÆSONIA [*sobbing*]: Cruel.

CALIGULA [*still beating the gong*]: Cold and ruthless.

CÆSONIA: Ruthless.

CALIGULA: And you will suffer, too.

CÆSONIA: Yes, yes—oh, no, please . . . I'm—I'm going mad, I think! [*Some patricians enter, followed by members of the palace staff. All look bewildered and perturbed.* CALIGULA *bangs the gong for the last time, raises his mallet, swings round and summons them in a shrill, half-crazy voice.*]

CALIGULA: Come here. All of you. Nearer. Nearer still. [*He is quivering with impatience.*] Your Emperor commands you to come nearer. [*They come forward, pale with terror.*] Quickly. And you, Cæsonia, come beside me. [*He takes her hand, leads her to the mirror, and with a wild sweep of his mallet effaces a reflection on its surface. Then gives a sudden laugh.*] All gone. You see, my dear? An end of memories; no more masks. Nothing, nobody left. Nobody? No, that's not true. Look, Cæsonia. Come here, all of you, and *look* . . .

[*He plants himself in front of the mirror in a grotesque attitude.*]

CÆSONIA [*staring, horrified, at the mirror*]: Caligula! [CALIGULA *lays a finger on the glass. His gaze steadies abruptly and when he speaks his voice has a new, proud ardor.*]

CALIGULA: Yes . . . Caligula.

CURTAIN

ACT II

Three years later.
A room in Cherea's house, where the patricians have met in secret.

FIRST PATRICIAN: It's outrageous, the way he's treating us.

THE OLD PATRICIAN: He calls me "darling"! In public, mind you—just to make a laughingstock of me. Death's too good for him.

FIRST PATRICIAN: And fancy making us run beside his litter when he goes into the country.

SECOND PATRICIAN: He says the exercise will do us good.

THE OLD PATRICIAN: Conduct like that is quite inexcusable.

THIRD PATRICIAN: You're right. That's precisely the sort of thing one can't forgive.

FIRST PATRICIAN: He confiscated your property, Patricius. He killed your father, Scipio. He's taken your wife from you, Octavius, and forced her to work in his public brothel. He has killed your son, Lepidus. I ask you, gentlemen, can you endure this? I, anyhow, have made up my mind. I know the risks, but I also know this life of abject fear is quite unbearable. Worse than death, in fact. Yes, as I said, my mind's made up.

SCIPIO: He made my mind up for me when he had my father put to death.

FIRST PATRICIAN: Well? Can you still hesitate?

A KNIGHT: No. We're with you. He's transferred our

stalls at the Circus to the public, and egged us on to fight with the rabble—just to have a pretext for punishing us, of course.

THE OLD PATRICIAN: He's a coward.

SECOND PATRICIAN: A bully.

THIRD PATRICIAN: A buffoon.

THE OLD PATRICIAN: He's impotent—that's his trouble, I should say.

[*A scene of wild confusion follows, weapons are brandished, a table is overturned, and there is a general rush toward the door. Just at this moment* CHEREA *strolls in, composed as usual, and checks their onrush.*]

CHEREA: What's all this about? Where are you going?

A PATRICIAN: To the palace.

CHEREA: Ah, yes. And I can guess why. But do you think you'll be allowed to enter?

THE PATRICIAN: There's no question of asking leave.

CHEREA: Lepidus, would you kindly shut that door? [*The door is shut.* CHEREA *goes to the overturned table and seats himself on a corner of it. The others turn toward him.*] It's not so simple as you think, my friends. You're afraid, but fear can't take the place of courage and deliberation. In short, you're acting too hastily.

A KNIGHT: If you're not with us, go. But keep your mouth shut.

CHEREA: I suspect I'm with you. But make no mistake. Not for the same reasons.

A VOICE: That's enough idle talk.

CHEREA [*standing up*]: I agree. Let's get down to facts. But, first, let me make myself clear. Though I am *with* you, I'm not *for* you. That, indeed, is why I think you're going about it the wrong way. You haven't taken your enemy's measure; that's obvious, since you attribute petty motives to him. But there's nothing petty about Caligula, and you're

riding for a fall. You'd be better placed to fight him
if you would try to see him as he really is.

A VOICE: We see him as he is—a crazy tyrant.

CHEREA: No. We've had experience of mad emperors.
But this one isn't mad enough. And what I loathe in
him is this: that he knows what he wants.

FIRST PATRICIAN: And we, too, know it; he wants to
murder us all.

CHEREA: You're wrong. Our deaths are only a side
issue. He's putting his power at the service of a
loftier, deadlier passion; and it imperils everything
we hold most sacred. True, it's not the first time
Rome has seen a man wielding unlimited power;
but it's the first time he sets no limit to his use of it,
and counts mankind, and the world we know, for
nothing. That's what appalls me in Caligula; that's
what I want to fight. To lose one's life is no great
matter; when the time comes I'll have the courage
to lose mine. But what's intolerable is to see one's
life being drained of meaning, to be told there's no
reason for existing. A man can't live without some
reason for living.

FIRST PATRICIAN: Revenge is a good reason.

CHEREA: Yes, and I propose to share it with you. But
I'd have you know that it's not on your account, or
to help you to avenge your petty humiliations. No,
if I join forces with you, it's to combat a big idea—
an ideal, if you like—whose triumph would mean
the end of everything. I can endure your being
made a mock of, but I cannot endure Caligula's
carrying out his theories to the end. He is convert-
ing his philosophy into corpses and—unfortunately
for us—it's a philosophy that's logical from start to
finish. And where one can't refute, one strikes.

A VOICE: Yes. We must *act*.

CHEREA: We must take action, I agree. But a frontal
attack's quite useless when one is fighting an im-

perial madman in the full flush of his power. You
can take arms against a vulgar tyrant, but cunning is
needed to fight down disinterested malice. You can
only urge it on to follow its bent, and bide your
time until its logic founders in sheer lunacy. As you
see, I prefer to be quite frank, and I warn you I'll
be with you only for a time. Afterward, I shall do
nothing to advance your interests; all I wish is to
regain some peace of mind in a world that has
regained a meaning. What spurs me on is not ambition but fear, my very reasonable fear of that inhuman vision in which my life means no more than
a speck of dust.

FIRST PATRICIAN [*approaching him*]: I have an inkling of what you mean, Cherea. Anyhow, the great
thing is that you, too, feel that the whole fabric of
society is threatened. You, gentlemen, agree with
me, I take it, that our ruling motive is of a moral
order. Family life is breaking down, men are losing
their respect for honest work, a wave of immorality
is sweeping the country. Who of us can be deaf to
the appeal of our ancestral piety in its hour of
danger? Fellow conspirators, will you tolerate a
state of things in which patricians are forced to run,
like slaves, beside the Emperor's litter?

THE OLD PATRICIAN: Will you allow them to be
addressed as "darling"?

A VOICE: And have their wives snatched from them?

ANOTHER VOICE: And their money?

ALL TOGETHER: No!

FIRST PATRICIAN: Cherea, your advise is good, and
you did well to calm our passion. The time is not
yet ripe for action; the masses would still be against
us. Will you join us in watching for the best moment to strike—and strike hard?

CHEREA: Yes—and meanwhile let Caligula follow his
dream. Or, rather, let's actively encourage him to

carry out his wildest plans. Let's put method into
his madness. And then, at last, a day will come when
he's alone, a lonely man in an empire of the dead
and kinsmen of the dead.

[*A general uproar. Trumpet calls outside. Then
silence, but for whispers of a name:* "CALIGULA!"
CALIGULA *enters with* CÆSONIA, *followed by* HELICON
and some soldiers. Pantomime. CALIGULA *halts and
gazes at the conspirators. Without a word he moves
from one to the other, straightens a buckle on one
man's shoulder, steps back to contemplate another,
sweeps them with his gaze, then draws his hand
over his eyes and walks out, still without a word.*]

CÆSONIA [*ironically, pointing to the disorder of the
room*]:   Were you having a fight?

CHEREA: Yes, we were fighting.

CÆSONIA [*in the same tone*]:   Really? Might I know
what you were fighting about?

CHEREA: About . . . nothing in particular.

CÆSONIA: Ah? Then it isn't true.

CHEREA: What isn't true?

CÆSONIA: You were *not* fighting.

CHEREA: Have it your own way. We weren't fighting.

CÆSONIA [*smiling*]:   Perhaps you'd do better to tidy
up the place. Caligula hates untidiness.

HELICON [*to the* OLD PATRICIAN]:   You'll end by
making him do something out of character.

THE OLD PATRICIAN: Pardon . . . I don't follow.
What have we done to him?

HELICON: Nothing. Just nothing. It's fantastic being
futile to that point; enough to get on anybody's
nerves. Try to put yourselves in Caligula's place. [*A
short pause.*] I see; doing a bit of plotting, weren't
you now?

THE OLD PATRICIAN: Really, that's too absurd. I hope
Caligula doesn't imagine . . .

HELICON: He doesn't imagine. He *knows*. But, I suppose, at bottom, he rather wants it. . . . Well, we'd better set to tidying up.

[*All get busy.* CALIGULA *enters and watches them.*]

CALIGULA [*to the* OLD PATRICIAN]: Good day, darling. [*To the others*] Gentlemen, I'm on my way to an execution. But I thought I'd drop in at your place, Cherea, for a light meal. I've given orders to have food brought here for all of us. But send for your wives first. [*A short silence.*] Rufius should thank his stars that I've been seized with hunger. [*Confidentially*] Rufius, I may tell you, is the knight who's going to be executed. [*Another short silence.*] What's this? None of you asks me why I've sentenced him to death? [*No one speaks. Meanwhile slaves lay the table and bring food.*] Good for you! I see you're growing quite intelligent. [*He nibbles an olive.*] It has dawned on you that a man needn't have done anything for him to die. [*He stops eating and gazes at his guests with a twinkle in his eye.*] Soldiers, I am proud of you. [*Three or four women enter.*] Good! Let's take our places. Anyhow. No order of precedence today. [*All are seated.*] There's no denying it, that fellow Rufius is in luck. But I wonder if he appreciates this short reprieve. A few hours gained on death, why, they're worth their weight in gold! [*He begins eating; the others follow suit. It becomes clear that* CALIGULA's *table manners are deplorable. There is no need for him to flick his olive stones onto his neighbors' plates, or to spit out bits of gristle over the dish, or to pick his teeth with his nails, or to scratch his head furiously. However, he indulges in these practices throughout the meal, without the least compunction. At one moment he stops eating, stares at* LEPIDUS, *one of the guests, and says roughly*] You're looking grumpy, Lepidus.

I wonder, can it be because I had your son killed?

LEPIDUS [*thickly*]: Certainly not, Caius. Quite the contrary.

CALIGULA [*beaming at him*]: "Quite the contrary!" It's always nice to see a face that hides the secrets of the heart. Your face is sad. But what about your heart? Quite the contrary—isn't that so, Lepidus?

LEPIDUS [*doggedly*]: Quite the contrary, Cæsar.

CALIGULA [*more and more enjoying the situation*]: Really, Lepidus, there's no one I like better than you. Now let's have a laugh together, my dear friend. Tell me a funny story.

LEPIDUS [*who has overrated his endurance*]: Please . . .

CALIGULA: Good! Very good! Then it's I who'll tell the story. But you'll laugh, won't you, Lepidus? [*With a glint of malice.*] If only for the sake of your other son. [*Smiling again.*] In any case, as you've just told us, you're not in a bad humor. [*He takes a drink, then says in the tone of a teacher prompting a pupil*] Quite . . . quite the . . .

LEPIDUS [*wearily*]: Quite the contrary, Cæsar.

CALIGULA: Splendid! [*Drinks again.*] Now listen. [*In a gentle, faraway tone*] Once upon a time there was a poor young emperor whom nobody loved. He loved Lepidus, and to root out of his heart his love for Lepidus, he had his youngest son killed. [*In a brisker tone*] Needless to say, there's not a word of truth in it. Still it's a funny story, eh? But you're not laughing. Nobody's laughing. Now listen! [*In a burst of anger*] I insist on everybody's laughing. You, Lepidus, shall lead the chorus. Stand up, every one of you, and laugh. [*He thumps the table.*] Do you hear what I say? I wish to see you laughing, all of you. [*All rise to their feet. During this scene all the players, CALIGULA and CÆSONIA excepted, behave like marionettes in a puppet play.*

CALIGULA *sinks back on his couch, beaming with delight, and bursts into a fit of laughter.*] Oh, Cæsonia! Just look at them! The game is up; honor, respectability, the wisdom of the nations, gone with the wind! The wind of fear has blown them all away. Fear, Cæsonia—don't you agree?—is a noble emotion, pure and simple, self-sufficient, like no other; it draws its patent of nobility straight from the guts. [*He strokes his forehead and drinks again. In a friendly tone*] Well, well, let's change the subject. What have you to say, Cherea? You've been very silent.

CHEREA: I'm quite ready to speak, Caius. When you give me leave.

CALIGULA: Excellent. Then—keep silent. I'd rather have a word from our friend Mucius.

MUCIUS [*reluctantly*]: As you will, Caius.

CALIGULA: Then tell us something about your wife. And begin by sending her to this place, on my right. [MUCIUS' WIFE *seats herself beside* CALIGULA.] Well, Mucius? We're waiting.

MUCIUS [*hardly knowing what he says*]: My wife . . . but . . . I'm very fond of her.
[*General laughter.*]

CALIGULA: Why, of course, my friend, of course. But how ordinary of you! So unoriginal! [*He is leaning toward her, tickling her shoulder playfully with his tongue.*] By the way, when I came in just now, you were hatching a plot, weren't you? A nice bloody little plot?

OLD PATRICIAN: Oh, Caius, how can you . . . ?

CALIGULA: It doesn't matter in the least, my pet. Old age will be served. I won't take it seriously. Not one of you has the spunk for an heroic act. . . . Ah, it's just come to my mind, I have some affairs of state to settle. But, first, let the imperious desires that nature creates in us have their way.

[*He rises and leads* MUCIUS' WIFE *into an adjoining room.* MUCIUS *starts up from his seat.*]

CÆSONIA [*amiably*]:   Please, Mucius. Will you pour me out another glass of this excellent wine. [MUCIUS *complies; his movement of revolt is quelled. Everyone looks embarrassed. Chairs creak noisily. The ensuing conversation is in a strained tone.* CÆSONIA *turns to* CHEREA.] Now, Cherea, suppose you tell me why you people were fighting just now?

CHEREA [*coolly*]:   With pleasure, my dear Cæsonia. Our quarrel arose from a discussion whether poetry should be bloodthirsty or not.

CÆSONIA: An interesting problem. Somewhat beyond my feminine comprehension, of course. Still it surprises me that your passion for art should make you come to blows.

CHEREA [*in the same rather stilted tone*]:   That I can well understand. But I remember Caligula's telling me the other day that all true passion has a spice of cruelty.

CÆSONIA [*helping herself from the dish in front of her*]:   There's truth in that. Don't you agree, gentlemen?

THE OLD PATRICIAN: Ah, yes. Caligula has a rare insight into the secret places of the heart.

FIRST PATRICIAN: And how eloquently he spoke just now of courage!

SECOND PATRICIAN: Really, he should put his ideas into writing. They would be most instructive.

CHEREA: And, what's more, it would keep him busy. It's obvious he needs something to occupy his leisure.

CÆSONIA [*still eating*]:   You'll be pleased to hear that Caligula shares your views; he's working on a book. Quite a big one, I believe.

[CALIGULA *enters, accompanied by* MUCIUS' WIFE.]

CALIGULA: Mucius, I return your wife, with many thanks. But excuse me, I've some orders to give.

[*He hurries out.* MUCIUS *has gone pale and risen to his feet.*]

CÆSONIA [*to* MUCIUS, *who is standing*]: This book of his will certainly rank among our Latin Classics. Are you listening, Mucius?

MUCIUS [*his eyes still fixed on the door by which* CALIGULA *went out*]: Yes. And what's the book about, Cæsonia?

CÆSONIA [*indifferently*]: Oh, it's above my head, you know.

CHEREA: May we assume it deals with the murderous power of poetry?

CÆSONIA: Yes, something of that sort, I understand.

THE OLD PATRICIAN [*cheerfully*]: Well anyhow, as our friend Cherea said, it will keep him busy.

CÆSONIA: Yes, my love. But I'm afraid there's one thing you won't like quite so much about this book, and that's its title.

CHEREA: What is it?

CÆSONIA: *Cold Steel.*

[*Caligula hurries in.*]

CALIGULA: Excuse me, but I've some urgent public work in hand. [*To the* INTENDANT] Intendant, you are to close the public granaries. I have signed a decree to that effect; you will find it in my study.

INTENDANT: But, sire . . .

CALIGULA: Famine begins tomorrow.

INTENDANT: But . . . but heaven knows what may happen—perhaps a revolution.

CALIGULA [*firmly and deliberately*]: I repeat; famine begins tomorrow. We all know what famine means —a national catastrophe. Well, tomorrow there will be a catastrophe, and I shall end it when I choose. After all, I haven't so many ways of proving I am free. One is always free at someone else's expense.

Absurd perhaps, but so it is. [*With a keen glance at* MUCIUS] Apply this principle to your jealousy— and you'll understand better. [*In a meditative tone*] Still, what an ugly thing is jealousy! A disease of vanity and the imagination. One pictures one's wife. . . . [MUCIUS *clenches his fists and opens his mouth to speak. Before he can get a word out,* CALIGULA *cuts in*] Now, gentlemen, let's go on with our meal. . . . Do you know, we've been doing quite a lot of work, with Helicon's assistance? Putting the final touches to a little monograph on execution—about which you will have much to say.

HELICON: Assuming we ask your opinion.

CALIGULA: Why not be generous, Helicon, and let them into our little secrets? Come now, give them a sample. Section Three, first paragraph.

HELICON [*standing, declaims in a droning voice*]: "Execution relieves and liberates. It is universal, tonic, just in precept and in practice. A man dies because he is guilty. A man is guilty because he is one of Caligula's subjects. Now all men are Caligula's subjects. *Ergo,* all men are guilty and shall die. It is only a matter of time and patience."

CALIGULA [*laughing*]: There's logic for you, don't you agree? That bit about patience was rather neat, wasn't it? Allow me to tell you, that's the quality I most admire in you . . . your patience. Now, gentlemen, you can disperse. Cherea doesn't need your presence any longer. Cæsonia, I wish you to stay. You too, Lepidus. Also our old friend Mereia. I want to have a little talk with you about our National Brothel. It's not functioning too well; in fact, I'm quite concerned about it.

[*The others file out slowly.* CALIGULA *follows* MUCIUS *with his eyes.*]

CHEREA: At your orders, Caius. But what's the trouble? Are the staff unsatisfactory?

CALIGULA: No, but the takings are falling off.

MEREIA: Then you should raise the entrance fee.

CALIGULA: There, Mereia, you missed a golden opportunity of keeping your mouth shut. You're too old to be interested in the subject, and I don't want your opinion.

MEREIA: Then why ask me to stay?

CALIGULA: Because, presently, I may require some cool, dispassionate advice.

[MEREIA *moves away*.]

CHEREA: If you wish to hear my views on the subject, Caius, I'd say, neither coolly nor dispassionately, that it would be a blunder to raise the scale of charges.

CALIGULA: Obviously. What's needed is a bigger turnover. I've explained my plan of campaign to Cæsonia, and she will tell you all about it. As for me, I've had too much wine, I'm feeling sleepy.

[*He lies down and closes his eyes.*]

CÆSONIA: It's very simple. Caligula is creating a new order of merit.

CHEREA: Sorry, I don't see the connection.

CÆSONIA: No? But there is one. It will be called the Badge of Civic Merit and awarded to those who have patronized Caligula's National Brothel most assiduously.

CHEREA: A brilliant idea!

CÆSONIA: I agree. Oh, I forgot to mention that the badge will be conferred each month, after checking the admission tickets. Any citizen who has not obtained the badge within twelve months will be exiled, or executed.

CHEREA: Why "or executed"?

CÆSONIA: Because Caligula says it doesn't matter which—but it's important he should have the right of choosing.

CHEREA: Bravo! The Public Treasury will wipe out
its deficit in no time.

[CALIGULA *has half opened his eyes and is watching
old* MEREIA *who, standing in a corner, has produced
a small flask and is sipping its contents.*]

CALIGULA [*still lying on the couch*]: What's that
you're drinking, Mereia?

MEREIA: It's for my asthma, Caius.

CALIGULA [*rises, and thrusting the others aside, goes up
to* MEREIA *and sniffs his mouth*]: No, it's an
antidote.

MEREIA: What an idea, Caius! You must be joking.
I have choking fits at night and I've been in the
doctor's hands for months.

CALIGULA: So you're afraid of being poisoned?

MEREIA: My asthma . . .

CALIGULA: No. Why beat about the bush? You're
afraid I'll poison you. You suspect me. You're keeping an eye on me.

MEREIA: Good heavens, no!

CALIGULA: You suspect me. I'm not to be trusted,
eh?

MEREIA: Caius!

CALIGULA [*roughly*]: Answer! [*In a cool, judicial
tone*] If you take an antidote, it follows that you
credit me with the intention of poisoning you.
Q.E.D.

MEREIA: Yes . . . I mean . . . no!

CALIGULA: And thinking I intend to poison you, you
take steps to frustrate my plan. [*He falls silent.
Meanwhile* CÆSONIA *and* CHEREA *have moved away,
backstage.* LEPIDUS *is watching the speakers with an
air of consternation.*] That makes two crimes,
Mereia, and a dilemma from which you can't escape.
Either I have no wish to cause your death; in
which case you are unjustly suspecting me, your

emperor. *Or else* I desire your death; in which case, vermin that you are, you're trying to thwart my will. [*Another silence.* CALIGULA *contemplates the old man gloatingly.*] Well, Mereia, what have you to say to my logic?

MEREIA: It . . . it's sound enough, Caius. Only it doesn't apply to the case.

CALIGULA: A third crime. You take me for a fool. Now sit down and listen carefully. [*To* LEPIDUS] Let everyone sit down. [*To* MEREIA] Of these three crimes only one does you honor; the second one—because by crediting me with a certain wish and presuming to oppose it you are deliberately defying me. You are a rebel, a leader of revolt. And that needs courage. [*Sadly*] I've a great liking for you Mereia. And that is why you'll be condemned for crime number two, and not for either of the others. You shall die nobly, a rebel's death. [*While he talks* MEREIA *is shrinking together on his chair.*] Don't thank me. It's quite natural. Here. [*Holds out a phial. His tone is amiable.*] Drink this poison. [MEREIA *shakes his head. He is sobbing violently.* CALIGULA *shows signs of impatience.*] Don't waste time. Take it. [MEREIA *makes a feeble attempt to escape. But* CALIGULA *with a wild leap is on him, catches him in the center of the stage and after a brief struggle pins him down on a low couch. He forces the phial between his lips and smashes it with a blow of his fist. After some convulsive movements* MEREIA *dies. His face is streaming with blood and tears.* CALIGULA *rises, wipes his hands absentmindedly, then hands* MEREIA'S *flask to* CÆSONIA.] What was it? An antidote?

CÆSONIA [*calmly*]: No, Caligula. A remedy for asthma.

[*A short silence.*]

CALIGULA [*gazing down at* MEREIA]: No matter. It

all comes to the same thing in the end. A little
sooner, a little later. . . .

[*He goes out hurriedly, still wiping his hands.*]

LEPIDUS [*in a horrified tone*]:   What . . . what shall
we do?

CÆSONIA [*coolly*]:   Remove that body to begin with,
I should say. It's rather a beastly sight.

[CHEREA *and* LEPIDUS *drag the body into the wings.*]

LEPIDUS [*to* CHEREA]:   We must act quickly.

CHEREA: We'll need to be two hundred.

[*Young* SCIPIO *enters. Seeing* CÆSONIA, *he makes as
if to leave.*]

CÆSONIA: Come.

SCIPIO: What do you want?

CÆSONIA: Come nearer. [*She pushes up his chin and
looks him in the eyes. A short silence. Then, in a
calm, unemotional voice*] He killed your father,
didn't he?

SCIPIO: Yes.

CÆSONIA: Do you hate him?

SCIPIO: Yes.

CÆSONIA: And you'd like to kill him?

SCIPIO: Yes.

CÆSONIA [*withdrawing her hand*]:   But—why tell me
this?

SCIPIO: Because I fear nobody. Killing him or being
killed—either way out will do. And anyhow you
won't betray me.

CÆSONIA: That's so. I won't betray you. But I want
to tell you something—or, rather, I'd like to speak to
what is best in you.

SCIPIO: What's best in me is—my hatred.

CÆSONIA: Please listen carefully to what I'm going
to say. It may sound hard to grasp, but it's as clear
as daylight, really. And it's something that would
bring about the one real revolution in this world of
ours, if people would only take it in.

SCIPIO: Yes? What is it?

CÆSONIA: Wait! Try to call up a picture of your father's death, of the agony on his face as they were tearing out his tongue. Think of the blood streaming from his mouth, and recall his screams, like a tortured animal's.

SCIPIO: Yes.

CÆSONIA: And now think of Caligula.

SCIPIO [*his voice rough with hatred*]: Yes.

CÆSONIA: Now listen. *Try to understand him.*

[*She goes out, leaving* SCIPIO *gaping after her in bewilderment.* HELICON *enters.*]

HELICON: Caligula will be here in a moment. Suppose you go for your meal, young poet?

SCIPIO: Helicon, help me.

HELICON: Too dangerous, my lamb. And poetry means nothing to me.

SCIPIO: You can help me. You know . . . so many things.

HELICON: I know that the days go by—and growing boys should have their meals on time . . . I know, too, that you could kill Caligula . . . and he wouldn't greatly mind it.

[HELICON *goes out.* CALIGULA *enters.*]

CALIGULA: Ah, it's you, Scipio. [*He pauses. One has the impression that he is somewhat embarrassed.*] It's quite a long time since I saw you last. [*Slowly approaches* SCIPIO.] What have you been up to? Writing more poems, I suppose. Might I see your latest composition?

SCIPIO [*likewise ill at ease, torn between hatred and some less defined emotion*]: Yes, Cæsar, I've written some more poems.

CALIGULA: On what subject?

SCIPIO: Oh, on nothing in particular. Well, on Nature in a way.

CALIGULA: A fine theme. And a vast one. And what
has Nature done for you?

SCIPIO [*pulling himself together, in a somewhat truc-
ulent tone*]:   It consoles me for not being Cæsar.

CALIGULA: Really? And do you think Nature could
console me for being Cæsar?

SCIPIO [*in the same tone*]:   Why not? Nature has
healed worse wounds than that.

CALIGULA [*in a curiously young, unaffected voice*]:
Wounds, you said? There was anger in your voice.
Because I put your father to death? . . . That word
you used—if you only knew how apt it is! My
wounds! [*In a different tone*] Well, well, there's
nothing like hatred for developing the intelligence.

SCIPIO [*stiffly*]:   I answered your question about
Nature.

[CALIGULA *sits down, gazes at* SCIPIO, *then brusquely
grips his wrists and forces him to stand up. He
takes the young man's face between his hands.*]

CALIGULA: Recite your poem to me, please.

SCIPIO: No, please, don't ask me that.

CALIGULA: Why not?

SCIPIO: I haven't got it on me.

CALIGULA: Can't you remember it?

SCIPIO: No.

CALIGULA: Anyhow you can tell me what it's about.

SCIPIO [*still hostile; reluctantly*]:   I spoke of a . . .
a certain harmony . . .

CALIGULA [*breaking in; in a pensive voice*]:   . . . between one's feet and the earth.

SCIPIO [*looking surprised*]:   Yes, it's almost that . . .
and it tells of the wavy outline of the Roman hills
and the sudden thrill of peace that twilight brings
to them . . .

CALIGULA: And the cries of swifts winding through
the green dusk.

SCIPIO [*yielding more and more to his emotion*]: Yes, yes! And that fantastic moment when the sky all flushed with red and gold swings round and shows its other side, spangled with stars.

CALIGULA: And the faint smell of smoke and trees and streams that mingles with the rising mist.

SCIPIO [*in a sort of ecstasy*]: Yes, and the chirr of crickets, the coolness veining the warm air, the rumble of carts and the farmers' shouts, dogs barking . . .

CALIGULA: And the roads drowned in shadow winding through the olive groves . . .

SCIPIO: Yes, yes. That's it, exactly. . . . But how did you know?

CALIGULA [*drawing* SCIPIO *to his breast*]: I wonder! Perhaps because the same eternal truths appeal to us both.

SCIPIO [*quivering with excitement, burying his head on* CALIGULA's *breast*]: Anyhow, what does it matter! All I know is that everything I feel or think of turns to love.

CALIGULA [*stroking his hair*]: That, Scipio, is a privilege of noble hearts—and how I wish I could share your . . . your limpidity! But my appetite for life's too keen; Nature can never sate it. You belong to quite another world, and you can't understand. You are single-minded for good; and I am single-minded—for evil.

SCIPIO: I *do* understand.

CALIGULA: No. There's something deep down in me—an abyss of silence, a pool of stagnant water, rotting weeds. [*With an abrupt change of manner*] Your poem sounds very good indeed, but, if you really want my opinion. . . .

SCIPIO [*his head on* CALIGULA's *breast, murmurs*]: Yes?

CALIGULA: All that's a bit . . . anemic.

SCIPIO [*recoiling abruptly, as if stung by a serpent, and gazing, horrified, at* CALIGULA, *he cries hoarsely*]: Oh, you brute! You loathsome brute! You've fooled me again. I know! You were playing a trick on me, weren't you? And now you're gloating over your success.

CALIGULA [*with a hint of sadness*]: There's truth in what you say. I *was* playing a part.

SCIPIO [*in the same indignant tone*]: What a foul, black heart you have! And how all that wickedness and hatred must make you suffer!

CALIGULA [*gently*]: That's enough.

SCIPIO: How I loathe you! And how I pity you!

CALIGULA [*angrily*]: Enough, I tell you.

SCIPIO: And how horrible a loneliness like yours must be!

CALIGULA [*in a rush of anger, gripping the boy by the collar, and shaking him*]: Loneliness! What do *you* know of it? Only the loneliness of poets and weaklings. You prate of loneliness, but you don't realize that one is *never* alone. Always we are attended by the same load of the future and the past. Those we have killed are always with us. But *they* are no great trouble. It's those we have loved, those who loved us and whom we did not love; regrets, desires, bitterness and sweetness, whores and gods, the celestial gang! Always, always with us! [*He releases* SCIPIO *and moves back to his former place*.] Alone! Ah, if only in this loneliness, this ghoul-haunted wilderness of mine, I could know, but for a moment, real solitude, real silence, the throbbing stillness of a tree! [*Sitting down, in an access of fatigue*.] Solitude? No, Scipio, mine is full of gnashings of teeth, hideous with jarring sounds and voices. And when I am with the women I make mine and darkness falls on us and I think, now my body's had its fill, that I can feel myself my own at last, poised between death and life—ah, then my solitude is fouled by the stale smell of pleasure from the woman sprawling at my side.

[*A long silence.* CALIGULA *seems weary and despondent.* SCIPIO *moves behind him and approaches hesitantly. He slowly stretches out a hand toward him, from behind, and lays it on his shoulder. Without looking round,* CALIGULA *places his hand on* SCIPIO'S.]

SCIPIO: All men have a secret solace. It helps them to endure, and they turn to it when life has wearied them beyond enduring.

CALIGULA: Yes, Scipio.

SCIPIO: Have you nothing of the kind in your life, no refuge, no mood that makes the tears well up, no consolation?

CALIGULA: Yes, I have something of the kind.

SCIPIO: What is it?

CALIGULA [*very quietly*]: Scorn.

CURTAIN

ACT III

A room in the imperial palace.
*Before the curtain rises a rhythmic clash of cymbals
and the thudding of a drum have been coming from
the stage, and when it goes up we see a curtained-off
booth, with a small proscenium in front, such as
strolling players use at country fairs. On the little
stage are* CÆSONIA *and* HELICON, *flanked by cymbal
players. Seated on benches, with their backs to the
audience, are some patricians and young* SCIPIO.

HELICON [*in the tone of a showman at a fair*]: Walk
up! Walk up! [*A clash of cymbals.*] Once more
the gods have come to earth. They have assumed
the human form of our heaven-born emperor,
known to men as Caligula. Draw near, mortals of
common clay; a holy miracle is taking place before
your eyes. By a divine dispensation peculiar to
Caligula's hallowed reign, the secrets of the gods
will be revealed to you. [*Cymbals.*]

CÆSONIA: Come, gentlemen. Come and adore him—
and don't forget to give your alms. Today heaven
and its mysteries are on show, at a price to suit
every pocket.

HELICON: For all to see, the secrets of Olympus,
revelations in high places, featuring gods in undress,
their little plots and pranks. Step this way! The
whole truth about your gods! [*Cymbals.*]

CÆSONIA: Adore him, and give your alms. Come
near, gentlemen. The show's beginning.
[*Cymbals. Slaves are placing various objects on the
platform.*]

HELICON: An epoch-making reproduction of the life celestial, warranted authentic in every detail. For the first time the pomp and splendor of the gods are presented to the Roman public. You will relish our novel, breathtaking effects: flashes of lightning [*slaves light Greek fires*], peals of thunder [*they roll a barrel filled with stones*], the divine event on its triumphal way. Now watch with all your eyes. [*He draws aside the curtain. Grotesquely attired as Venus,* CALIGULA *beams down on them from a pedestal.*]

CALIGULA [*amiably*]: I'm Venus today.

CÆSONIA: Now for the adoration. Bow down. [*All but* SCIPIO *bend their heads.*] And repeat after me the litany of Venus called Caligula.

"Our Lady of pangs and pleasures . . ."

THE PATRICIANS: "Our Lady of pangs and pleasures . . ."

CÆSONIA: "Born of the waves, bitter and bright with seafoam . . ."

THE PATRICIANS: "Born of the waves, bitter and bright with seafoam . . ."

CÆSONIA: "O Queen whose gifts are laughter and regrets . . ."

THE PATRICIANS: "O Queen whose gifts are laughter and regrets . . ."

CÆSONIA: "Rancors and raptures . . ."

THE PATRICIANS: "Rancors and raptures . . ."

CÆSONIA: "Teach us the indifference that kindles love anew . . ."

THE PATRICIANS: "Teach us the indifference that kindles love anew . . ."

CÆSONIA: "Make known to us the truth about this world—which is that it has none . . ."

THE PATRICIANS: "Make known to us the truth about this world—which is that it has none . . ."

CÆSONIA: "And grant us strength to live up to this verity of verities."

THE PATRICIANS: "And grant us strength to live up to this verity of verities."

CÆSONIA: Now, pause.

THE PATRICIANS: Now, pause.

CÆSONIA [*after a short silence*]: "Bestow your gifts on us, and shed on our faces the light of your impartial cruelty, your wanton hatred; unfold above our eyes your arms laden with flowers and murders . . ."

THE PATRICIANS: ". . . your arms laden with flowers and murders."

CÆSONIA: "Welcome your wandering children home, to the bleak sanctuary of your heartless, thankless love. Give us your passions without object, your griefs devoid of reason, your raptures that lead nowhere . . ."

THE PATRICIANS: ". . . your raptures that lead nowhere . . ."

CÆSONIA [*raising her voice*]: "O Queen, so empty yet so ardent, inhuman yet so earthly, make us drunk with the wine of your equivalence, and surfeit us forever in the brackish darkness of your heart."

THE PATRICIANS: "Make us drunk with the wine of your equivalence, and surfeit us forever in the brackish darkness of your heart." [*When the patricians have said the last response,* CALIGULA, *who until now has been quite motionless, snorts and rises.*]

CALIGULA [*in a stentorian voice*]: Granted, my children. Your prayer is heard. [*He squats cross-legged on the pedestal. One by one the patricians make obeisance, deposit their alms, and line up on the right. The last, in his flurry, forgets to make an offering.* CALIGULA *bounds to his feet.*] Steady! Steady on! Come here, my lad. Worship's very well, but almsgiving is better. Thank you. We are appeased. Ah, if the gods had no wealth other than the love you mortals give them, they'd be as poor as poor Caligula. Now, gentlemen, you may go, and spread abroad the glad tidings of the miracle you've been allowed to witness. You have seen Venus, seen her godhead with your fleshly eyes, and Venus herself has spoken to you. Go, most favored gentlemen. [*The patricians begin to move away.*] Just a moment. When you leave, mind you take the exit on your left. I have posted sentries in the others, with orders to kill you.

[*The patricians file out hastily, in some disorder. The slaves and musicians leave the stage.*]

HELICON [*pointing a threatening finger at* SCIPIO]: Naughty boy, you've been playing the anarchist again.

SCIPIO [*to* CALIGULA]: You spoke blasphemy, Caius.

CALIGULA: Blasphemy? What's that?

SCIPIO: You're befouling heaven, after bloodying the earth.

HELICON: How this youngster loves big words!

[*He stretches himself on a couch.*]

CÆSONIA [*composedly*]: You should watch your tongue, my lad. At this moment men are dying in Rome for saying much less.

SCIPIO: Maybe—but I've resolved to tell Caligula the truth.

CÆSONIA: Listen to him, Caligula! That was the one thing missing in your Empire—a bold young moralist.

CALIGULA [*giving* SCIPIO *a curious glance*]: Do you really believe in the gods, Scipio?

SCIPIO: No.

CALIGULA: Then I fail to follow. If you don't believe, why be so keen to scent out blasphemy?

SCIPIO: One may deny something without feeling

called on to besmirch it, or deprive others of the
right of believing in it.

CALIGULA: But that's humility, the real thing, unless
I'm much mistaken. Ah, my dear Scipio, how glad
I am on your behalf—and a trifle envious, too.
Humility's the one emotion I may never feel.

SCIPIO: It's not I you're envious of; it's the gods.

CALIGULA: If you don't mind, that will remain our
secret—the great enigma of our reign. Really, you
know, there's only one thing for which I might be
blamed today—and that's this small advance I've
made upon the path of freedom. For someone who
loves power the rivalry of the gods is rather irksome.
Well, I've proved to these imaginary gods that any
man, without previous training, if he applies his
mind to it, can play their absurd parts to perfection.

SCIPIO: That, Caius, is what I meant by blasphemy.

CALIGULA: No, Scipio, it's clear-sightedness. I've
merely realized that there's only one way of getting
even with the gods. All that's needed is to be as
cruel as they.

SCIPIO: All that's needed is to play the tyrant.

CALIGULA: Tell me, my young friend. What exactly
is a tyrant?

SCIPIO: A blind soul.

CALIGULA: That's a moot point. I should say the real
tyrant is a man who sacrifices a whole nation to his
ideal or his ambition. But I have no ideal, and there's
nothing left for me to covet by way of power or
glory. If I use this power of mine, it's to compensate.

SCIPIO: For what?

CALIGULA: For the hatred and stupidity of the gods.

SCIPIO: Hatred does not compensate for hatred.
Power is no solution. Personally I know only one
way of countering the hostility of the world we
live in.

CALIGULA: Yes? And what is it?

SCIPIO: Poverty.

CALIGULA [*bending over his feet and scrutinizing his toes*]: I must try that, too.

SCIPIO: Meanwhile many men round you are dying.

CALIGULA: Oh, come! Not so many as all that. Do you know how many wars I've refused to embark on?

SCIPIO: No.

CALIGULA: Three. And do you know why I refused?

SCIPIO: Because the grandeur of Rome means nothing to you.

CALIGULA: No. Because I respect human life.

SCIPIO: You're joking, Caius.

CALIGULA: Or, anyhow, I respect it more than I respect military triumphs. But it's a fact that I don't respect it more than I respect my own life. And if I find killing easy, it's because dying isn't hard for me. No, the more I think about it, the surer I feel that I'm no tyrant.

SCIPIO: What does it matter, if it costs us quite as dear as if you were one?

CALIGULA [*with a hint of petulance*]: If you had the least head for figures you'd know that the smallest war a tyrant—however levelheaded he might be—indulged in would cost you a thousand times more than all my vagaries (shall we call them?) put together.

SCIPIO: Possibly. But at least there'd be *some* sense behind a war; it would be understandable—and to understand makes up for much.

CALIGULA: There's no understanding fate; therefore I choose to play the part of fate. I wear the foolish, unintelligible face of a professional god. And that is what the men who were here with you have learned to adore.

SCIPIO: That, too, Caius, is blasphemy.

CALIGULA: No, Scipio, it's dramatic art. The great mistake you people make is not to take the drama

seriously enough. If you did, you'd know that any
man can play lead in the divine comedy and become
a god. All he needs do is to harden his heart.

SCIPIO: You may be right, Caius. But I rather think
you've done everything that was needed to rouse up
against you a legion of human gods, ruthless as yourself, who will drown in blood your godhead of a day.

CÆSONIA: Really, Scipio!

CALIGULA [*peremptorily*]: No, don't stop him, Cæsonia. Yes, Scipio, you spoke truer than you knew;
I've done everything needed to that end. I find it
hard to picture the event you speak of—but I sometimes dream it. And in all those faces surging up out
of the angry darkness, convulsed with fear and
hatred, I see, and I rejoice to see, the only god I've
worshipped on this earth; foul and craven as the
human heart. [*Irritably*] Now go. I've had enough
of you, more than enough. [*In a different tone*] I
really must attend to my toenails; they're not nearly
red enough, and I've no time to waste. [*All go, with
the exception of* HELICON. *He hovers round* CALIG-
ULA, *who is busy examining his toes.*] Helicon!

HELICON: Yes?

CALIGULA: Getting on with your task?

HELICON: What task?

CALIGULA: You know . . . the moon.

HELICON: Ah yes, the moon. . . . It's a matter of
time and patience. But I'd like to have a word with
you.

CALIGULA: I might have patience; only I have not
much time. So you must make haste.

HELICON: I said I'd do my utmost. But, first, I **have**
something to tell you. Very serious news.

CALIGULA [*as if he has not heard*]: Mind you, I've
had her already.

HELICON: Whom?

CALIGULA: The moon.

HELICON: Yes, yes. . . . Now listen, please. Do you know there's a plot being hatched against your life?

CALIGULA: What's more, I had her thoroughly. Only two or three times, to be sure. Still, I had her all right.

HELICON: For the last hour I've been trying to tell you about it, only—

CALIGULA: It was last summer. I'd been gazing at her so long, and stroking her so often on the marble pillars in the gardens that evidently she'd come to understand.

HELICON: Please stop trifling, Caius. Even if you refuse to listen, it's my duty to tell you this. And if you shut your ears, it can't be helped.

CALIGULA [*applying red polish to his toenails*]: This varnish is no good at all. But, to come back to the moon—it was a cloudless August night. [HELICON *looks sulkily away, and keeps silence.*] She was coy, to begin with. I'd gone to bed. First she was blood-red, low on the horizon. Then she began rising, quicker and quicker, growing brighter and brighter all the while. And the higher she climbed, the paler she grew, till she was like a milky pool in a dark wood rustling with stars. Slowly, shyly she approached, through the warm night air, soft, light as gossamer, naked in beauty. She crossed the threshold of my room, glided to my bed, poured herself into it, and flooded me with her smiles and sheen. . . . No, really this new varnish is a failure. . . . So you see, Helicon, I can say, without boasting, that I've had her.

HELICON: Now will you listen, and learn the danger that's threatening you?

CALIGULA [*ceasing to fiddle with his toes, and gazing at him fixedly*]: All I want, Helicon, is—the moon. For the rest, I've always known what will

kill me. I haven't yet exhausted all that is to keep
me living. That's why I want the moon. And you
must not return till you have secured her for
me.

HELICON: Very well. . . . Now I'll do my duty and
tell you what I've learned. There's a plot against you.
Cherea is the ringleader. I came across this tablet
which tells you all you need to know. See, I put it
here.

[*He places the tablet on one of the seats and moves
away.*]

CALIGULA: Where are you off to, Helicon?

HELICON [*from the threshold*]:   To get the moon for
you.

[*There is a mouselike scratching at the opposite
door.* CALIGULA *swings round and sees the* OLD PA-
TRICIAN.]

THE OLD PATRICIAN [*timidly*]:   May I, Caius . . .

CALIGULA [*impatiently*]:   Come in! Come in! [*Gazes
at him.*] So, my pet, you've returned to have another
look at Venus.

THE OLD PATRICIAN: Well . . . no. It's not quite that.
Ssh! Oh, sorry, Caius! I only wanted to say. . . .
You know I'm very, very devoted to you—and my
one desire is to end my days in peace.

CALIGULA: Be quick, man. Get it out!

THE OLD PATRICIAN: Well, it's . . . it's like this.
[*Hurriedly*] It's terribly serious, that's what I meant
to say.

CALIGULA: No, it isn't serious.

THE OLD PATRICIAN: But—I don't follow. *What* isn't
serious?

CALIGULA: But what are we talking about, my love?

THE OLD PATRICIAN [*glancing nervously round the
room*]:   I mean to say. . . . [*Wriggles, shuffles,
then bursts out with it.*] There's a plot afoot, against
you.

CALIGULA: There! You see. Just as I said; it isn't serious.

THE OLD PATRICIAN: But, Caius, they mean to kill you.

CALIGULA [*approaching him and grasping his shoulders*]: Do you know why I can't believe you?

THE OLD PATRICIAN [*raising an arm, as if to take an oath*]: The gods bear witness, Caius, that . . .

CALIGULA [*gently but firmly pressing him back toward the door*]: Don't swear. I particularly ask you not to swear. Listen, instead. Suppose it were true, what you are telling me—I'd have to assume you were betraying your friends, isn't that so?

THE OLD PATRICIAN [*flustered*]: Well, Caius, considering the deep affection I have for you . . .

CALIGULA [*in the same tone as before*]: And I cannot assume *that*. I've always loathed baseness of that sort so profoundly that I could never restrain myself from having a betrayer put to death. But I know the man you are, my worthy friend. And I'm convinced you neither wish to play the traitor nor to die.

THE OLD PATRICIAN: Certainly not, Caius. Most certainly not.

CALIGULA: So you see I was right in refusing to believe you. You wouldn't stoop to baseness, would you?

THE OLD PATRICIAN: Oh, no, indeed!

CALIGULA: Nor betray your friends?

THE OLD PATRICIAN: I need hardly tell you that, Caius.

CALIGULA: Therefore it follows that there isn't any plot. It was just a joke—between ourselves, rather a silly joke—what you've just been telling me, eh?

THE OLD PATRICIAN [*feebly*]: Yes, yes. A joke, merely a joke.

CALIGULA: Good. So now we know where we are. Nobody wants to kill me

THE OLD PATRICIAN: Nobody. That's it. Nobody at all.
CALIGULA [*drawing a deep breath; in measured tones*]:
Then—leave me, sweetheart. A man of honor is an
animal so rare in the present-day world that I
couldn't bear the sight of one too long. I must be left
alone to relish this unique experience. [*For some
moments he gazes, without moving, at the tablet. He
picks it up and reads it. Then, again, draws a deep
breath. Then summons a palace guard.*]
CALIGULA: Bring Cherea to me. [*The man starts to
leave.*] Wait! [*The man halts.*] Treat him politely.
[*The man goes out.* CALIGULA *falls to pacing the
room. After a while he approaches the mirror.*]
You decided to be logical, didn't you, poor simpleton? Logic for ever! The question now is: Where
will that take you? [*Ironically*] Suppose the moon
were brought here, everything would be different.
That was the idea, wasn't it? Then the impossible
would become possible, in a flash the Great Change
come, and all things be transfigured. After all, why
shouldn't Helicon bring it off? One night, perhaps,
he'll catch her sleeping in a lake, and carry her here,
trapped in a glistening net, all slimy with weeds and
water, like a pale bloated fish drawn from the depths.
Why not, Caligula? Why not, indeed? [*He casts a
glance round the room.*] Fewer and fewer people
round me; I wonder why. [*Addressing the mirror,
in a muffled voice*] Too many dead, too many
dead—that makes an emptiness. . . . No, even if
the moon were mine, I could not retrace my way.
Even were those dead men thrilling again under the
sun's caress, the murders wouldn't go back underground for that. [*Angrily*] Logic, Caligula; follow
where logic leads. Power to the uttermost; willful-
ness without end. Ah, I'm the only man on earth
to know the secret—that power can never be com-

plete without a total self-surrender to the dark impulse of one's destiny. No, there's no return. I must go on and on, until the consummation.

[CHEREA *enters.* CALIGULA *is slumped in his chair, the cloak drawn tightly round him.*]

CHEREA: You sent for me, Caius?

CALIGULA [*languidly*]: Yes, Cherea.

[*A short silence.*]

CHEREA: Have you anything particular to tell me?

CALIGULA: No, Cherea.

[*Another silence.*]

CHEREA [*with a hint of petulance*]: Are you sure you really need my presence?

CALIGULA: Absolutely sure, Cherea. [*Another silence. Then, as if suddenly recollecting himself*] I'm sorry for seeming so inhospitable. I was following up my thoughts, and—Now do sit down, we'll have a friendly little chat. I'm in a mood for some intelligent conversation. [CHEREA *sits down. For the first time since the play began,* CALIGULA *gives the impression of being his natural self.*] Do you think, Cherea, that it's possible for two men of much the same temperament and equal pride to talk to each other with complete frankness—if only once in their lives? Can they strip themselves naked, so to speak, and shed their prejudices, their private interests, the lies by which they live?

CHEREA: Yes, Caius, I think it possible. But I don't think you'd be capable of it.

CALIGULA: You're right. I only wished to know if you agreed with me. So let's wear our masks, and muster up our lies. And we'll talk as fencers fight, padded on all the vital parts. Tell me, Cherea, why don't you like me?

CHEREA: Because there's nothing likable about you, Caius. Because such feelings can't be had to order. And because I understand you far too well. One cannot like an aspect of oneself which one always tries to keep concealed.

CALIGULA: But why is it you hate me?

CHEREA: There, Caius, you're mistaken. I do not hate you. I regard you as noxious and cruel, vain and selfish. But I cannot hate you, because I don't think you are happy. And I cannot scorn you, because I know you are no coward.

CALIGULA: Then why wish to kill me?

CHEREA: I've told you why; because I regard you as noxious, a constant menace. I like, and need, to feel secure. So do most men. They resent living in a world where the most preposterous fancy may at any moment become a reality, and the absurd transfix their lives, like a dagger in the heart. I feel as they do; I refuse to live in a topsy-turvy world. I want to know where I stand, and to stand secure.

CALIGULA: Security and logic don't go together.

CHEREA: Quite true. My plan of life may not be logical, but at least it's sound.

CALIGULA: Go on.

CHEREA: There's no more to say. I'll be no party to your logic. I've a very different notion of my duties as a man. And I know that the majority of your subjects share my view. You outrage their deepest feelings. It's only natural that you should . . . disappear.

CALIGULA: I see your point, and it's legitimate enough. For most men, I grant you, it's obvious. But *you*, I should have thought, would have known better. You're an intelligent man, and given intelligence, one has a choice: either to pay its price or to disown it. Why do you shirk the issue and neither disown it nor consent to pay its price?

CHEREA: Because what I want is to live, and to be happy. Neither, to my mind, is possible if one pushes the absurd to its logical conclusions. As you see,

I'm quite an ordinary sort of man. True, there are moments when, to feel free of them, I desire the death of those I love, or I hanker after women from whom the ties of family or friendship debar me. Were logic everything, I'd kill or fornicate on such occasions. But I consider that these passing fancies have no great importance. If everyone set to gratifying them, the world would be impossible to live in, and happiness, too, would go by the board. And these, I repeat, are the things that count, for me.

CALIGULA: So, I take it, you believe in some higher principle?

CHEREA: Certainly I believe that some actions are— shall I say?—more praiseworthy than others.

CALIGULA: And *I* believe that all are on an equal footing.

CHEREA: I know it, Caius, and that's why I don't hate you. I understand, and, to a point, agree with you. But you're pernicious, and you've got to go.

CALIGULA: True enough. But why risk your life by telling me this?

CHEREA: Because others will take my place, and because I don't like lying.

[*A short silence.*]

CALIGULA: Cherea!

CHEREA: Yes, Caius?

CALIGULA: Do you think that two men of similar temperament and equal pride can, if only once in their lives, open their hearts to each other?

CHEREA: That, I believe, is what we've just been doing.

CALIGULA: Yes, Cherea. But you thought I was incapable of it.

CHEREA: I was wrong, Caius. I admit it, and I thank you. Now I await your sentence.

CALIGULA: My sentence? Ah, I see. [*Producing the*

tablet from under his cloak.] You know what this is, Cherea?

CHEREA: I knew you had it.

CALIGULA [*passionately*]: You knew I had it! So your frankness was all a piece of play acting. The two friends did *not* open their hearts to each other. Well, well! It's no great matter. Now we can stop playing at sincerity, and resume life on the old footing. But first I'll ask you to make just one more effort; to bear with my caprices and my tactlessness a little longer. Listen well, Cherea. This tablet is the one and only piece of evidence against you.

CHEREA: Caius, I'd rather go. I'm sick and tired of all these antics. I know them only too well, and I've had enough. Let me go, please.

CALIGULA [*in the same tense, passionate voice*]: No, stay. This tablet is the only evidence. Is that clear?

CHEREA: Evidence? I never knew you needed evidence to send a man to his death.

CALIGULA: That's true. Still, for once I wish to contradict myself. Nobody can object to that. It's so pleasant to contradict oneself occasionally; so restful. And I need rest, Cherea.

CHEREA: I don't follow . . . and, frankly, I've no taste for these subtleties.

CALIGULA: I know, Cherea, I know. You're not like me; you're an ordinary man, sound in mind and body. And naturally you've no desire for the extraordinary. [*With a burst of laughter*] You want to live and to be happy. That's all!

CHEREA: I think, Caius, we'd better leave it at that. . . . Can I go?

CALIGULA: Not yet. A little patience, if you don't mind—I shall not keep you long. You see this thing —this piece of evidence? I choose to assume that I can't sentence you to death without it. That's my idea . . . and my repose. Well! See what becomes of evidence in an emperor's hands. [*He holds the tablet to a torch.* CHEREA *approaches. The torch is between them. The tablet begins to melt.*] You see, conspirator! The tablet's melting, and as it melts a look of innocence is dawning on your face. What a handsome forehead you have, Cherea! And how rare, how beautiful a sight is an innocent man! Admire my power. Even the gods cannot restore innocence without first punishing the culprit. But your emperor needs only a torch flame to absolve you and give you a new lease of hope. So carry on, Cherea; follow out the noble precepts we've been hearing, wherever they may take you. Meanwhile your emperor awaits his repose. It's his way of living and being happy.

[CHEREA *stares, dumfounded, at* CALIGULA. *He makes a vague gesture, seems to understand, opens his mouth to speak—and walks abruptly away. Smiling, holding the tablet to the flame,* CALIGULA *follows the receding figure with his gaze.*]

CURTAIN

ACT IV

A room in the imperial palace.
The stage is in semidarkness. CHEREA *and* SCIPIO *enter.*
CHEREA *crosses to the right, then comes back left to*
SCIPIO.

SCIPIO [*sulkily*]: What do you want of me?

CHEREA: There's no time to lose. And we must know our minds, we must be resolute.

SCIPIO: Who says I'm not resolute?

CHEREA: You didn't attend our meeting yesterday.

SCIPIO [*looking away*]: That's so, Cherea.

CHEREA: Scipio, I am older than you, and I'm not in the habit of asking others' help. But, I won't deny it, I need you now. This murder needs honorable men to sponsor it. Among all these wounded vanities and sordid fears, our motives only, yours and mine, are disinterested. Of course I know that, if you leave us, we can count on your silence. But that is not the point. What I want is—for you to stay with us.

SCIPIO: I understand. But I can't, oh, no, I *cannot* do as you wish.

CHEREA: So you are with him?

SCIPIO: No. But I cannot be against him. [*Pauses; then in a muffled voice*] Even if I killed him, my heart would still be with him.

CHEREA: And yet—he killed your father!

SCIPIO: Yes—and that's how it all began. But that, too, is how it ends.

CHEREA: He denies what you believe in. He tramples on all that you hold sacred.

SCIPIO: I know, Cherea. And yet something inside me is akin to him. The same fire burns in both our hearts.

CHEREA: There are times when a man must make his choice. As for me, I have silenced in my heart all that might be akin to him.

SCIPIO: But—*I*—I cannot make a choice. I have my own sorrow, but I suffer with him, too; I share his pain. I understand all—that is my trouble.

CHEREA: So that's it. You have chosen to take his side.

SCIPIO [*passionately*]: No, Cherea. I beg you, don't think that. I can never, never again take anybody's side.

CHEREA [*affectionately; approaching* SCIPIO]: Do you know, I hate him even more for having made of you —what he has made.

SCIPIO: Yes, he has taught me to expect everything of life.

CHEREA: No, he has taught you despair. And to have instilled despair into a young heart is fouler than the foulest of the crimes he has committed up to now. I assure you, *that* alone would justify me in killing him out of hand.

[*He goes toward the door.* HELICON *enters.*]

HELICON: I've been hunting for you high and low, Cherea. Caligula's giving a little party here, for his personal friends only. Naturally he expects you to attend it. [*To* SCIPIO] You, my boy, aren't wanted. Off you go!

SCIPIO [*looking back at* CHEREA *as he goes out*]: Cherea.

CHEREA [*gently*]: Yes, Scipio?

SCIPIO: Try to understand.

CHEREA [*in the same gentle tone*]: No, Scipio.

[SCIPIO *and* HELICON *go out. A clash of arms in the*

wings. Two soldiers enter at right, escorting the
OLD PATRICIAN *and the* FIRST PATRICIAN, *who show*
signs of alarm.]

FIRST PATRICIAN [*to one of the soldiers, in a tone*
which he vainly tries to steady]: But . . . but
what *can* he want with us at this hour of the
night?

SOLDIER: Sit there. [*Points to the chairs on the right.*]

FIRST PATRICIAN: If it's only to have us killed—like
so many others—why all these preliminaries?

SOLDIER: Sit down, you old mule.

THE OLD PATRICIAN: Better do as he says. It's clear he
doesn't know anything.

SOLDIER: Yes, darling, quite clear. [*Goes out.*]

FIRST PATRICIAN: We should have acted sooner; I
always said so. Now we're in for the torture cham-
ber.

[*The* SOLDIER *comes back with* CHEREA, *then goes*
out.]

CHEREA [*seating himself. He shows no sign of appre-*
hension]: Any idea what's happening?

FIRST PATRICIAN AND THE OLD PATRICIAN [*speaking*
together]: He's found out about the conspiracy.

CHEREA: Yes? And then?

THE OLD PATRICIAN [*shuddering*]: The torture cham-
ber for us all.

CHEREA [*still unperturbed*]: I remember that Caligula
once gave eighty-one thousand sesterces to a slave
who, though he was tortured nearly to death,
wouldn't confess to a theft he had committed.

FIRST PATRICIAN: A lot of consolation that is—for us!

CHEREA: Anyhow, it shows that he appreciates courage. You ought to keep that in mind. [*To the* OLD
PATRICIAN] Would you very much mind not chatter-
ing with your teeth? It's a noise I particularly dislike.

THE OLD PATRICIAN: I'm sorry, but—

FIRST PATRICIAN: Enough trifling! Our lives are at stake.

CHEREA [*coolly*]: Do you know Caligula's favorite remark?

THE OLD PATRICIAN [*on the verge of tears*]: Yes. He says to the executioner: "Kill him slowly, so that he feels what dying's like!"

CHEREA: No, there's a better one. After an execution he yawns, and says quite seriously: "What I admire most is my imperturbability."

FIRST PATRICIAN: Do you hear . . . ?

[*A clanking of weapons is heard off stage.*]

CHEREA: That remark betrays a weakness in his make-up.

THE OLD PATRICIAN: Would you be kind enough to stop philosophizing? It's something I particularly dislike.

[*A slave enters and deposits a sheaf of knives on a seat.*]

CHEREA [*who has not noticed him*]: Still, there's no denying it's remarkable, the effect this man has on all with whom he comes in contact. He forces one to think. There's nothing like insecurity for stimulating the brain. That, of course, is why he's so much hated.

THE OLD PATRICIAN [*pointing a trembling finger*]: Look!

CHEREA [*noticing the knives, in a slightly altered tone*]: Perhaps you were right.

FIRST PATRICIAN: Yes, waiting was a mistake. We should have acted at once.

CHEREA: I agree. Wisdom's come too late.

THE OLD PATRICIAN: But it's . . . it's crazy. I don't want to die.

[*He rises and begins to edge away. Two soldiers appear, and, after slapping his face, force him back onto his seat. The* FIRST PATRICIAN *squirms in his chair.* CHEREA *utters some inaudible words. Suddenly a queer music begins behind the curtain at the back of the stage; a thrumming and tinkling of zithers and cymbals. The patricians gaze at each other in silence. Outlined on the illuminated curtain, in shadow play,* CALIGULA *appears, makes some grotesque dance movements, and retreats from view. He is wearing ballet dancer's skirts and his head is garlanded with flowers. A moment later a* SOLDIER *announces gravely:* "Gentlemen, the performance is over." *Meanwhile* CÆSONIA *has entered soundlessly behind the watching patricians. She speaks in an ordinary voice, but none the less they give a start on hearing it.*]

CÆSONIA: Caligula has instructed me to tell you that, whereas in the past he always summoned you for affairs of state, today he invited you to share with him an artistic emotion. [*A short pause. Then she continues in the same tone*] He added, I may say, that anyone who has not shared in it will be beheaded. [*They keep silent.*] I apologize for insisting, but I must ask you if you found that dance beautiful.

FIRST PATRICIAN [*after a brief hesitation*]: Yes, Cæsonia. It was beautiful.

THE OLD PATRICIAN [*effusively*]: Lovely! Lovely!

CÆSONIA: And you, Cherea?

CHEREA [*icily*]: It was . . . very high art.

CÆSONIA: Good. Now I can describe your artistic emotions to Caligula.

[CÆSONIA *goes out.*]

CHEREA: And now we must act quickly. You two stay here. Before the night is out there'll be a hundred of us.

[*He goes out.*]

THE OLD PATRICIAN: No, no. *You* stay. Let me go, instead. [*Sniffs the air.*] It smells of death here.

FIRST PATRICIAN: And of lies. [*Sadly*] I said that dance was beautiful!

THE OLD PATRICIAN [*conciliatingly*]: And so it was, in a way. Most original.

[*Some patricians and knights enter hurriedly.*]

SECOND PATRICIAN: What's afoot? Do you know anything? The Emperor's summoned us here.

THE OLD PATRICIAN [*absent-mindedly*]: For the dance, maybe.

SECOND PATRICIAN: What dance?

THE OLD PATRICIAN: Well, I mean . . . er . . . the artistic emotion.

THIRD PATRICIAN: I've been told Caligula's very ill.

FIRST PATRICIAN: He's a sick man, yes. . . .

THIRD PATRICIAN: What's he suffering from? [*In a joyful tone*] By God, is he going to die?

FIRST PATRICIAN: I doubt it. His disease is fatal—to others only.

THE OLD PATRICIAN: That's one way of putting it.

SECOND PATRICIAN: Quite so. But hasn't he some other disease less serious, and more to our advantage?

FIRST PATRICIAN: No. That malady of his excludes all others.

[*He goes out.* CÆSONIA *enters. A short silence.*]

CÆSONIA [*in a casual tone*]: If you want to know, Caligula has stomach trouble. Just now he vomited blood.

[*The patricians crowd round her.*]

SECOND PATRICIAN: O mighty gods, I vow, if he recovers, to pay the Treasury two hundred thousand sesterces as a token of my joy.

THIRD PATRICIAN [*with exaggerated eagerness*]: O Jupiter, take my life in place of his!

[CALIGULA *has entered, and is listening.*]

CALIGULA [*going up to the* SECOND PATRICIAN]: I accept your offer, Lucius. And I thank you. My Treasurer will call on you tomorrow. [*Goes to the*

THIRD PATRICIAN *and embraces him.*] You can't
imagine how touched I am. [*A short silence. Then,
tenderly*] So you love me, Cassius, as much as that?

THIRD PATRICIAN [*emotionally*]:   Oh, Cæsar, there's
nothing, nothing I wouldn't sacrifice for your sake.

CALIGULA [*embracing him again*]:   Ah, Cassius, this
is really too much; I don't deserve all this love.
[CASSIUS *makes a protesting gesture.*] No, no, really
I don't! I'm not worthy of it. [*He beckons to two
soldiers.*] Take him away. [*Gently, to* CASSIUS]
Go, dear friend, and remember that Caligula has
lost his heart to you.

THIRD PATRICIAN [*vaguely uneasy*]:   But—where are
they taking me?

CALIGULA: Why, to your death, of course. Your generous offer was accepted, and I feel better already.
Even that nasty taste of blood in my mouth has
gone. You've cured me, Cassius. It's been miracu-
lous, and how proud you must feel of having worked
the miracle by laying your life down for your
friend—especially when that friend's none other
than Caligula! So now you see me quite myself
again, and ready for a festive night.

THIRD PATRICIAN [*shrieking, as he is dragged away*]:
No! No! I don't want to die. You can't be serious!

CALIGULA [*in a thoughtful voice, between the shrieks*]:
Soon the sea roads will be golden with mimosas.
The women will wear their lightest dresses. And
the sky! Ah, Cassius, what a blaze of clean, swift
sunshine! The smiles of life. [CASSIUS *is near the
door.* CALIGULA *gives him a gentle push. Suddenly
his tone grows serious*] Life, my friend, is something to be cherished. Had you cherished it enough,
you wouldn't have gambled it away so rashly.
[CASSIUS *is led off.* CALIGULA *returns to the table.*]
The loser must pay. There's no alternative. [*A short
silence.*] Come, Cæsonia. [*He turns to the others*]

By the way, an idea has just waylaid me, and it's such an apt one that I want to share it with you. Until now my reign has been too happy. There's been no world-wide plague, no religious persecution, not even a rebellion—nothing in fact to make us memorable. And that, I'd have you know, is why I try to remedy the stinginess of fate. I mean—I don't know if you've followed me—that, well [*he gives a little laugh*], it's I who replace the epidemics that we've missed. [*In a different tone*] That's enough. I see Cherea's coming. Your turn, Cæsonia. [CALIGULA *goes out.* CHEREA *and the* FIRST PATRICIAN *enter.* CÆSONIA *hurries toward* CHEREA.]

CÆSONIA: Caligula is dead.

[*She turns her head, as if to hide her tears; her eyes are fixed on the others, who keep silence. Everyone looks horrified, but for different reasons.*]

FIRST PATRICIAN: You . . . you're *sure* this dreadful thing has happened? It seems incredible. Only a short while ago he was dancing.

CÆSONIA: Quite so—and the effort was too much for him. [CHEREA *moves hastily from one man to the other. No one speaks.*] You've nothing to say, Cherea?

CHEREA [*in a low voice*]: It's a great misfortune for us all, Cæsonia.

[CALIGULA *bursts in violently and goes up to* CHEREA.]

CALIGULA: Well played, Cherea. [*He spins round and stares at the others. Petulantly*] Too bad! It didn't come off. [*To* CÆSONIA] Don't forget what I told you.

[CALIGULA *goes out.* CÆSONIA *stares after him without speaking.*]

THE OLD PATRICIAN [*hoping against hope*]: Is he ill, Cæsonia?

CÆSONIA [*with a hostile look*]: No, my pet. But

what you don't know is that the man never has more
than two hours' sleep and spends the best part of
the night roaming about the corridors in his palace.
Another thing you don't know—and you've never
given a thought to—is what may pass in this man's
mind in those deadly hours between midnight and
sunrise. Is he ill? No, not ill—unless you invent a
name and medicine for the black ulcers that fester
in his soul.

CHEREA [*seemingly affected by her words*]: You're
right, Cæsonia. We all know that Caius . . .

CÆSONIA [*breaking in emotionally*]: Yes, you know
it—in your fashion. But, like all those who have
none, you can't abide anyone who has too much
soul. Healthy people loathe invalids. Happy people
hate the sad. Too much soul! That's what bites you,
isn't it? You prefer to label it a disease; that way all
the dolts are justified and pleased. [*In a changed
tone*] Tell me, Cherea. Has love ever meant anything to you?

CHEREA [*himself again*]: I'm afraid we're too old
now, Cæsonia, to learn the art of love-making. And
anyhow it's highly doubtful if Caligula will give us
time to do so.

CÆSONIA [*who has recovered her composure*]: True
enough. [*She sits down.*] Oh, I was forgetting. . . .
Caligula asked me to impart some news to you. You
know, perhaps, that it's a red-letter day today,
consecrated to art.

THE OLD PATRICIAN: According to the calendar?

CÆSONIA: No, according to Caligula. He's convoked
some poets. He will ask them to improvise a poem
on a set theme. And he particularly wants those of
you who are poets to take part in the competition.
He specially mentioned young Scipio and Metellus.

METELLUS: But we're not ready.

CÆSONIA [*in a level tone, as if she has not heard him*]:
Needless to say there are prizes. There will be
penalties, too. [*Looks of consternation.*] Between
ourselves, the penalties won't be so very terrible.
[CALIGULA *enters, looking gloomier than ever.*]

CALIGULA: All ready?

CÆSONIA: Yes. [*To a soldier*] Bring in the poets.
[*Enter, two by two, a dozen poets, keeping step;
they line up on the right of the stage.*]

CALIGULA: And the others?

CÆSONIA: Metellus! Scipio!
[*They cross the stage and take their stand beside
the poets.* CALIGULA *seats himself, backstage on the
left, with* CÆSONIA *and the patricians. A short
silence.*]

CALIGULA: Subject: death. Time limit: one minute.
[*The poets scribble feverishly on their tablets.*]

THE OLD PATRICIAN: Who will compose the jury?

CALIGULA: I. Isn't that enough?

THE OLD PATRICIAN: Oh, yes, indeed. Quite enough.

CHEREA: Won't you take part in the competition,
Caius?

CALIGULA: Unnecessary. I made my poem on that
theme long ago.

THE OLD PATRICIAN [*eagerly*]: Where can one get a
copy of it?

CALIGULA: No need to get a copy. I recite it every
day, after my fashion. [CÆSONIA *eyes him nervously.* CALIGULA *rounds on her almost savagely*]
Is there anything in my appearance that displeases
you?

CÆSONIA [*gently*]: I'm sorry. . . .

CALIGULA: No meekness, please. For heaven's sake,
no meekness. You're exasperating enough as it is,
but if you start being humble . . . [CÆSONIA
slowly moves away. CALIGULA *turns to* CHEREA.] I
continue. It's the only poem I have made. And it's

proof that I'm the only true artist Rome has known
—the only one, believe me—to match his inspiration with his deeds.

CHEREA: That's only a matter of having the power.

CALIGULA: Quite true. Other artists create to compensate for their lack of power. I don't need to
make a work of art; I *live* it. [*Roughly*] Well, poets,
are you ready?

METELLUS: I think so.

THE OTHERS: Yes.

CALIGULA: Good. Now listen carefully. You are to
fall out of line and come forward one by one. I'll
whistle. Number One will start reading his poem.
When I whistle, he must stop, and the next begin.
And so on. The winner, naturally, will be the one
whose poem hasn't been cut short by the whistle.
Get ready. [*Turning to* CHEREA, *he whispers*] You
see, organization's needed for everything, even for
art.

[*Blows his whistle.*]

FIRST POET: Death, when beyond thy darkling
shore . . .

[*A blast of the whistle. The poet steps briskly to
the left. The others will follow the same procedure.
these movements should be made with mechanical
precision.*]

SECOND POET: In their dim cave, the Fatal Sisters
Three . . .

[*Whistle.*]

THIRD POET: Come to me death, beloved . . .

[*A shrill blast of the whistle. The* FOURTH POET
*steps forward and strikes a dramatic posture. The
whistle goes before he has opened his mouth.*]

FIFTH POET: When I was in my happy infancy . . .

CALIGULA [*yelling*]:   Stop that! What earthly connection has a blockhead's happy infancy with the theme
I set? The connection! Tell me the connection!

FIFTH POET: But, Caius, I've only just begun, and
. . . [*Shrill blast.*]

SIXTH POET [*in a high-pitched voice*]: Ruthless, he
goes his hidden ways . . .
[*Whistle*]

SEVENTH POET [*mysteriously*]: Oh, long, abstruse
orison . . .
[*Whistle, broken off as* SCIPIO *comes forward without a tablet.*]

CALIGULA: You haven't a tablet?

SCIPIO: I do not need one.

CALIGULA: Well, let's hear you. [*He chews at his
whistle.*]

SCIPIO [*standing very near* CALIGULA, *he recites list-
lessly, without looking at him*]:
  Pursuit of happiness that purifies the heart,
  Skies rippling with light,
  O wild, sweet, festal joys, frenzy without hope!

CALIGULA [*gently*]: Stop, please. The others needn't
compete. [*To* SCIPIO] You're very young to understand so well the lessons we can learn from death.

SCIPIO [*gazing straight at* CALIGULA]: I was very
young to lose my father.

CALIGULA [*turning hastily*]: Fall in, the rest of you.
No, really a sham poet is too dreadful an infliction.
Until now I'd thought of enrolling you as my allies;
I sometimes pictured a gallant band of poets de-
fending me in the last ditch. Another illusion gone!
I shall have to relegate you to my enemies. So now
the poets are against me—and that looks much like
the end of all. March out in good order. As you go
past you are to lick your tablets so as to efface the
atrocities you scrawled on them. Attention! Forward! [*He blows his whistle in short rhythmic
jerks. Keeping step, the poets file out by the right,
tonguing their immortal tablets.* CALIGULA *adds in a
lower tone*] Now leave me, everyone.

[*In the doorway, as they are going out,* CHEREA *touches the* FIRST PATRICIAN's *shoulder, and speaks in his ear.*]

CHEREA: Now's our opportunity.

[SCIPIO, *who has overheard, halts on the threshold and walks back to* CALIGULA.]

CALIGULA [*acidly*]:   Can't you leave me in peace— as your father's doing?

SCIPIO: No, Caius, all that serves no purpose now. For now I know, I *know* that you have made your choice.

CALIGULA: Won't you leave me in peace!

SCIPIO: Yes, you shall have your wish; I am going to leave you, for I think I've come to understand you. There's no way out left to us, neither to you nor to me—who am like you in so many ways. I shall go away, far away, and try to discover the meaning of it all. [*He gazes at* CALIGULA *for some moments. Then, with a rush of emotion*] Good-by, dear Caius. When all is ended, remember that I loved you. [*He goes out.* CALIGULA *makes a vague gesture. Then, almost savagely, he pulls himself together and takes some steps toward* CÆSONIA.]

CÆSONIA: What did he say?

CALIGULA: Nothing you'd understand.

CÆSONIA: What are thinking about?

CALIGULA: About him. And about you, too. But it amounts to the same thing.

CÆSONIA: What is the matter?

CALIGULA [*staring at her*]:   Scipio has gone. I am through with his friendship. But you, I wonder why you are still here. . . .

CÆSONIA: Why, because you're fond of me.

CALIGULA: No. But I think I'd understand—if I had you killed.

CÆSONIA: Yes, that would be a solution. Do so, then. . . . But why, oh, why can't you relax, if only for a moment, and live freely, without constraint?

CALIGULA: I have been doing that for several years; in fact I've made a practice of it.

CÆSONIA: I don't mean that sort of freedom. I mean —Oh, don't you realize what it can be to live and love quite simply, naturally, in . . . in purity of heart?

CALIGULA: This purity of heart you talk of—every man acquires it, in his own way. Mine has been to follow the essential to the end. . . . Still all that needn't prevent me from putting you to death. [*Laughs.*] It would round off my career so well, the perfect climax. [*He rises and swings the mirror round toward himself. Then he walks in a circle, letting his arms hang limp, almost without gestures; there is something feral in his gait as he continues speaking.*] How strange! When I don't kill, I feel alone. The living don't suffice to people my world and dispel my boredom. I have an impression of an enormous void when you and the others are here, and my eyes see nothing but empty air. No, I'm at ease only in the company of my dead. [*He takes his stand facing the audience, leaning a little forward. He has forgotten* CÆSONIA's *presence.*] Only the dead are real. They are of my kind. I see them waiting for me, straining toward me. And I have long talks with this man or that, who screamed to me for mercy and whose tongue I had cut out.

CÆSONIA: Come. Lie down beside me. Put your head on my knees. [CALIGULA *does so.*] That's better, isn't it? Now rest. How quiet it is here!

CALIGULA: Quiet? You exaggerate, my dear. Listen! [*Distant metallic tinklings, as of swords or armor.*] Do you hear those thousands of small sounds all around us, hatred stalking its prey? [*Murmuring voices, footsteps.*]

CÆSONIA: Nobody would dare. . . .

CALIGULA: Yes, stupidity.

CÆSONIA: Stupidity doesn't kill. It makes men slow to act.

CALIGULA: It can be murderous, Cæsonia. A fool stops at nothing when he thinks his dignity offended. No, it's not the men whose sons or fathers I have killed who'll murder me. *They*, anyhow, have understood. They're with me, they have the same taste in their mouths. But the others—those I made a laughingstock of—I've no defense against their wounded vanity.

CÆSONIA [*passionately*]: *We* will defend you. There are many of us left who love you.

CALIGULA: Fewer every day. It's not surprising. I've done all that was needed to that end. And then— let's be fair—it's not only stupidity that's against me. There's the courage and the simple faith of men who ask to be happy.

CÆSONIA [*in the same tone*]: No, *they* will not kill you. Or, if they tried, fire would come down from heaven and blast them, before they laid a hand on you.

CALIGULA: From heaven! There is no heaven, my poor dear woman! [*He sits down.*] But why this sudden access of devotion? It wasn't provided for in our agreement, if I remember rightly.

CÆSONIA [*who has risen from the couch and is pacing the room*]: Don't you understand? Hasn't it been enough to see you killing others, without my also knowing you'll be killed as well? Isn't it enough to feel you hard and cruel, seething with bitterness, when I hold you in my arms; to breathe a reek of murder when you lie on me? Day after day I see all that's human in you dying out, little by little. [*She turns toward him.*] Oh, I know. I know I'm getting old, my beauty's on the wane. But it's you only

I'm concerned for now; so much so that I've ceased troubling whether you love me. I only want you to get well, quite well again. You're still a boy, really; you've a whole life ahead of you. And, tell me, what greater thing can you want than a whole life?

CALIGULA [*rising, looks at her fixedly*]: You've been with me a long time now, a very long time.

CÆSONIA: Yes. . . . But you'll keep me, won't you?

CALIGULA: I don't know. I only know that, if you're with me still, it's because of all those nights we've had together, nights of fierce, joyless pleasure; it's because you alone know me as I am. [*He takes her in his arms, bending her head back a little with his right hand.*] I'm twenty-nine. Not a great age really. But today when none the less my life seems so long, so crowded with scraps and shreds of my past selves, so complete in fact, you remain the last witness. And I can't avoid a sort of shameful tenderness for the old woman that you soon will be.

CÆSONIA: Tell me that you mean to keep me with you.

CALIGULA: I don't know. All I know—and it's the most terrible thing of all—is that this shameful tenderness is the one sincere emotion that my life has given up to now. [CÆSONIA *frees herself from his arms.* CALIGULA *follows her. She presses her back to his chest and he puts his arms round her.*] Wouldn't it be better that the last witness should disappear?

CÆSONIA: That has no importance. All I know is: I'm happy. What you've just said has made me very happy. But why can't I share my happiness with you?

CALIGULA: Who says I'm unhappy?

CÆSONIA: Happiness is kind. It doesn't thrive on bloodshed.

CALIGULA: Then there must be two kinds of happiness, and I've chosen the murderous kind. For I *am* happy. There was a time when I thought I'd reached the extremity of pain. But, no, one can go farther yet. Beyond the frontier of pain lies a splendid, sterile happiness. Look at me. [*She turns toward him.*] It makes me laugh, Cæsonia, when I think how for years and years all Rome carefully avoided uttering Drusilla's name. Well, all Rome was mistaken. Love isn't enough for me; I realized it then. And I realize it again today, when I look at you. To love someone means that one's willing to grow old beside that person. That sort of love is right outside my range. Drusilla old would have been far worse than Drusilla dead. Most people imagine that a man suffers because out of the blue death snatches away the woman he loves. But his real suffering is less futile; it comes from the discovery that grief, too, cannot last. Even grief is vanity.

You see, I had no excuses, not the shadow of a real love, neither bitterness nor profound regret. Nothing to plead in my defense! But today—you see me still freer than I have been for years; freed as I am from memories and illusion. [*He laughs bitterly.*] I know now that nothing, *nothing* lasts. Think what that knowledge means! There have been just two or three of us in history who really achieved this freedom, this crazy happiness. Well, Cæsonia, you have seen out a most unusual drama. It's time the curtain fell, for you.

[*He stands behind her again, linking his forearm round* CÆSONIA'S *neck.*]

CÆSONIA [*terrified*]: No, it's impossible! How can you call it happiness, this terrifying freedom?

CALIGULA [*gradually tightening his grip on* CÆSONIA'S *throat*]: Happiness it is, Cæsonia; I know what I'm saying. But for this freedom I'd have been a contented man. Thanks to it, I have won the god-like enlightenment of the solitary. [*His exaltation grows as little by little he strangles* CÆSONIA, *who puts up no resistance, but holds her hands half opened, like a suppliant's, before her. Bending his head, he goes on speaking, into her ear*] I live, I kill, I exercise the rapturous power of a destroyer, compared with which the power of a creator is merest child's play. And this, *this* is happiness; this and nothing else—this intolerable release, devastating scorn, blood, hatred all around me; the glorious isolation of a man who all his life long nurses and gloats over the ineffable joy of the unpunished murderer; the ruthless logic that crushes out human lives [*he laughs*], that's crushing yours out, Cæsonia, so as to perfect at last the utter loneliness that is my heart's desire.

CÆSONIA [*struggling feebly*]: Oh, Caius . . .

CALIGULA [*more and more excitedly*]: No. No sentiment. I must have done with it, for the time is short. My time is very short, dear Cæsonia. [CÆSONIA *is gasping, dying.* CALIGULA *drags her to the bed and lets her fall on it. He stares wildly at her; his voice grows harsh and grating.*] You, too, were guilty. But killing is not the solution. [*He spins round and gazes crazily at the mirror.*] Caligula! You, too; you, too, are guilty. Then what of it—a little more, a little less? Yet who can condemn me in this world where there is no judge, where nobody is innocent? [*He brings his eyes close to his reflected face. He sounds genuinely distressed*] You see, my poor friend. Helicon has failed you. I won't have the moon. Never, never, never! But how bitter it is to know all, and to have to go through to the consummation! Listen! That was a sound of weapons. Innocence arming for the fray—and innocence will triumph. Why am I not in their place, among them?

And I'm afraid. That's cruelest of all, after despising
others, to find oneself as cowardly as they. Still, no
matter. Fear, too, has an end. Soon I shall attain
that emptiness beyond all understanding, in which
the heart has rest. [*He steps back a few paces, then
returns to the mirror. He seems calmer. When he
speaks again his voice is steadier, less shrill.*]
Yet, really, it's quite simple. If I'd had the moon, if
love were enough, all might have been different.
But where could I quench this thirst? What human
heart, what god, would have for me the depth of a
great lake? [*Kneeling, weeping*] There's nothing
in this world, or in the other, made to my stature.
And yet I know, and you, too, know [*still weeping,
he stretches out his arms toward the mirror*] that
all I need is for the impossible to be. The impossible!
I've searched for it at the confines of the world, in
the secret places of my heart. I've stretched out my
hands [*his voice rises to a scream*]; see, I stretch
out my hands, but it's always you I find, you only,
confronting me, and I've come to hate you. I have
chosen a wrong path, a path that leads to nothing.
My freedom isn't the right one. . . . Nothing,
nothing yet. Oh, how oppressive is this darkness!
Helicon has not come; we shall be forever guilty.
The air tonight is heavy as the sum of human
sorrows. [*A clash of arms and whisperings are heard
in the wings.* CALIGULA *rises, picks up a stool, and
returns to the mirror, breathing heavily. He contemplates himself, makes a slight leap forward, and,
watching the symmetrical movement of his reflected self, hurls the stool at it, screaming*] To
history, Caligula! Go down to history! [*The mirror
breaks and at the same moment armed conspirators
rush in.* CALIGULA *swings round to face them with a
mad laugh.* SCIPIO *and* CHEREA, *who are in front,
fling themselves at him and stab his face with their*

daggers. CALIGULA's *laughter turns to gasps. All strike him, hurriedly, confusedly. In a last gasp, laughing and choking,* CALIGULA *shrieks*] I'm still alive!

C U R T A I N

THE MIS-UNDERSTANDING

A PLAY IN THREE ACTS

To my friends of the THÉÂTRE DE L'ÉQUIPE

CHARACTERS IN THE PLAY

THE OLD MANSERVANT

MARTHA

THE MOTHER

JAN

MARIA

LE MALENTENDU (THE MISUNDERSTANDING) *was*
presented for the first time at the
THÉÂTRE DES MATHURINS, *Paris, in 1944*

ACT I

Noon. The clean, brightly lit public room of an inn. Everything is very spick and span.

THE MOTHER: He'll come back.

MARTHA: Did he tell you so?

THE MOTHER: Yes.

MARTHA: Alone?

THE MOTHER: That I can't say.

MARTHA: He doesn't look like a poor man.

THE MOTHER: No, and he never asked what our charges were.

MARTHA: A good sign, that. But usually rich men don't travel alone. Really it's *that* makes things so difficult. You may have to wait ages when you're looking out for a man who is not only rich but quite alone.

THE MOTHER: Yes, we don't get so many opportunities.

MARTHA: It means, of course, that we've had many slack times these last few years. This place is often empty. Poor people who stop here never stay long, and it's mighty seldom rich ones come.

THE MOTHER: Don't grumble about that, Martha. Rich people give a lot of extra work.

MARTHA [*looking hard at her*]: But they pay well. [*A short silence.*] Tell me, mother; what's come over you? For some time I've noticed that you weren't quite . . . quite your usual self.

THE MOTHER: I'm tired, my dear, that's all. What I need is a long rest.

MARTHA: Listen, mother. I can take over the household work you're doing now. Then you'll have your days free.

THE MOTHER: That wasn't quite the sort of rest I meant. Oh, I suppose it's just an old woman's fancy. All I'm longing for is peace—to be able to relax a little. [*She gives a little laugh.*] I know it sounds silly, Martha, but some evenings I feel almost like taking to religion.

MARTHA: You're not so very old, mother; you haven't come to that yet. And, anyhow, I should say *you* could do better.

THE MOTHER: Of course I was only joking, my dear. All the same . . . at the end of one's life, it's not a bad idea to take things easy. One can't be always on the go, as you are, Martha. And it isn't natural for a woman of your age, either. I know plenty of girls who were born the same year as you, and they think only of pleasure and excitements.

MARTHA: Their pleasures and excitements are nothing compared to ours, don't you agree, mother?

THE MOTHER: I'd rather you didn't speak of that.

MARTHA [*thoughtfully*]: Really one would think that nowadays some words burn your tongue.

THE MOTHER: What can it matter to you—provided I don't shrink from acts? But that has no great importance. What I really meant was that I'd like to see you smile now and again.

MARTHA: I do smile sometimes, I assure you.

THE MOTHER: Really? I've never seen you.

MARTHA: That's because I smile when I'm by myself, in my bedroom.

THE MOTHER [*looking closely at her*]: What a hard face you have, Martha!

MARTHA [*coming closer; calmly*]: Ah, so you don't approve of my face?

THE MOTHER [*after a short silence, still looking at her*]:
I wonder . . . Yes, I think I do.

MARTHA [*emotionally*]:   Oh, mother, can't you understand? Once we have enough money in hand, and I
can escape from this shut-in valley; once we can say
good-by to this inn and this dreary town where it's
always raining; once we've forgotten this land of
shadows—ah, then, when my dream has come true,
and we're living beside the sea, *then* you will see me
smile. Unfortunately one needs a great deal of
money to be able to live in freedom by the sea. That
is why we mustn't be afraid of words; that is why
we must take trouble over this man who's come to
stay here. If he is rich enough, perhaps my freedom
will begin with him.

THE MOTHER: If he's rich enough, and if he's by himself.

MARTHA: That's so. He has to be by himself as well.
Did he talk much to you, mother?

THE MOTHER: No, he said very little.

MARTHA: When he asked for his room, did you notice how he looked?

THE MOTHER: No. My sight's none too good, you
know, and I didn't really look at his face. I've
learned from experience that it's better not to look
at them too closely. It's easier to kill what one
doesn't know. [*A short silence.*] There! That should
please you. You can't say now that I'm afraid of
words.

MARTHA: Yes, and I prefer it so. I've no use for hints
and evasions. Crime is crime, and one should know
what one is doing. And, from what you've just said,
it looks as if you had it in mind when you were
talking to that traveler.

THE MOTHER: No, I wouldn't say I had it in mind—it
was more from force of habit.

MARTHA: Habit? But you said yourself that these opportunities seldom come our way.

THE MOTHER: Certainly. But habit begins with the second crime. With the first nothing starts, but something ends. Then, too, while we have had few opportunities, they have been spread out over many years, and memory helps to build up habits. Yes, it was force of habit that made me keep my eyes off that man when I was talking to him, and, all the same, convinced me he had the look of a victim.

MARTHA: Mother, we must kill him.

THE MOTHER [*in a low tone*]: Yes, I suppose we'll have to.

MARTHA: You said that in a curious way.

THE MOTHER: I'm tired, that's all. Anyhow, I'd like this one to be the last. It's terribly tiring to kill. And, though really I care little where I die—beside the sea or here, far inland—I do hope we will get away together, the moment it's over.

MARTHA: Indeed we shall—and what a glorious moment that will be! So, cheer up, mother, there won't be much to do. You know quite well there's no question of killing. He'll drink his tea, he'll go to sleep, and he'll be still alive when we carry him to the river. Some day, long after, he will be found jammed against the weir, along with others who didn't have his luck and threw themselves into the water with their eyes open. Do you remember last year when we were watching them repair the sluices, how you said that ours suffered least, and life was crueler than we? So don't lose heart, you'll be having your rest quite soon and I'll be seeing what I've never seen.

THE MOTHER: Yes, Martha, I won't lose heart. And it was quite true, what you said about "ours." I'm always glad to think they never suffered. Really, it's hardly a crime, only a sort of intervention, a flick

of the finger given to unknown lives. And it's also
quite true that, by the look of it, life is crueler than
we. Perhaps that is why I can't manage to feel
guilty. I can only just manage to feel tired.

[*The* OLD MANSERVANT *comes in. He seats himself
behind the bar and remains there, neither moving
nor speaking, until* JAN'S *entrance.*]

MARTHA: Which room shall we put him in?

THE MOTHER: Any room, provided it's on the first
floor.

MARTHA: Yes, we had a lot of needless trouble last
time, with the two flights of stairs. [*For the first
time she sits down.*] Tell me, mother, is it true that
down on the coast the sand's so hot it scorches one's
feet?

THE MOTHER: As you know, Martha, I've never been
there. But I've been told the sun burns everything
up.

MARTHA: I read in a book that it even burns out
people's souls and gives them bodies that shine like
gold but are quite hollow, there's nothing left inside.

THE MOTHER: Is that what makes you want to go
there so much?

MARTHA: Yes, my soul's a burden to me, I've had
enough of it. I'm eager to be in that country, where
the sun kills every question. I don't belong here.

THE MOTHER: Unfortunately we have much to do
beforehand. Of course, when it's over, I'll go there
with you. But I am not like you; I shall not have
the feeling of going to a place where I belong.
After a certain age one knows there is no resting
place anywhere. Indeed there's something to be
said for this ugly brick house we've made our home
and stocked with memories; there are times when
one can fall asleep in it. But, naturally it would
mean something, too, if I could have sleep and

forgetfulness together. [*She rises and walks toward the door.*] Well, Martha, get everything ready. [*Pauses.*] If it's really worth the effort.

[MARTHA *watches her go out. Then she, too, leaves by another door. For some moments only the* OLD MANSERVANT *is on the stage.* JAN *enters, stops, glances round the room, and sees the old man sitting behind the counter.*]

JAN: Nobody here? [*The old man gazes at him, rises, crosses the stage, and goes out.* MARIA *enters.* JAN *swings round on her.*] So you followed me!

MARIA: Forgive me—I couldn't help it. I may not stay long. Only please let me look at the place where I'm leaving you.

JAN: Somebody may come, and your being here will upset all my plans.

MARIA: Do please let us take the chance of someone's coming and my telling who you are. I know you don't want it, but—[*He turns away fretfully. A short silence.* MARIA *is examining the room.*] So this is the place?

JAN: Yes. That's the door I went out by, twenty years ago. My sister was a little girl. She was playing in that corner. My mother didn't come to kiss me. At the time I thought I didn't care.

MARIA: Jan, I can't believe they failed to recognize you just now. A mother's bound to recognize her son; it's the least she can do.

JAN: Perhaps. Still, twenty years' separation makes a difference. Life has been going on since I left. My mother's grown old, her sight is failing. I hardly recognized her myself.

MARIA [*impatiently*]: I know. You came in; you said "Good day"; you sat down. This room wasn't like the one you remembered.

JAN: Yes, my memory had played me false. They received me without a word. I was given the glass of beer I asked for. I was looked at, but I wasn't *seen*. Everything was more difficult than I'd expected.

MARIA: You know quite well it needn't have been difficult; you had only to speak. On such occasions one says "It's I," and then it's all plain sailing.

JAN: True. But I'd been imagining—all sorts of things. I'd expected a welcome like the prodigal son's. Actually I was given a glass of beer, against payment. It took the words out of my mouth, and I thought I'd better let things take their course.

MARIA: There was nothing to take its course. It was another of those ideas of yours—and a word would have been enough.

JAN: It wasn't an idea of mine, Maria; it was the force of things. What's more, I'm not in such a hurry. I have come here to bring them my money, and if I can, some happiness. When I learned about my father's death I realized I had duties toward these two women and now, as a result, I'm doing what it's right for me to do. But evidently it is not so easy as people think, coming back to one's old home, and it takes time to change a stranger into a son.

MARIA: But why not let them know the truth at once? There are situations in which the normal way of acting is obviously the best. If one wants to be recognized, one starts by telling one's name; that's common sense. Otherwise, by pretending to be what one is not, one simply muddles everything. How could you expect not to be treated as a stranger in a house you entered under false colors? No, dear, there's something . . . something morbid about the way you're doing this.

JAN: Oh, come, Maria! It's not so serious as that. And, mind you, it suits my plan. I shall take this opportunity of seeing them from the outside. Then

I'll have a better notion of what to do to make them happy. Afterwards, I'll find some way of getting them to recognize me. It's just a matter of choosing one's words.

MARIA: No, there's only one way, and it's to do what any ordinary mortal would do—to say "It's I," and to let one's heart speak for itself.

JAN: The heart isn't so simple as all that.

MARIA: But it uses simple words. Surely there was no difficulty in saying: "I'm your son. This is my wife. I've been living with her in a country we both love, a land of endless sunshine beside the sea. But something was lacking there to complete my happiness, and now I feel I need you."

JAN: Don't be unfair, Maria. I don't need them; but I realized they may need me, and a man doesn't live only for himself.

[*A short silence.* MARIA *looks away from him.*]

MARIA: Perhaps you are right. I'm sorry for what I said. But I have grown terribly suspicious since coming to this country where I've looked in vain for a single happy face. This Europe of yours is so sad. Since we've been here, I haven't once heard you laugh, and, as for me, I feel my nerves on edge all the time. Oh, why did you make me leave my country? Let's go away, Jan; we shall not find happiness here.

JAN: It's not happiness we've come for. We had happiness already.

MARIA [*passionately*]: Then why not have been satisfied with it?

JAN: Happiness isn't everything; there is duty, too. Mine was to come back to my mother and my own country. [MARIA *makes a protesting gesture and is about to answer.* JAN *checks her. Footsteps can be heard.*] Someone's coming. Do please go, Maria.

MARIA: No, I can't, I can't! Not yet, anyhow!

JAN [*as the footsteps approach*]:   Go there. [*He gently pushes her toward the door at the back. The* OLD MANSERVANT *crosses the room without seeing* MARIA, *and goes out by the other door.*] Now, leave at once. You see, luck is on my side.

MARIA: Please, let me stay. I promise not to speak a word, only to stay beside you till you're recognized.

JAN: No. You'd give me away.

[*She turns away, then comes back and looks him in the eyes.*]

MARIA: Jan, we've been married for five years.

JAN: Yes, almost five years.

MARIA [*lowering her eyes*]:   And this will be the first night we spend apart. [*He says nothing and she looks up, gazing earnestly at him.*] I've always loved everything about you, even what I didn't understand, and I know that really I wouldn't wish you to be other than you are. I'm not a very troublesome wife, am I? But here I'm scared of the empty bed you are sending me to, and I'm afraid, too, of your forsaking me.

JAN: Surely you can trust my love better than that?

MARIA: I do trust it. But besides your love there are your dreams—or your duties; they're the same thing. They take you away from me so often, and at those moments it's as if you were having a holiday from me. But I can't take a holiday from you, and tonight [*She presses herself to him, weeping*], this night without you—oh, I shall never be able to bear it!

JAN [*clasping her tightly*]:   But this is childishness, my dear!

MARIA: Of course it's childish. But . . . but we were so happy over there, and it's not my fault if the nights in this country terrify me. I don't want to be alone tonight.

JAN: But do try to understand, my dear; I've a promise to keep, and it's most important.

MARIA: What promise?

JAN: The one I made to myself on the day I understood my mother needed me.

MARIA: You've another promise to keep.

JAN: Yes?

MARIA: The promise you made me on the day you joined your life to mine.

JAN: But surely I can keep both promises. What I'm asking of you is nothing very terrible. Nor is it a mere caprice. Only one evening and one night in which to take my bearings here, get to know better these two women who are dear to me, and to secure their happiness.

MARIA [*shaking her head*]: A separation always means a lot to people who love each other—with the right kind of love.

JAN: But, you romantic little creature, you know quite well I love you with the right kind of love.

MARIA: No, Jan. Men do not know how real love should be. Nothing they have can ever satisfy them. They're always dreaming dreams, building up new duties, going to new countries and new homes. Women are different; they know that life is short and one must make haste to love, to share the same bed, embrace the man one loves, and dread every separation. When one loves one has no time for dreams.

JAN: But, really, dear, aren't you exaggerating? It's such a simple thing I'm doing; trying to get in touch again with my mother, to help her and bring her happiness. As for my dreams and duties, you'll have to take them as they are. Without them I'd be a mere shadow of myself; indeed you'd love me less, were I without them.

MARIA [*turning her back to him abruptly*]: Oh,

I know you can talk me round, you can always find good reasons for anything you want to do. But I refuse to listen, I stop my ears when you start speaking in that special voice I know so well. It's the voice of your loneliness, not of love.

JAN [*standing behind her*]: Let's not talk of that now, Maria. All I'm asking is to be left here by myself, so that I can clear up certain things in my mind. Really it's nothing so very terrible, or extraordinary, my sleeping under the same roof as my mother. God will see to the rest and He knows, too, that in acting thus I'm not forgetting you. Only—no one can be happy in exile or estrangement. One can't remain a stranger all one's life. It is quite true that a man needs happiness, but he also needs to find his true place in the world. And I believe that coming back to my country, making happy those I love, will help me to do this. I don't look any farther.

MARIA: Surely you could do it without all these . . . these complications? No, Jan, I'm afraid you are going the wrong way about it.

JAN: It's the right way, because it's the only way of finding out whether or not I did well to have those dreams.

MARIA: I hope you'll find that you did well. But I have only one dream—of that country where we were happy together; and only one duty—toward you.

JAN [*embracing her*]: Let me have my way, dear. I'll find the things to say that will put everything right.

MARIA [*in an access of emotion*]: Then follow your dream, dear. Nothing matters, if only I keep your love. Usually I can't be unhappy when you hold me in your arms. I bide my time, I wait till you come down from the clouds; and then my hour begins. What makes me so unhappy today is that, though I'm quite sure of your love, I'm no less sure you will not let me stay with you. That's why men's love is so cruel, so heart-rending. They can't prevent themselves from leaving what they value most.

JAN [*holding her face between his hands, and smiling*]: Quite true, my dear. But come now! Look at me! I'm not in any danger, as you seem to fear. I'm carrying out my plan, and I know all will be well. You're entrusting me for just one night to my mother and my sister; there's nothing so alarming about that, is there?

MARIA [*freeing herself*]: Then—good-by! And may my love shield you from harm. [*She goes to the door, and holds out her hands.*] See how poor I am; they're empty! You—you're going forward to adventure. I can only wait.

[*After a momentary hesitation she goes out.* JAN *sits down.* MARTHA *enters.*]

JAN: Good afternoon. I've come about the room.

MARTHA: I know. It's being made ready. But, first, I must enter you in our register.

[*She goes out and comes back with the register.*]

JAN: I must say, your servant is a very queer fellow.

MARTHA: This is the first time we've had any complaint about him. He always carries out his duties quite satisfactorily.

JAN: Oh, I wasn't complaining. I only meant that he seemed a bit of a character. Is he dumb?

MARTHA: It's not that.

JAN: Ah! then he does speak.

MARTHA: As little as possible and only when really necessary.

JAN: Anyhow, he doesn't seem to hear what one says.

MARTHA: It's not so much that he doesn't hear; only

he hears badly. Now I must ask you for your name
and Christian names.

JAN: Hasek, Karl.

MARTHA: Only Karl?

JAN: Yes.

MARTHA: Date and place of birth?

JAN: I'm thirty-eight.

MARTHA: Yes, but where were you born?

JAN [*after a brief hesitation*]: Oh, in . . . in Bohemia.

MARTHA: Profession?

JAN: None.

MARTHA: One has to be very rich, or very poor, to
travel, when one does no work.

JAN [*smiling*]: I'm not very poor and, for several reasons, I'm glad it's so.

MARTHA [*in a different tone*]: You're a Czech, I
suppose?

JAN: Certainly.

MARTHA: Your usual residence?

JAN: In Bohemia.

MARTHA: Have you come from there?

JAN: No, I've come from the south. [*She looks at
him questioningly.*] From across the sea.

MARTHA: Ah, yes. [*A short silence.*] Do you go
there often?

JAN: Fairly often.

MARTHA [*she seems lost in thought for some moments before continuing*]: And where are you
going?

JAN: I've not decided. It will depend on a lot of
things.

MARTHA: Then do you propose to stay here?

JAN: I don't know. It depends on what I find here.

MARTHA: That doesn't matter. Is no one here expecting you?

JAN: No, I couldn't say anyone's expecting me.

MARTHA: You have your identity papers, I suppose?

JAN: Yes, I can show you them.

MARTHA: Don't trouble. I've only got to write down whether you have an identity card or a passport.

JAN [*producing a passport from his pocket*]: I've a passport. Here it is. Will you have a look at it? [*She takes it, but her thoughts are obviously elsewhere. She seems to be weighing it in her palm; then she hands it back.*]

MARTHA: No, keep it. When you're over there, do you live near the sea?

JAN: Yes.

[*She gets up, seems about to put the book away; then, changing her mind, holds it open in front of her.*]

MARTHA [*with sudden harshness*]: Ah, I was forgetting. Have you a family?

JAN: Well, I had one once. But I left them many years ago.

MARTHA: No, I meant, are you married?

JAN: Why do you ask that? I've never had the question put to me in any other hotel.

MARTHA: It's one of the questions on the list given us by the police.

JAN: You surprise me. . . . Yes, I'm married. Didn't you notice my wedding ring?

MARTHA: No, I didn't. It's none of my business to look at your hands; I'm here to fill in your registration form. Your wife's address, please.

JAN: Well, she . . . as a matter of fact, she's stayed behind, in her country.

MARTHA: Ah! Very good. [*Closes the book.*] Shall I bring you a drink now, while your room's being made ready?

JAN: No, thanks. But, if you don't mind, I'll stay here. I hope I won't be in your way.

MARTHA: Why should you be in my way? This is a
public room, for the use of our customers.

JAN: Yes, but someone by himself can be more of a
nuisance than a crowd of people.

MARTHA [*busying herself about the room*]:   Why?
I presume you don't intend to waste my time with
idle chatter. I've no use for people who come here
and try to play the fool—and you should have
guessed that. The people hereabouts have learned it,
anyhow, and you'll very soon see for yourself that
this is a quiet inn, and you'll have all the calm you
want. Hardly anybody comes here.

JAN: That can't be very good for business.

MARTHA: We may lose some, but we make up for it
in peace, and peace is something for which you
can't pay too high a price. And don't forget that
one good customer is better than a roaring trade; so
that's what we are out for—the right kind of visitor.

JAN: But. . . . [*He hesitates.*] Isn't your life here
a bit dull at times? Don't you and your mother find
it very lonely?

MARTHA [*rounding on him angrily*]:   I decline to
answer such questions. You had no business to ask
them, and you should have known it. I can see I'll
have to warn you how things stand. As a guest at
this inn you have the rights and privileges of a
guest, but nothing more. Still, don't be afraid, you
will have every attention you're entitled to. You will
be very well looked after and I shall be greatly surprised if you ever complain of your reception here.
But I fail to see why we should go out of our way
to give you special reasons for satisfaction. That's
why your questions are out of place. It has nothing
to do with you whether or not we feel lonely; just
as you need not trouble yourself whether you cause
us inconvenience or ask too much of us. By all

means stand upon your rights as a guest. But do not go beyond them.

JAN: I beg your pardon. Nothing was further from my intention than to offend you; I only wanted to show my good will. I had a feeling that perhaps we weren't quite so remote from each other as you seem to think; no more than that.

MARTHA: I can see I must repeat what I was saying. There can be no question of offending me or not offending me. Since you seem determined to adopt an attitude that you have no right to adopt, I prefer to make things clear. I can assure you I'm not in the least vexed. Only it is in our interest, yours and mine, that we should keep our distance. If you persist in talking in a manner unbecoming a guest, there's no alternative; we must refuse to have you here. But if you will understand, as I cannot doubt you will, that two women who let you a room in their hotel are under no obligation to treat you as a friend into the bargain, all will go smoothly.

JAN: I quite agree; and it was inexcusable, my giving you an impression that I failed to understand this.

MARTHA: Oh, there's no great harm done. You are not the first who's tried to take that line. But I always made it pretty clear how we felt about such matters, and that settled it.

JAN: Yes, you certainly have made it clear, and I suppose I'd better say no more—for the present.

MARTHA: Not at all. There's nothing to prevent your talking as a guest should talk.

JAN: And how should a guest talk?

MARTHA: Most of our guests talk about all sorts of things: politics, their travels, and so forth. Never about my mother or myself—and that is as it should be. Some of them even talk about their private lives or their jobs. And that, too, is within their rights. After all, one of the services for which we're paid is listening to our customers. But it goes without saying that the charges made for board and lodging don't oblige hotelkeepers to answer personal questions. My mother may do so sometimes, out of indifference; but I make a principle of refusing. Once you've grasped this, we shall not only be on excellent terms, but you'll discover you have many things to tell us, and that sometimes it's quite pleasant to be listened to when one's talking about oneself.

JAN: I'm afraid you won't find me much good at talking about myself. But, really, that won't be necessary. If I stay here only a short time, there will be no point in your getting to know me. And if I make a long stay, you'll have plenty of opportunity of knowing who I am, without my speaking.

MARTHA: I hope you will not bear me any malice for what I've told you. There'd be no reason for it, anyhow. I've always found it better to be quite frank, and I had to stop your talking in a tone that was bound to lead to strained relations. Really, I'm asking nothing out of the way. Until today there was nothing in common between us, and some very special reasons would be needed for our suddenly becoming intimate. And you must forgive me if I fail to see, so far, anything in the least resembling a reason of that kind.

JAN: I'd forgiven you already. Indeed, I quite agree that intimacy isn't come by at a moment's notice; one has to earn it. So, if you now consider that everything's been cleared up between us, I can only say I'm very glad of it.

[*The* MOTHER *enters.*]

THE MOTHER: Good afternoon, sir. Your room is ready now.

JAN: Thanks very much, madame.

[*The* MOTHER *sits down.*]

THE MOTHER [*to* MARTHA]: Have you filled in the form?

MARTHA: Yes, I've done that.

THE MOTHER: May I have a look? You must excuse me, sir, but the police here are very strict. . . . Yes, I see my daughter's not put down whether you've come here on business, or for reasons of health, or as a tourist.

JAN: Well, let's say as a tourist.

THE MOTHER: To see the monastery, no doubt? It's very highly thought of, I'm told.

JAN: Yes, indeed; I've heard a lot about it. Also I wanted to see this place again. It has very pleasant memories for me.

THE MOTHER: Did you ever live here?

JAN: No, but a long time ago I happened to come this way, and I've never forgotten that visit.

THE MOTHER: Still, this is just an ordinary little country town.

JAN: That's so. But I'm much attached to it. In fact, ever since I came here I've been feeling almost at home.

THE MOTHER: Will you be staying long?

JAN: Really, I don't know. I imagine that surprises you, but it's the truth. I don't know. To stay in a place you need to have reasons—friendships, the presence of people you are fond of. Otherwise there'd be no point in staying there rather than elsewhere. And since it's hard to know if one will be made welcome, it's natural for me to be uncertain about my plans.

THE MOTHER: That sounds a little vague, if I may say so.

JAN: I know, but I can't express myself better, I'm afraid.

THE MOTHER: Anyhow, I expect you'll soon have had enough of this place.

JAN: No, I've a faithful heart, and I soon build up
   memories and attachments, if I'm given a chance.

MARTHA [*impatiently*]:   A faithful heart, indeed!
   Hearts count for mighty little here!

JAN [*seeming not to have heard her; to the
   MOTHER*]:   You seem terribly disillusioned. Have
   you been living long in this hotel?

THE MOTHER: For years and years. So many years
   that I have quite forgotten when it began and the
   woman I was then. This girl is my daughter. She's
   kept beside me all through those years, and probably that's why I know she is my daughter. Otherwise I might have forgotten her, too.

MARTHA: Really, mother! You've no reason to tell
   him all that.

THE MOTHER: You're right, Martha.

JAN [*hastily*]:   Please don't say any more. But
   how well I understand your feelings, madame;
   they're what one comes to at the end of a long,
   hard-working life. Yet perhaps it might have been
   quite different if you'd been helped, as every
   woman should be helped, and given the support of
   a man's arm.

THE MOTHER: Oh, once upon a time I had it—but
   there was too much work to do. My husband and I,
   together, could hardly cope with it. We didn't even
   have time to think of each other; I believe I had
   forgotten him even before he died.

JAN: That, too, I can understand. But [*He hesitates
   for a moment.*]—perhaps if a son had been here to
   give you a helping hand, you wouldn't have forgotten *him?*

MARTHA: Mother, you know we've a lot of work to
   do.

THE MOTHER: A son? Oh, I'm too old, too old! Old
   women forget to love even their sons. Hearts wear
   out, sir.

JAN: That's so. But he, I'm sure, doesn't forget.

MARTHA [*standing between them; peremptorily*]: If a son came here, he'd find exactly what an ordinary guest can count on: amiable indifference, no more and no less. All the men we have had here received that, and it satisfied them. They paid for their rooms and were given a key. They didn't talk about their hearts. [*A short silence.*] That simplified our work.

THE MOTHER: Don't talk about that.

JAN [*reflectively*]: Did they stay here long?

MARTHA: Some of them, a very long time. We did all that was needed for them to stay. Those who weren't so well off left after the first night. We didn't do anything for them.

JAN: I've plenty of money and I propose to stay some little time in this hotel—if you're willing to keep me. I forgot to mention that I can pay you in advance.

THE MOTHER: Oh, we never ask people to do that.

MARTHA: If you are rich, so much the better. But no more talk about your heart, please. We can do nothing about that. In fact your way of speaking got so much on my nerves that I very nearly asked you to go. Take your key and make yourself comfortable in your room. But remember you are in a house where the heart isn't catered to. Too many bleak years have passed over this little spot of Central Europe, and they've drained all the warmth out of this house. They have killed any desire for friendliness, and, let me repeat it, you won't find anything in the least like intimacy here. You will get what the few travelers who lodge with us are used to getting and it has nothing to do with sentiment. So take your key and bear this well in mind: we're accepting you as a guest, in our quiet way, for interested

motives, and if we keep you it will be in our quiet
way, for interested motives.

[JAN *takes the key and watches her go out.*]

THE MOTHER: Don't pay too much attention to what
she says. But it's a fact there's some things she
never could bear talking about. [*She starts to rise.
He comes forward to help her.*] Don't trouble, my
son; I'm not a cripple yet. Look at my hands;
they're still quite strong. Strong enough to hold up
a man's legs. [*A short silence. He is gazing at the
key.*] Is it what I just said that you're thinking
about?

JAN: No. I'm sorry, I hardly heard it. But, tell me,
why did you say "my son" just now?

THE MOTHER: Oh, I shouldn't have done that, sir. I
didn't mean to take liberties. It was just . . . a
manner of speaking.

JAN: I understand. Now I'll have a look at my room.

THE MOTHER: Certainly, sir. Our old manservant is
waiting for you in the passage. [*He gazes at her, on
the brink of speaking.*] Is there anything you want?

JAN [*hesitantly*]:   Well . . . no, madame. Except
that I'd like to thank you for your welcome.

[*He goes out. Left to herself, the* MOTHER *sits down
again, lays her hands on the table, and contemplates
them.*]

THE MOTHER: That was a queer thing I did just now,
talking about my hands. Still, if he had really looked
at them, perhaps he'd have guessed what he refused
to understand in Martha's words. But why must
this man be so much bent on dying, and I so little
on killing? If only he'd leave—then I could have
another long night's rest! I'm too old. Too old to
lock my hands again on a man's ankles and feel the
body swaying, swaying, all the way down to the
river. Too old for that last effort when we launch

him into the water. It will leave me gasping for breath, and every muscle aching, with my arms hanging limp, without even the strength to wipe off the drops that splash up when the sleeping body plunges into the eddies. Too old, too old! . . . Well, well, since I must, I must! He is the perfect victim and it's for me to give him the sleep I wanted for my own night. And so . . .

[MARTHA *enters abruptly.*]

MARTHA: There you are, daydreaming again! And yet—we've much to do.

THE MOTHER: I was thinking of that man. No, really I was thinking of myself.

MARTHA: You'd do better to think about tomorrow. What good was it, not looking at that man, if you can't keep your thoughts off him? You said yourself, it's easier to kill what one doesn't know. Do be *sensible*.

THE MOTHER: That was one of your father's favorite words, I remember. But I'd like to feel sure this is the last time we'll have to be . . . sensible. It's odd. When your father used that word it was to drive away the fear of being found out, but when you tell me to be sensible it's only to quench the little spark of goodness that was kindling in my heart.

MARTHA: What you call a spark of goodness is merely sleepiness. But, only postpone your languor till tomorrow, and then you'll be able to take things easy for the rest of your days.

THE MOTHER: You're right, I know. But why should chance have sent us a victim who is so . . . so unsuitable?

MARTHA: Chance doesn't enter into it. But I admit this traveler is really too confiding, his innocence is too much of a good thing. What would the world come to if condemned men started unbosoming their sentimental troubles to the hangman? It's un-

sound in principle. But it aggravates me, too, and
when I'm dealing with him, I'll bring to bear some
of the anger I always feel at the stupidity of men.

THE MOTHER: That, too, is unsound. In the past we
brought neither anger nor pity to our task; only the
indifference it needed. But tonight I am tired, and
you, I see, are angered. Are we really obliged to go
through with it under these conditions, and to over-
ride everything for the sake of a little more money?

MARTHA: Not for money, but for a home beside the
sea, and forgetfulness of this hateful country. You
may be tired of living, but I, too, am tired, tired to
death of these narrow horizons. I feel I couldn't
endure another month here. Both of us are sick of
this inn and everything to do with it. You, who are
old, want no more than to shut your eyes and to
forget. But I can still feel in my heart some of the
absurd desires I had when I was twenty, and I
want to act in such a way as to have done with them
forever—even if, for that, we must go a little
further with the life we want to leave. And really
it's your duty to help me; it was you who brought
me into the world in a land of clouds and mist, instead of a land of sunshine.

THE MOTHER: Martha, I almost wonder if it wouldn't
be better for me to be forgotten, as I've been forgotten by your brother, than to hear you speaking
to me in that tone, the tone of an accuser.

MARTHA: You know well I did not mean to wound
you. [*A short silence; then passionately*] What
could I do without you? What would become of me
if you were far away? I, anyhow, could never,
never forget you, and if at times the strain of this
life we lead makes me fail in the respect I owe you,
I beg you, mother, to forgive me.

THE MOTHER: You are a good daughter, Martha, and
I can well believe that an old woman is sometimes

hard to understand. But, I feel this is the moment to tell you what I've been trying all this time to say: "Not tonight."

MARTHA: What! Are we to wait till tomorrow? You know quite well you've never had such an idea before; and it would never do for him to have time to meet people here. No, we must act while we have him to ourselves.

THE MOTHER: Perhaps. I don't know. But not tonight. Let him be for this one night. It will give us a reprieve. And perhaps it's through him we shall save ourselves.

MARTHA: Save ourselves? Why should we want to do that, and what an absurd thing to say! All you can hope for is to gain by what you do tonight the right to sleep your fill, once it's over.

THE MOTHER: That's what I meant by "saving ourselves." To retain the hope of sleep.

MARTHA: Good! Then I swear it's in our hands to work out our salvation. Mother, we must have done with indecision. Tonight it shall be; or not at all.

C U R T A I N

ACT II

A bedroom at the inn. Dusk is falling. JAN *is gazing out of the window.*

JAN: Maria was right. This evening hour tells on the nerves. [*A short pause.*] I wonder what her thoughts are, what she is up to, in that other hotel bedroom. I picture her huddled up in a chair; she's not crying, but her heart's like ice. Over there the nightfall brought a promise of happiness. But here. . . . [*Looks round the room.*] Nonsense! I've no reason for feeling this uneasiness. When a man starts something, he has no business to look back. It's in this room everything will be settled.

[*A sharp rap on the door.* MARTHA *comes in.*]

MARTHA: I hope I'm not disturbing you. I only wanted to change the towels and fill your jug.

JAN: Oh, I thought it had been done.

MARTHA: No. The old man who works for us sometimes forgets things like that.

JAN: They're only details, anyhow. . . . But I hardly dare to tell you that you're not disturbing me.

MARTHA: Why?

JAN: I'm not sure that's allowed for in our . . . our agreement.

MARTHA: You see! You can't answer like any ordinary person, even when you want to make things easy.

JAN [*smiling*]: Sorry. I shall have to train myself. Only you must give me a little time.

MARTHA [*busy with the room*]: Yes, that's the whole

point. [*He turns and looks out of the window. She studies him. His back is to her. She continues speaking as she works.*] I'm sorry, sir, that this room is not as comfortable as you might wish.

JAN: It's spotlessly clean, and that is something one appreciates. Unless I'm much mistaken, you had it done up not very long ago.

MARTHA: Quite true. But how can you tell that?

JAN: Oh, by some details.

MARTHA: Anyhow, many of our guests grumble because there isn't running water, and I can hardly blame them. Also, there should be a lamp above the bed; for some time we've been meaning to have one installed. It must be rather a nuisance for people who're used to reading in bed to have to get up to switch the light off.

JAN [*turning toward her*]: That's so. I hadn't noticed. Still it's not a very serious drawback.

MARTHA: It's kind of you to take it like that. I am glad the defects of our hotel don't trouble you; in fact you seem to notice them less than we do. I've known people whom they'd have been enough to drive away.

JAN: I hope you'll let me make a remark that goes beyond our pact—and say that you're a very surprising person. One certainly doesn't expect hotel-keepers to go out of their way to point out defects in the accommodation. Really it almost looks as if you wanted to make me leave.

MARTHA: That wasn't quite what I had in mind. [*Coming to a sudden decision.*] But it's a fact that mother and I are rather reluctant to have you here.

JAN: I must say I noticed that you weren't doing much to keep me. Still, I can't imagine why. You have no reason to doubt my solvency, and I hardly think I give the impression of someone with a crime on his conscience.

MARTHA: Certainly not. If you must know, not only
don't you look in the least like a criminal, but you
produce the opposite effect—of complete innocence. Our reasons were quite different from what
you think. We intend to leave this hotel shortly
and we've been meaning every day to close down,
so as to start preparing for the move. That had no
difficulties, as we get so few visitors. But we could
never quite make up our minds. It's your coming
that has made us realize how thoroughly we'd abandoned any idea of going on with the business.

JAN: Am I to understand you definitely want to see
me go?

MARTHA: As I said, we can't decide; I, especially,
can't decide. Actually everything depends on me
and I haven't made up my mind yet, one way or
the other.

JAN: Please remember this; I don't want to be a
burden on you and I shall behave exactly as you
wish. However, I'd like to say that it will suit me
if I can stay here for one or two days. I have some
problems to thrash out before moving on, and I
counted on finding here the peace and quietness I
need.

MARTHA: I quite understand your desire, I assure
you, and, if you like, I'll reconsider the matter.
[A short silence. She takes some steps hesitantly toward the door.] Am I right in thinking you'll go
back to the country from which you've come?

JAN: Yes—if necessary.

MARTHA: It's a pretty country, isn't it?

JAN [looking out of the window]: Yes, a very
pretty country.

MARTHA: Is it true that there are long stretches of
the coast where you never meet a soul?

JAN: Quite true. There's nothing to remind you that
men exist. Sometimes at dawn you find the traces

of birds' feet on the sand. Those are the only signs
of life. And in the evenings . . .

MARTHA [*softly*]: Yes? What are the evenings like?

JAN: Marvelous, indescribable! Yes, it's a lovely
country.

MARTHA [*in a tone she has not used before*]: I've
thought of it, often and often. Travelers have told
me things, and I've read what I could. And often, in
the harsh, bleak spring we have here, I dream of
the sea and the flowers over there. [*After a short
silence, in a low, pensive voice*] And what I picture
makes me blind to everything around me.

[*After gazing at her thoughtfully for some moments,* JAN *sits down facing her.*]

JAN: I can understand that. Spring over there grips
you by the throat and flowers burst into bloom by
thousands, above the white walls. If you roamed
the hills that overlook my town for only an hour
or so, you'd bring back in your clothes a sweet,
honeyed smell of yellow roses.

[MARTHA, *too, sits down.*]

MARTHA: How wonderful that must be! What we
call spring here is one rose and a couple of buds
struggling to keep alive in the monastery garden.
[*Scornfully*] And that's enough to stir the hearts of
the men in this part of the world. Their hearts are
as stingy as that rose tree. A breath of richer air
would wilt them; they have the springtime they
deserve.

JAN: You're not quite fair; you have the autumn,
too.

MARTHA: What's the autumn?

JAN: A second spring when every leaf's a flower.
[*He looks at her keenly.*] Perhaps it's the same
thing with some hearts; perhaps they'd blossom if
you helped them with your patience.

MARTHA: I've no patience for this dreary Europe,

where autumn has the face of spring and the spring
smells of poverty. No, I prefer to picture those
other lands over which summer breaks in flame,
where the winter rains flood the cities, and where
. . . things are what they are. [*A short silence.* JAN
*gazes at her with growing interest. She notices this
and rises abruptly from the chair.*] Why are you
looking at me like that?

JAN: Sorry. But since we seem to have dropped our
convention for the present, I don't see why I
shouldn't tell you. It strikes me that, for the first
time, you've been talking to me with—shall I say?
—some human feeling.

MARTHA [*violently*]: Don't be too sure of that.
And even if I have been, you've no cause for re-
joicing. What you call human feeling is not the
nicest part of me. What is human in me is what I
desire, and to get what I desire, I'd stick at nothing,
I'd sweep away every obstacle on my path.

JAN: I can understand that sort of violence. And I
have no cause to let it frighten me, as I'm not an
obstacle on your path, and I've no motive for opposing your desires.

MARTHA: Certainly you have no reason to oppose
them. But it's equally true you have no reason for
furthering them, and, in some cases, that might
bring things to a head.

JAN: Why be so sure I have no reason for furthering
them?

MARTHA: Common sense tells me that; also my wish
to keep you outside my plans.

JAN: Ah! That means, I take it, that we've returned
to our conventions?

MARTHA: Yes, and we did wrong to depart from
them—you can see that for yourself. Now it remains for me to thank you for having spoken of that
country where you lived, and I must excuse myself

for having, perhaps, wasted your time. [*She is on her way to the door.*] Still, let me tell you, the time was not wholly wasted. Our talk roused desires in me that were beginning to fall asleep. If you're really bent on staying here you've won your case without knowing it. When I entered this room I had almost decided to ask you to leave, but, as you see, you've played on my human feelings; now I hope you'll stay. And so my longing for the sea and sunshine will be the gainer by it.

[*He gazes at her without speaking for a moment.*]

JAN [*thoughtfully*]: You have a very strange way of talking. Still, if I may, and if your mother, too, has no objection, I'll stay on.

MARTHA: My mother's desires are weaker than mine; that's only natural. She doesn't think enough about the sea and those lonely beaches to make her realize you have got to stay. So she hasn't the same motives for wanting to keep you. But, at the same time, she hasn't any really strong motive for opposing me; and that will settle it.

JAN: So, if I've not misunderstood, one of you will let me stay for the sake of money, and the other through indifference.

MARTHA: What more can a traveler expect? But there's truth in what you said.

[*She opens the door.*]

JAN: Well, I suppose I should be glad of that. Still perhaps you'll let me say that everything here strikes me as very strange; the people and their way of speaking. Really this is a queer house.

MARTHA: Perhaps that's only because you are behaving queerly in it.

[*She goes out.*]

JAN [*looking toward the door*]: Maybe she's right. I wonder, though. [*Goes to the bed and sits down.*] Really the one wish that girl has given me is the wish to leave at once, to return to Maria and our happiness together. I've been behaving stupidly. What business have I to be here? . . . No, I have a reason, a good reason; I owe a duty to my mother and sister. I've neglected them too long. It's up to me to do something for them, to atone for my neglect. It's not enough in such cases to declare oneself: "It's I." One has to make oneself loved, as well. [*He rises.*] Yes, this is the room in which all will be decided. A wretchedly cold room, by the way. I can't recognize anything in it. Everything's been changed, and now it might be a bedroom in any one of those commercial hotels where men by themselves stay a night in passing. I've had experience of them, and I always used to think there was something they had to say—something like an answer or a message. Perhaps I shall get the answer here, tonight. [*He looks out of the window.*] Clouding up, I see. It's always like this in a hotel bedroom; the evenings are depressing for a lonely man. I can feel it again, that vague uneasiness I used to feel in the old days—here, in the hollow of my chest—like a raw place that the least movement irritates. . . . And I know what it is. It's fear, fear of the eternal loneliness, fear that there is no answer. And who could there be to answer in a hotel bedroom? [*He has moved to the bell; after some hesitation he puts his finger on the bell push. For a while there is silence; then one hears approaching footsteps, a knock. The door opens. The* OLD MANSERVANT *is standing on the threshold. He neither moves nor speaks.*] It's nothing. Sorry to have disturbed you. I only wanted to see if the bell was working and anyone would answer. [*The old man stares at him, then closes the door. Receding footsteps.*] The bell works, but *he* doesn't speak. That's no answer. [*He looks at the sky.*] The clouds are banking up still. A solid mass of darkness that will burst and fall upon the earth. What should I do? Which is right: Maria or my dreams? [*Two knocks on the door.* MARTHA *enters with a tray.*] What's this?

MARTHA: The tea you ordered.

JAN: But—I didn't order anything.

MARTHA: Oh? The old man must have heard wrong. He often understands badly. Still, as the tea is here, I suppose you'll have it? [*She puts the tray on the table.* JAN *makes a vague gesture.*] It won't go on the bill.

JAN: No, it isn't that. But I'm glad you brought me some tea. Very kind of you.

MARTHA: Please don't mention it. What we do is in our interests.

JAN: I can see you're determined not to leave me any illusions! But frankly I don't see where your interest comes in, in this case.

MARTHA: It does, I assure you. Sometimes a cup of tea's enough to keep our guests here.

[*She goes out.* JAN *picks up the cup, stares at it, puts it down again.*]

JAN: So the prodigal son's feast is continuing. First, a glass of beer—but in exchange for my money; then a cup of tea—because it encourages the visitor to stay on. But I'm to blame, too; I cannot strike the right note. When I'm confronted by that girl's almost brutal frankness, I search in vain for the words that would put things right between us. Of course, her part is simpler; it's easier to find words for a rebuff than those which reconcile. [*He picks up the cup, is silent for some moments, then continues in a low, tense voice*] O God, give me the power to find the right words, or else make me abandon this vain attempt and return to Maria's love. And then give me the strength, once I have chosen, to abide by my choice. [*He raises the cup to his lips.*] The feast of the returning prodigal. The least I can do is to do it honor; and so I shall have played my part until I leave this place. [*He drinks. Loud knocking at the door.*] Who's there?

[*The door opens. The* MOTHER *enters.*]

THE MOTHER: I'm sorry to disturb you, sir, but my daughter tells me she brought you some tea.

JAN: There it is.

THE MOTHER: Have you drunk it?

JAN: Yes. Why do you ask?

THE MOTHER: Excuse me, I've come to fetch the tray.

JAN [*smiling*]:   I'm sorry this cup of tea is causing so much trouble.

THE MOTHER: It isn't quite that. But, as a matter of fact, that tea was not meant for you.

JAN: Ah, there's the explanation. It was brought without my having ordered it.

THE MOTHER [*wearily*]:   Yes, that's it. It would have been better if. . . . Anyhow that hasn't any great importance, whether you've drunk it or not.

JAN [*in a puzzled tone*]:   I'm exceedingly sorry, I assure you, but your daughter insisted on leaving it, and I never imagined. . . .

THE MOTHER: I'm sorry, too. But please don't excuse yourself. It was just a mistake.

[*She puts the cup and saucer on the tray and moves toward the door.*]

JAN: Madame!

THE MOTHER: Yes?

JAN: I must apologize again. I've just come to a decision. I think I'll leave this evening, after dinner. Naturally I'll pay for the room, for the night. [*She gazes at him in silence.*] I quite understand your looking surprised. But please don't imagine you are in any way responsible for my sudden change of plan. I have a great regard for you, a very great regard. But, to be candid, I don't feel at ease here, and I'd rather not stay the night.

THE MOTHER: That's quite all right, sir. Of course you can do exactly as you wish. Still, perhaps you may change your mind between now and dinnertime. Sometimes one yields to a passing impression, but later on things settle themselves and one gets used to new conditions.

JAN: I doubt it, madame. However, I would not like you to believe I am leaving because I'm dissatisfied with you. On the contrary, I am very grateful to you for welcoming me as you have done. For, I must say, I seemed to notice you had a certain . . . friendliness toward me.

THE MOTHER: That was only natural, sir, and I'm sure you understand I had no personal reasons for showing any ill will.

JAN [*with restrained emotion*]: That may be so— I hope so. But, if I told you that, it is because I want us to part on good terms. Later on, perhaps, I'll come back. In fact I'm sure I shall. And then things will certainly go better, and I've no doubt we shall find pleasure in meeting again. But just now I feel that I have made a mistake, I have no business being here. In a word—though this may strike you as an odd way of putting it—I have a feeling that this house isn't for me.

THE MOTHER: I know what you mean, sir. But usually one feels that sort of thing immediately; you have been rather slow, it seems to me, to discover it.

JAN: I agree. But just now I'm rather at sea. I've come to Europe on some urgent business, and it's always a bit disconcerting, returning to a country after years and years of absence. I trust you understand what I mean.

THE MOTHER: Yes, I do understand, and I'd have
   liked things to turn out as you wished. But I think
   that, as far as we're concerned, there's nothing more
   we can do about it.

JAN: So it seems, I admit. Still, really, one never can
   be sure.

THE MOTHER: Anyhow, I think we have done everything needed to have you stay with us.

JAN: Indeed you have, and I've nothing to complain
   of. The truth is that you are the first people I have
   met since my return, so it's natural my first taste of
   the difficulties ahead should come when I'm with
   you. Obviously I alone am to blame for this; I
   haven't found my feet yet.

THE MOTHER: It's often like that in life; one makes a
   bad start, and nobody can do anything about it. In
   a way it's quite true that what has happened vexes
   me as well. But I tell myself that, after all, I've no
   reason to attach importance to it.

JAN: Well, it's something that you share my discom-
   fort and that you try to understand me. I can hardly
   tell you how touched I am by your attitude, and
   how much I appreciate it. [*He stretches his hand toward her.*] Really I . . .

THE MOTHER: Oh, what you call my attitude's quite
   natural, really. It's our duty to make ourselves
   agreeable to our guests.

JAN [*in a disappointed tone*]:   That's so. [*A short
   silence.*] So it comes to this: all I owe you is an
   apology and, if you think fit, some compensation.
   [*He draws his hand over his forehead. He seems exhausted and is speaking less easily.*] You may have
   made preparations, gone to some expense; so it's
   only fair. . . .

THE MOTHER: The only preparations we've made are
   those we always make in such cases. And I can as-

sure you that you owe us no compensation. It was not on our account that I was regretting your indecision, but on yours.

JAN [*leaning against the table*]: Oh, that doesn't matter. The great thing is that we understand each other and I won't leave you with too bad an impression of myself. Personally I shall not forget this house—be sure of that—and I hope that when I return I'll be in a better mood to appreciate it. [*She goes to the door without speaking.*] Madame! [*She turns. He speaks with some difficulty, but ends more easily than he began.*] I'd like. . . . Excuse me, but my journey's tired me. [*Sits on the bed.*] I'd like anyhow to thank you for the tea, and for the welcome you have given me. And I'd also like you to know that I won't leave this house feeling like a stranger.

THE MOTHER: Really, sir, being thanked for something due to a mistake is always embarrassing.

[*She goes out.* JAN *watches her, makes as if to move, but one can see he is feeling limp. Then, leaning his elbow on the pillow, he seems to abandon himself to his growing lethargy.*]

JAN: Yes, I must handle it quite simply, quite straight forwardly. Tomorrow I'll come here with Maria and I shall say "It's I." There's nothing to prevent my making them happy. Maria was right; I can see that now. [*He sighs and leans back on the pillow.*] I don't like the feel of this evening; everything seems so far away. [*He stretches himself full-length on the bed, murmuring almost inaudibly.*] Yes, or no? [*After tossing about a little,* JAN *falls asleep. The room is in almost complete darkness. A long silence. The door opens. The two women enter with a lamp.*]

MARTHA [*after holding the lamp above the sleeping man; in a whisper*]: All's well.

THE MOTHER [*in a low voice at first, but gradually raising it*]:   No, Martha! I dislike having my hand forced like this. I'm being dragged into this act; you began it so that I'd have no chance of drawing back. I don't like your way of riding rough-shod over my reluctance.

MARTHA: It is a way that simplifies everything. If you had given me any clear reason for your reluctance, I'd have been bound to consider it. But as you couldn't make up your mind, it was right for me to help you by taking the first step.

THE MOTHER: I know, of course, that it does not greatly matter; this man or some other, today or some later day, tonight or tomorrow—it had to come to that. None the less, I don't feel pleased about it.

MARTHA: Come, mother! Think of tomorrow in-stead, and let's get busy. Our freedom will begin when this night ends.

[*She unbuttons* JAN's *coat, extracts his wallet, and counts the notes.*]

THE MOTHER: How soundly he's sleeping!

MARTHA: He's sleeping as they all slept. . . . Now let's start.

THE MOTHER: Wait a little, please. Isn't it strange how helpless and defenseless men look when they're asleep?

MARTHA: It's an attitude they assume. They always wake up eventually. . . .

THE MOTHER [*meditatively*]:   No, men aren't quite so remarkable as you seem to think. But of course you, Martha, don't know what I mean.

MARTHA: No, mother, I don't. But I do know that we are wasting time.

THE MOTHER [*with a sort of weary irony*]:   Oh, there's no such hurry. On the contrary, this is the moment we can relax, now that the main thing's done. Why work yourself up like this? Is it really worth while?

MARTHA: Nothing's worth while, the moment one talks about it. It's better to get on with the work in hand and ask no questions of oneself.

THE MOTHER [*calmly*]: Let's sit down, Martha.

MARTHA: Here? Beside him?

THE MOTHER: Certainly. Why not? He has entered on a sleep that will take him far, and it's not likely he will wake up and inquire what we're doing here. As for the rest of the world—it stops short at that closed door. Why shouldn't we enjoy this little breathing space in peace?

MARTHA: You're joking, and it's my turn to tell you I don't appreciate your way of talking.

THE MOTHER: You're wrong. I don't feel in the least like joking. I'm merely showing calmness, while you are letting your nerves run wild. No, Martha, sit down [*She gives a curious laugh*] and look at that man who's even more innocent in sleep than in his talk. He, anyhow, is through with the world. From now on, everything will be easy for him. He will pass from a dreamful sleep into dreamless sleep. And what for others is a cruel wrench will be for him no more than a protracted rest.

MARTHA: Innocence has the sleep that innocence deserves. And this man, anyhow, I had no reason for hating. So I'm glad he is being spared any pain. But I've no reason, either, for looking at him, and I think it a bad idea of yours, staring like that a man whom presently you'll have to carry.

THE MOTHER [*shaking her head; in a low voice*]: When the hour comes we shall carry him. But we still have time in hand and perhaps it won't be such a bad idea—for him at any rate—if we look at him attentively. For it's not too late yet; sleep isn't death. Yes, Martha, look at him. He is living through a

moment when he has no say in his fate; when his
hopes of life are made over to indifferent hands.
Let these hands stay as they are, folded in my lap,
until the dawn, and without his knowing anything,
he'll have entered on a new lease of life. But if they
move toward him and form a hard ring round his
ankles, he will lie in an unremembered grave for
ever.

MARTHA [*rising brusquely*]:   Mother, you're forgetting that all nights end, and we have much to do.
First, we must look through the papers in his pockets
and carry him downstairs. Then we'll have to put
out all the lights and keep watch in the doorway
as long as need be.

THE MOTHER: Yes, there is much for us to do, and
that is where we are in a different case from his;
he, at least, is free now of the burden of his life.
He has done with the anxiety of making decisions,
with thoughts of work that must be done, with
strain and stress. A cross is lifted from his shoulders;
the cross of that inner life which allows of no repose, no weakness, no relaxing. At this moment
he exacts nothing of himself, and old and tired as I
am, I almost think that there lies happiness.

MARTHA: We've no time for wondering where happiness lies. When I have kept watch as long as need
be, there will still be much to do. We shall have to
go down to the river and make sure some drunk
man isn't sleeping on the bank. Then we'll have to
carry him down there as quickly as we can—and
you know the effort that means. We shall have to do
it in several stages and, once we are on the bank,
swing him out as far as possible into midstream. And
let me remind you again that nights don't last for
ever.

THE MOTHER: Yes, all that lies before us, and the mere
thought of it makes me tired, with a tiredness that

has lasted so long that my old blood can't cope with it. And, meanwhile, this man has no suspicion; he is enjoying his repose. If we let him wake he'll have to start life again, and from what I've seen of him, I know he is much like other men and cannot live in peace. Perhaps that is why we must take him there and hand him over to the mercy of the dark water. [*She sighs.*] But it's a sad thing so much effort should be needed to rid a man of his follies and put him in the way of peace.

MARTHA: I can only think, mother, that your wits are wandering. I repeat, we have much to do. Once he's thrown in, we shall have to efface the marks on the riverbank, blur our footsteps on the path, destroy his clothes and baggage—make him vanish from the face of the earth, in fact. Time's passing and soon it will be too late to carry all this out with the composure that it needs. Really I cannot understand what has come over you, to be sitting at that man's bedside and staring at him, though you can hardly see him, and persisting in this absurd, useless talk.

THE MOTHER: Tell me, Martha. Did you know that he meant to leave this evening?

MARTHA: No, I didn't. But if I'd known, it wouldn't have changed anything, once I had made up my mind.

THE MOTHER: He told me that just now, and I didn't know how to answer him.

MARTHA: Ah! So you had a talk with him?

THE MOTHER: Yes, when you said you'd brought his tea, I came here. I'd have stopped him from drinking it, if I had been in time. As it was, once I knew the beginning had been made, I felt we'd better let things take their course; really it hadn't much importance.

MARTHA: If you still feel like that, there's no reason for dawdling here. So please get up from that chair

and help me finish off this business—which is getting on my nerves.

THE MOTHER [*rising*]:   Yes, I suppose I'll end by
helping you. Only you might allow a few minutes
more to an old woman whose blood doesn't flow as
fast as yours. You've been on the rush ever since this
morning, and you expect me to keep pace with
you! Even that man there couldn't manage it; before he had framed the thought of leaving, he'd
drunk the tea you gave him.

MARTHA: If you must know, it was he who made up
my mind for me. You talked me into sharing your
reluctance. But then he started telling me about
those countries where I've always longed to go, and
by working on my feelings hardened my heart
against him. Thus innocence is rewarded.

THE MOTHER: And yet he'd come to understand. He
said he felt that this house was not his home.

MARTHA [*violently and impatiently*]:   Of course it is
not his home. For that matter it is nobody's home.
No one will ever find warmth or comfort or con-
tentment in this house. Had he realized that sooner,
he'd have been spared, and spared us, too. He would
have spared our having to teach him that this room
is made for sleeping in, and this world for dying
in. Come, mother, and for the sake of the God you
sometimes call on, let's have done with it.

[*The* MOTHER *takes a step toward the bed.*]

THE MOTHER: Very well, Martha, we'll begin. But I
have a feeling that tomorrow's dawn will never
come.

CURTAIN

ACT III

The public room. The MOTHER, MARTHA *and the* MAN-
SERVANT *are on the stage. The old man is sweeping and
tidying up the room;* MARTHA, *standing behind the bar,
is drawing back her hair. The* MOTHER *is walking toward the door.*

MARTHA: Well, you see that dawn has come and
we've gotten through the night without mishap.

THE MOTHER: Yes. And tomorrow I'll be thinking it's
a good thing to have done with it. But, just now, all
I feel is that I'm dead tired and my heart's dried up
within me. Ah, it was a hard night indeed!

MARTHA: But this morning is the first for years when
I breathe freely. Never did a killing cost me less.
I almost seem to hear the waves already, and I feel
like crying out for joy.

THE MOTHER: So much the better, Martha. So much
the better. As for me, I feel so old this morning that
I can't share anything with you. But perhaps tomorrow I'll be in a better way.

MARTHA: Yes, and everything will, I hope, be better. But do please stop complaining and give me a
chance of relishing my new-found happiness. I'm
like a young girl again this morning; I feel my blood
flowing warm, and I want to run about and sing!
. . . Oh, mother, may I ask you something? . . .
[*Pauses.*]

THE MOTHER: What's come over you, Martha?
You're like a different person.

MARTHA: Mother. . . . [*Hesitates; then in a rush.*] Tell me, am I still pretty?

THE MOTHER: Yes, I think you're looking really pretty this morning. Some acts seem to have a good effect on you.

MARTHA: Oh, no! Those acts you mean lie on me so lightly. But this morning I feel as if I'd been born again, to a new life; at last I'm going to a country where I shall be happy.

THE MOTHER: No doubt, no doubt. And, once I've got over my tiredness, I, too, shall breathe freely. Even now, it makes up for all those sleepless nights of ours, to know they'll have brought you happiness. But this morning I must rest; all I'm conscious of is that the night has been a hard one.

MARTHA: What does last night matter? Today is a great day. [*To the servant.*] Keep your eyes open when you're sweeping; we dropped some of his papers on the way out and I couldn't stop to pick them up. They're on the floor somewhere. [*The* MOTHER *leaves the room. Sweeping under a table, the old man comes on* JAN's *passport, opens it, runs his eyes over it, and hands it, open, to* MARTHA.] I don't need to see it. Put it with the other things; we'll burn them all together. [*The old man goes on holding the passport to* MARTHA. *She takes it.*] What is it? [*The old man goes out.* MARTHA *reads the passport slowly, without showing any emotion; then calls in a voice that sounds completely calm.*] Mother!

THE MOTHER [*from the next room*]:   What do you want now?

MARTHA: Come here. [*The* MOTHER *returns.* MARTHA *gives her the passport.*] Read!

THE MOTHER: You know quite well my eyes are tired.

MARTHA: Read!

[*The* MOTHER *takes the passport, sits at the table,*

spreads it open, and reads. For a long while she stares at the page in front of her.]

THE MOTHER [*in a toneless voice*]:   Yes, I always knew it would turn out like this one day—and that would be the end. The end of all!

MARTHA [*coming from behind the bar and standing in front of it*]:   Mother!

THE MOTHER: No, Martha, let me have my way; I've lived quite long enough. I have lived many years more than my son. That isn't as it should be. Now I can go and join him at the bottom of the river, where the weeds already have covered up his face.

MARTHA: Mother! Surely you won't leave me alone?

THE MOTHER: You have been a great help to me, Martha, and I am sorry to leave you. If such words have any meaning left for us, I can honestly say you were a good daughter, in your fashion. You have always shown me the respect you owed me. But now I am very weary; my old heart, which seemed indifferent to everything, has learned again today what grief means, and I'm not young enough to come to terms with it. In any case, when a mother is no longer capable of recognizing her own son, it's clear her role on earth is ended.

MARTHA: No. Not if her daughter's happiness remains to be ensured. And, no less than my heart, my hopes are shattered when I hear you speaking in this new, amazing way—you who had taught me to respect nothing.

THE MOTHER [*in the same listless tone*]:   It only proves that in a world where everything can be denied, there are forces undeniable; and on this earth where nothing's sure we have our certainties. [*Bitterly*] And a mother's love for her son is now my certainty.

MARTHA: So you are not sure that a mother can love her daughter?

THE MOTHER: It's not now I'd want to wound you, Martha, but love for a daughter can never be the same thing. It strikes less deep. And how could I now live without my son's love?

MARTHA: A wonderful love—that forgot you utterly for twenty years!

THE MOTHER: Yes, it was a wonderful love that out-lasted twenty years of silence. Say what you will, that love is wonderful enough for me—since I can't live without it. [*She rises from her chair.*]

MARTHA: It's not possible you can talk like that, without any thought for your daughter, without the least stirring of revolt!

THE MOTHER: Hard as it is on you, it *is* possible. I have no thought for anything; still less any feeling of revolt. No doubt this is my punishment, and for all murderers a time comes when, like me, they are dried up within, sterile, with nothing left to live for. That's why society gets rid of them; they're good for nothing.

MARTHA: I can't bear to hear you talking like that, about crime and punishment; it's . . . despicable!

THE MOTHER: I'm not troubling to pick my words; I've ceased to have any preference. But it's true that by one act I have ruined everything. I have lost my freedom and my hell has begun.

MARTHA [*going up to her mother; fiercely*]:   You never spoke like that before. During all these years you've stood beside me, and your hands never flinched from gripping the legs of those who were to die. A lot you thought of hell or freedom in those days! It never occurred to you that you had no right to live, and you went on—doing as you did. What change can your son have brought to that?

THE MOTHER: I went on with it; that's true. But what I lived through then, I lived through by dint of habit, which is not so very different from death.

An experience of grief was enough to change all that, and my son's coming has brought that change. [MARTHA *makes a gesture and seems about to speak.*] Oh, I know, Martha, that doesn't make sense. What has a criminal to do with grief? But I'd have you notice that my grief is not the wild grief that mothers feel; I haven't raised my voice as yet. It's no more than the pain of feeling love rekindle in my heart; and yet it's too much for me. I know that this pain, too, doesn't make sense. [*In a changed tone.*] But then this world we live in doesn't make sense, and I have a right to judge it, since I've tested all it has to offer, from creation to destruction.

[*She walks resolutely toward the door.* MARTHA *slips in front of her and bars the way.*]

MARTHA: No, mother, you shall not leave me. Don't forget that it was I who stayed beside you, and *he* went away. For a whole lifetime I have been with you, and he left you in silence. That must come into the reckoning. That must be paid for. And it's your duty to come back to me.

THE MOTHER [*gently*]: That's true enough, Martha. But he, my son, was killed by me.

[MARTHA *has half turned away and seems to be gazing at the door.*]

MARTHA [*after a short silence, with rising emotion*]: All that life can give a man was given him. He left this country. He came to know far horizons, the sea, free beings. But I stayed here, eating my heart out in the shadows, small and insignificant, buried alive in a gloomy valley in the heart of Europe. Buried alive! No one has ever kissed my mouth and no one, not even you, has seen me naked. Mother, I swear to you, that *must* be paid for. And now, when at last I am to get what's due to me, you cannot, *must* not desert me on the vain pretext that a man is dead. Do try to understand that for a man who has lived his life death is a little thing. We can forget my brother and your son. What has happened to him has no importance; he had nothing more to get from life. But for me it's different, and you are defrauding me of everything, cheating me of the pleasures he enjoyed. Why must that man deprive me of my mother's love as well and drag you down with him into the icy darkness of the river? [*They gaze silently at each other;* MARTHA *lowers her eyes. She speaks now in a very low voice.*] I ask so little, so very little of life. Mother, there are words I never could bring myself to use, but—don't you think it would be soothing if we started our life again just as it used to be, you and I together?

THE MOTHER: Did you recognize him?

MARTHA: No, I didn't. I had not the slightest recollection of what he looked like, and everything happened as it was bound to happen. You said it yourself; this world doesn't make sense. But you weren't altogether wrong in asking me that question. For I know now that if I'd recognized him, it would have made no difference.

THE MOTHER: I prefer to think that isn't true. No soul is wholly criminal, and the wickedest murderers have moments when they lay down their arms.

MARTHA: I have such moments, too. But I would not have lowered my head to a brother whom I did not know and who meant nothing to me.

THE MOTHER: To whom then would you lower your head?

[MARTHA *lowers her head.*]

MARTHA: To you.

[*A short silence.*]

THE MOTHER [*quietly*]: Too late, Martha. I can do nothing more for you. [*Half averting her eyes.*] Oh, why did he keep silence? Silence is fatal. But

speaking is as dangerous; the little he said hurried it
on. [*Turns toward her daughter.*] Are you crying,
Martha? No, you wouldn't know how to cry. Can
you remember the time when I used to kiss you?

MARTHA: No, mother.

THE MOTHER: I understand. It was so long ago, and
I forgot so soon to hold out my arms to you. But I
never ceased loving you. [*She gently thrusts aside*
MARTHA, *who gradually makes way for her.*] I
know it now; now that your brother's coming has
brought to life again that intolerable love which I
now must kill—together with myself.

[*The doorway is free for her to pass.*]

MARTHA [*burying her face in her hands*]: But what,
oh, what can mean more to you than your daughter's grief?

THE MOTHER: Weariness, perhaps . . . and my longing for rest.

[*She goes out.* MARTHA *makes no effort to detain
her. Once her mother has left she runs to the door,
slams it to, and presses herself against it. She breaks
into loud, fierce cries.*]

MARTHA: No, no! What concern of mine was it to
look after my brother? None whatever! And yet
now I'm an outcast in my own home, there is no
place for me to lay my head, my own mother will
have none of me. No, it wasn't my duty to look
after him—oh, the unfairness of it all, the injustice
done to innocence! For he—he now has what he
wanted, while I am left lonely, far from the sea I
longed for. Oh, how I hate him! All my life was
spent waiting for this great wave that was to lift me
up and sweep me far away, and now I know it will
never come again. I am doomed to stay here with all
those other countries, other nations, on my left hand
and my right, before me and behind; all those plains
and mountains that are barriers to the salt winds

blowing from the sea, and whose chatterings and grumblings drown its low, unceasing summons. [*In a lower tone*] There are places to which, far as they may be from the sea, the evening wind brings sometimes a smell of seaweed. It tells of moist seabeaches, loud with the cries of seagulls, or of golden sands bathed in a sunset glow that has no limit. But the sea winds fail long before they reach this place. Never, never shall I have what's due to me. I may press my ear to the earth but I shall not hear the crash of icy breakers, or the measured breathing of a happy sea. I am too far from all I love, and my exile is beyond remedy. I hate him, yes, I hate him for having got what he wanted! My only home is in this gloomy, shut-in country where the sky has no horizons; for my hunger I have nothing but the sour Moravian sloes, for my thirst only the blood that I have shed. That is the price one must pay for a mother's love!

There is no love for me, so let her die. Let every door be shut against me; all I wish is to be left in peace with my anger, my very rightful anger. For I have no intention of rolling my eyes heavenward or pleading for forgiveness before I die. In that southern land, guarded by the sea, to which one can escape, where one can breathe freely, press one's body to another's body, roll in the waves—to that sea-guarded land the gods have no access. But here one's gaze is cramped on every side, everything is planned to make one look up in humble supplication. I hate this narrow world in which we are reduced to gazing up at God.

But I have not been given my rights and I am smarting from the injustice done me; I will not bend my knee. I have been cheated of my place on earth, cast away by my mother, left alone with my crimes, and I shall leave this world without being reconciled. [*A knock at the door.*] Who's there?

MARIA: A traveler.

MARTHA: We're not taking any guests now.

MARIA: But my husband's here. I have come to see him.

[MARIA *enters.*]

MARTHA [*staring at her*]: Your husband. Who's that?

MARIA: He came here yesterday evening and he promised to call for me this morning. I can't understand why he didn't come.

MARTHA: He said his wife was abroad.

MARIA: He had special reasons for that. But we'd arranged to meet this morning.

MARTHA [*who has kept her eyes fixed on* MARIA]: That may be difficult. Your husband's gone.

MARIA: Gone? I don't follow. Didn't he take a room here?

MARTHA: Yes, but he left it during the night.

MARIA: Really, I can't believe that. I know his reasons for wanting to stay in this house. But the way you speak alarms me. Please tell me frankly whatever you have to tell.

MARTHA: I have nothing to tell you, except that your husband is no longer here.

MARIA: I simply cannot understand; he would not have gone away without me. Did he say that he was going for good, or that he'd come back?

MARTHA: He has left us for good.

MARIA: Please listen. I can't bear to be kept in suspense any longer. Since yesterday I've been waiting, waiting, in this strange land, and now my anxiety has brought me to this house. I will not go away before I have seen my husband or been told where I can find him.

MARTHA: Your husband's whereabouts is your concern, not mine.

MARIA: You are wrong. You, too, are concerned in this, and closely. I don't know if my husband will

approve of my telling you this, but I'm sick and
tired of this futile game of make-believe. The man
who came here yesterday is the brother you'd heard
nothing of for years and years.

MARTHA: That's no news to me.

MARIA [*violently*]: Then—what can have happened?
If everything has been cleared up, how is it Jan's
not here? Did you not welcome him home, you and
your mother, and weren't you full of joy at his
return?

MARTHA: My brother is no longer here—because he
is dead.

[MARIA *gives a start and stares at* MARTHA *for some
moments without speaking. Then she takes a step
toward her, smiling.*]

MARIA: Ah, you're joking, of course. Jan's often told
me that when you were little you loved mystifying
people. You and I are almost sisters and—

MARTHA: Don't touch me. Stay where you are.
There is nothing in common between us. [*Pauses.*]
I can assure you I'm not joking; your husband died
last night. So there's no reason for you to stay here
any longer.

MARIA: But you're mad, stark staring mad! People
don't die like that—when one's arranged to meet
them, from one moment to the other, all of a sudden. I can't believe you. Let me see him and then I
may believe what I can't even imagine.

MARTHA: That impossible. He's at the bottom of the
river. [MARIA *stretches her hand toward her.*]
Don't touch me! Stay there. I repeat; he is at the
bottom of the river. My mother and I carried him
to the river last night, after putting him to sleep.
He didn't suffer, but he is dead sure enough, and it
was we, his mother and I, who killed him.

MARIA [*shrinking away*]: It must be I who am mad.
I'm hearing words that have never before been

said on this earth. I knew that no good would come
to me here, but this is sheer craziness and I will not
share in it. At the very moment when your words
strike death into my heart, it seems to me that you
are talking of some other man, not of the man who
shared my nights, and all this is a tale of long ago,
in which my love never had a part.

MARTHA: It's not for me to convince you; only to
tell you the truth. A truth which you will have to
recognize before long.

MARIA [*in a sort of reverie*]:   But why, *why* did you
do it?

MARTHA: What right have you to question me?

MARIA [*passionately*]:   What right? . . . My love
for him.

MARTHA: What does that word mean?

MARIA: It means—it means all that at this moment is
tearing, gnawing at my heart; it means this rush of
frenzy that makes my fingers itch for murder. It
means all my past joys, and this wild, sudden grief
you have brought me. Yes, you crazy woman, if it
wasn't that I've steeled my heart against believing,
you'd learn the meaning of that word, when you
felt my nails scoring your cheeks.

MARTHA: Again, you are using language I cannot
understand. Words like love and joy and grief are
meaningless to me.

MARIA [*making a great effort to speak calmly*]:
Listen, Martha—that's your name, isn't it? Let's
stop this game, if game it is, of cross purposes.
Let's have done with useless words. Tell me quite
clearly what I want to know quite clearly, before I
let myself break down.

MARTHA: Surely I made it clear enough. We did to
your husband last night what we had done to other
travelers before; we killed him and took his money.

MARIA: So his mother and sister were criminals?

MARTHA: Yes. But that's their business, and no one else's.

MARIA [*still controlling herself with an effort*]:   Had you learned he was your brother when you did it?

MARTHA: If you *must* know, there was a misunder-standing. And if you have any experience at all of the world, that won't surprise you.

MARIA [*going toward the table, her hands clenched on her breast; in a low, sad voice*]:   Oh, my God, I knew it! I knew this play acting was bound to end in tragedy and we'd be punished, he and I, for having lent ourselves to it. I felt danger in the very air one breathes in this country. [*She stops in front of the table and goes on speaking, without looking at* MARTHA.] He wanted to make his home-coming a surprise, to get you to recognize him and to bring you happiness. Only at first he couldn't find the words that were needed. And then, while he was groping for the words, he was killed. [*Weeping.*] And you, like two madwomen, blind to the marvel-ous son who had returned to you—for marvelous he was, and you will never know the greatheartedness, the noble soul, of the man you killed last night. . . . He might have been your pride, as he was mine. But, no, you were his enemy—oh, the pity of it!— for else how could you bring yourself to speak so calmly of what should make you rush into the street, screaming out your heart, like a wounded animal?

MARTHA: You have no right to sit in judgment without knowing all. By now my mother's lying with her son, pressed to the sluice-gate, and the current is beginning to gnaw their faces, and buffeting them against the rotting piles. Soon their bodies will be drawn up and buried together in the same earth. But I cannot see what there is even in this to set me screaming with pain. I have a very different idea of the human heart, and, to be frank, your tears revolt me.

MARIA [*swinging round on her fiercely*]: My tears are for the joys I've lost for ever; for a life's happiness stolen from me. And this is better for you than the tearless grief I shall have presently, which could kill you without the flutter of an eyelid.

MARTHA: Do not imagine talk like that affects me; really it would make little difference. For I, too, have seen and heard enough; I, too, have resolved to die. But I shall not join them; why, indeed, would I want their company? I shall leave them to their new-found love, to their dark embraces. Neither you nor I have any part in these; all that is ended and they are unfaithful to us—forever. Luckily I have my bedroom and its roof-beam is strong.

MARIA: What does it matter to me that you die or the whole world falls in ruins, if through you I have lost the man I love, and henceforth I am doomed to live in a dark night of loneliness, where every memory is a torture?

[MARTHA *comes behind her and speaks over her head.*]

MARTHA: Let's not exaggerate. You have lost your husband and I have lost my mother. We are even. But you have only lost him once, after enjoying his love for years and without his having cast you off. My lot is worse. First my mother cast me off, and now she is dead. I have lost her twice.

MARIA: Yes, perhaps I might be tempted to pity you and share my grief with you, if I did not know what was awaiting him, alone in his room last night, when you were plotting his death.

MARTHA [*her voice has a sudden accent of despair*]: I'm even with your husband, too, for I have suffered as he suffered. Like him, I thought I had made my

home sure for always; I thought that crime had
forged a bond between me and my mother that
nothing could ever break. And on whom in all the
world should I rely, if not on the woman who had
killed beside me? I was mistaken. Crime, too, means
solitude, even if a thousand people join together to
commit it. And it is fitting that I should die alone,
after having lived and killed alone. [MARIA *turns
toward her, tears streaming down her cheeks.*
MARIA *moves back, her voice grows hard again.*]
Stop! I told you not to touch me. At the mere
thought that a human hand could lay its warmth on
me before I die; at the mere thought that anything
at all resembling the foul love of men is dogging me
still, I feel the blood pulsing in my temples in a fury
of disgust.

[MARIA *has risen to her feet. The two women now
are face to face, standing very near each other.*]

MARIA: Have no fear. I shall do nothing to prevent
your dying as you wish. For with this hideous pain
that grips my body like a vise, I feel a sort of
blindness falling on my eyes and everything around
me is growing dim. Neither you nor your mother
will ever be more to me than vague, fleeting faces
that came and went in the course of a tragedy which
can never end. For you, Martha, I have no hatred
and no pity. I have lost the power of loving or
hating anybody. [*Suddenly she buries her face in
her hands.*] But then—I have hardly had time to
suffer or to rebel. My calamity was . . . too big
for me.

MARTHA [*who has taken some steps toward the door,
comes back toward* MARIA]:   But still not big
enough; it has left you eyes to weep with. And I
see that something remains for me to do before
leaving you for ever. I have yet to drive you to
despair.

MARIA [*gazing at her, horror-stricken*]: Oh, please leave me alone! Go away, and let me be!

MARTHA: Yes, I am going, and it will be a relief for me, as well. Your love and your tears are odious to me. But before I go to die, I must rid you of the illusion that you are right, that love isn't futile, and that what has happened was an accident. On the contrary, it's now that we are in the normal order of things, and I must convince you of it.

MARIA: What do you mean by that?

MARTHA: That in the normal order of things no one is ever recognized.

MARIA [*distractedly*]: Oh, what do I care? I only know that my heart is torn to shreds, and nothing, nothing matters to it except the man you killed.

MARTHA [*savagely*]: Be silent! I will not have you speak of that man; I loathe him. And he is nothing to you now. He has gone down into the bitter house of eternal exile. The fool! Well, he has got what he wanted; he is with the woman he crossed the sea to find. So all of us are served now, as we should be, in the order of things. But fix this in your mind; neither for him nor for us, neither in life nor in death, is there any peace or homeland. [*With a scornful laugh*] For you'll agree one can hardly call it a home, that place of clotted darkness underground, to which we go from here to feed blind animals.

MARIA [*weeping*]: I can't, oh, no, I can't bear to hear you talk like that. And I know he, too, wouldn't have borne it. It was to find another homeland that he crossed the sea.

MARTHA [*who has walked to the door, swings round on her*]: His folly has received its wages. And soon you will receive yours. [*Laughing as before*] We're cheated, I tell you. Cheated! What do they serve, those blind impulses that surge up in us, the yearnings that rack our souls? Why cry out for the sea, or for love? What futility! Your husband knows now what the answer is: that charnel house where in the end we shall lie huddled together, side by side. [*Vindictively*] A time will come when you, too, know it, and then, could you remember anything, you would recall as a delightful memory this day which seems to you the beginning of the cruelest of exiles. Try to realize that no grief of yours can ever equal the injustice done to man.

And now—before I go, let me give a word of advice; I owe it to you, since I killed your husband. Pray your God to harden you to stone. It's the happiness He has assigned Himself, and the one true happiness. Do as He does, be deaf to all appeals, and turn your heart to stone while there still is time. But if you feel you lack the courage to enter into this hard, blind peace—then come and join us in our common house. Good-by, my sister. As you see, it's all quite simple. You have a choice between the mindless happiness of stones and the slimy bed in which we are awaiting you.

[*She goes out.* MARIA, *who has been listening in horrified amazement, sways, stretching out her arms in front of her.*]

MARIA [*her voice rising to a scream*]: Oh, God, I cannot live in this desert! It is on You that I must call, and I shall find the words to say. [*She sinks on her knees.*] I place myself in your hands. Have pity, turn toward me. Hear me and raise me from the dust, O Heavenly Father! Have pity on those who love each other and are parted.

[*The door opens. The* OLD MANSERVANT *is standing on the threshold.*]

THE OLD MANSERVANT [*in a clear, firm tone*]: What's all this noise? Did you call me?

MARIA [*gazing at him*]: Oh! . . . I don't know. But

help me, help me, for I need help. Be kind and say that you will help me.

THE OLD MANSERVANT [*in the same tone*]:   No.

C U R T A I N

STATE
OF
SIEGE

A PLAY IN THREE PARTS

To JEAN-LOUIS BARRAULT

CHARACTERS IN THE PLAY

THE PLAGUE

THE SECRETARY

NADA

VICTORIA

THE JUDGE

THE JUDGES'S WIFE

THE JUDGE'S DAUGHTER

DIEGO

THE GOVERNOR

THE ALCALDE

WOMEN OF CADIZ

MEN OF CADIZ

AN OFFICER

A HERALD

A FISHERMAN

AN ASTROLOGER

AN ACTOR

A MERCHANT

A PRIEST

A BOATMAN

BEGGARS, GUARDS, TOWN CRIERS

L'ÉTAT DE SIÈGE (STATE OF SIEGE) *was presented for the first time at the* THÉÂTRE MARIGNY, *Paris, on October 27, 1948, by the* COMPAGNIE MADELEINE RENAUD-JEAN-LOUIS BARRAULT, *with incidental music by* ARTHUR HONEGGER.

FIRST PART
PROLOGUE

A musical overture built around a theme recalling the sound of an air-raid siren.

When the curtain rises the stage is in darkness.

The overture ends, but the drone of the siren persists in the background.

Suddenly a comet rises stage-right, then glides slowly across the blackness of the sky toward stage-left, showing up in outline the walls of a Spanish fortified city and the forms of some people standing with their backs to the audience and gazing up at the comet.

A clock strikes four. The dialogue that now begins is barely comprehensible, a muttering of broken phrases.

It's the end of the world.

Don't talk nonsense!

If the world is dying . . .

The world, maybe; not Spain.

Even Spain can die.

On your knees, and pray for mercy!

It's the comet of evil.

Not of Spain; there'll always be a Spain!

[*Two or three people turn their heads. Some shift their positions cautiously. Then all are motionless again, while the buzzing in the air grows louder, shriller, more insistent, and, taken up by the orchestra, acquires the tone of a threatening voice. The comet, too, swells prodigiously. Suddenly a woman screams; at her scream the music stops abruptly and the comet dwindles to its original size. Gasping for breath, the woman rushes away. There is a general movement of the crowd. The ensuing dialogue, pitched slightly higher than before, is easier to follow.*]

It's a sign of war.

That's sure.

It's nothing of the sort!

That depends.

Nonsense! It's only the heat.

The heat of Cadiz.

That's enough!

It's terrifying, the noise it makes.

It's deafening!

It means our city's doomed.

Alas, poor Cadiz! You're doomed!

Quiet! Quiet!

[*They are gazing again at the comet when a voice is clearly heard, that of an* OFFICER *of the Watch.*]

THE OFFICER: Go back home, all of you. You have seen what you have seen, and that's enough. Much to-do for nothing, and nothing will come of it. Cadiz is still Cadiz, after all.

A VOICE: Still, it's a warning. Signs in the heavens are sent to warn us.

A VOICE: O great and terrible God!

A VOICE: There's a war coming—it's a sign of war.

A VOICE: That's all old wives' tales, you dolt! We have too much intelligence nowadays, thank goodness, to believe such superstitious nonsense.

A VOICE: So you say! And that's the way one's sure of running into trouble. Stupid as pigs, that's what you clever folk are. And, don't forget, pigs end up with their throats slit.

THE OFFICER: Go back to your homes. War is our concern, not yours.

NADA: Ah! I only wish it was! But what happens

when there's a war? The officers die in their beds, and it's we who get it in the neck.

A VOICE: That's Nada. Listen to him! Nada the half-wit.

A VOICE: Tell us, Nada. You should know. What does that thing portend?

NADA [*he is a cripple*]: You never like what I have to tell you. You always laugh at me. Why not ask that medical student instead; he's going to be a doctor soon and *he* should know. . . . Me, I talk to my bottle. [*Raises a bottle to his lips.*]

A VOICE: Diego! Tell us what it means.

DIEGO: What does that matter to you? Keep stout hearts and all will be well.

A VOICE: Ask the officer what he thinks about it.

THE OFFICER: The officer thinks you people are committing a breach of the peace.

NADA: The officer is lucky. He does his job and has no use for highfalutin ideas.

DIEGO: Look! It's off again!

A VOICE: O great and terrible God!

[*The buzzing starts again, and the comet crosses the sky as before. Voices in the crowd.*]

Stop!

That's enough!

Poor Cadiz!

Listen! It's sizzling!

It means we're all done for.

Keep quiet, damn you!

[*A clock strikes five. The comet fades out. Day is breaking.*]

NADA [*seated on a milestone, chuckling ironically*]: So there you are! I, Nada, luminary of this city by grace of my superior wit and knowledge, drunkard out of disdain for everything and my loathing for your esteem, flouted by you because I alone have kept intact the freedom that comes of scorn—I,

Nada the prophet, am moved to give you, now that the fireworks are over, a warning, gratis and guaranteed correct. So let me tell you, we are in for it, definitely in for it—and we're going to be in it, up to the neck.

Mind you, we've been in for it quite a while; only it took a drunkard like myself to know that. For what? you ask me. That's for you to guess, my brainy friends. I formed my own opinion long ago, and I've no intention of departing from it. Life and death are one, and man's a faggot for the burning. Yes, you're heading for trouble, take my word for it; that comet was a bad omen, sure enough. A warning to you all.

Ah, you don't believe me? Just as I expected. Provided you eat your three meals, work your eight hours a day, and pay the keep of your two women, you think that all is well and you're in step. And so you are, marching in step like a chaingang, mighty pleased with yourselves, treading the good old beaten track. Only, my worthy friends, don't forget you're marching to calamity. Well, there you have my warning, *my* conscience anyhow is clear. But you need not worry; they are bearing you in mind up there. [*Points to the sky.*] And you know what that means. They're holy terrors.

JUDGE CASADO: That's enough, Nada. I will not permit blasphemy. You have been taking liberties— disgraceful liberties—with the Creator far too long.

NADA: Oh, come now, judge! Did I say anything about the Creator? I heartily approve of all He does. For I, too, am a judge in my own fashion. I've read in books that it's wiser to be hand in glove with Him than to be his victim. What's more, I doubt if God is really to blame. Once men start upsetting the applecart and slaughtering each other, you soon discover that God—though He, too, knows the ropes—is a mere amateur compared with them.

JUDGE CASADO: It's rascals of your sort who bring these celestial warnings. For, mark my words, that comet was a warning. But it was meant for those whose hearts are evil. And who of you can say his heart is pure? Therefore I bid you fear the worst and pray God to pardon your offenses. Down on your knees, then! On your knees! [*All kneel,* NADA *excepted.*] Fear, Nada! Fear and kneel!

NADA: It's no use asking me to kneel. My leg's too stiff. As for fearing—I'm prepared for everything, even the worst, by which I mean your precious piety.

JUDGE CASADO: So you believe in nothing, wretched man?

NADA: In nothing in the world, except wine. And in nothing in heaven.

JUDGE CASADO: O Lord, forgive him, for he knows not what he says, and spare this city of thy children.

NADA: *Ite, missa est.* Diego, stand me a bottle at the Sign of the Comet. And tell me how your love-affair's progressing.

DIEGO: I am engaged to the Judge's daughter, Nada, and I'll ask you to stop insulting her father. You're insulting me as well.

[*Trumpet call. A* HERALD *enters, accompanied by a group of the* Watch.]

THE HERALD: These are the Governor's orders. Let each of you withdraw from hence and return to his work. Good governments are governments under which nothing happens. Thus it is the Governor's will that nothing shall happen here, so that his government may remain benevolent as it has always been. Therefore we apprise you, the townsfolk of Cadiz, that nothing has occurred to justify alarm or discomposure. And accordingly, as from this sixth hour, each of you is ordered to deny that any comet has ever risen on the horizon of our city. All who disregard this order, any citizen who speaks of comets otherwise than as natural phenomena, past or to come, will be punished with the utmost rigor of the law.

[*Trumpet call. The* HERALD *withdraws.*]

NADA: Well, Diego, what do you think of that? Clever, ain't it?

DIEGO: Clever? I'd say ridiculous. Lying is always a fool's game.

NADA: No, it's good administration. What's more I heartily approve of it, since its object is to knock the bottom out of everything. Ah, how lucky we are to have such a Governor! If his budget shows a deficit or his good lady shares her bed with all and sundry, he just writes off the deficit and turns a blind eye to her goings-on. Cuckolds, your wives are faithful; cripples, you can walk; and you, the blind, can see. The hour of truth has struck!

DIEGO: Don't play the bird of ill omen, you old screech owl! For the hour of truth is the hour of the deathblow.

NADA: Exactly. Death to all the world, I say! Ah, if only I could have the whole world before me, tense and quivering like a bull in the arena, his small eyes red with fury and the foam on his pink muzzle like a frill of dirty lace! Old as it is, my arm wouldn't falter, I'd slit the spinal cord with one clean cut, and the huge brute would topple over and fall and fall through the abyss of space and time down to the crack of doom!

DIEGO: You despise too many things, Nada. Save up your scorn; some day you'll need it.

NADA: I need nothing. My scorn will see me through till my last hour. And nothing on this rotten earth

of ours, no king, no comet, no moral code, will ever
get me down.

DIEGO: Steady, Nada. Don't exalt yourself like that
or we shall like you less.

NADA: I am above everything now—I have ceased to
feel the need of anything.

DIEGO: No one is above honor.

NADA: And what, my son, is honor?

DIEGO: It is what holds my head up.

NADA: Honor is merely a natural phenomenon, past
or yet to come. So—cut it out!

DIEGO: Have it your own way, Nada. Anyhow, I
must be off; she's expecting me. That's why I
don't believe in your gloomy prophecies; I'm too
busy being happy. And that's a full-time occupation, which calls for peace and good will everywhere.

NADA: I have told you already, my son, that we are
in it already, up to the neck. So abandon hope, the
comedy is starting. In fact I've only just time
enough to hurry to the market and drink a bottle to
the triumph of death.

[*All lights go out.*]

END OF THE PROLOGUE

*After some moments the lights go up on a scene of
animation. Gestures are brisker, everyone moves to a
faster rhythm. Music. Shopkeepers take down their
shutters, thus clearing the foreground of obstructions,
and the market place comes into view. A* CHORUS,
*composed of the populace and headed by the fisher-
men, gradually fills it. Their voices are exultant.*

CHORUS: Nothing is happening, nothing will happen.
Fresh fish! Fresh fish! It's not disaster threatening,

but summer coming in. [*Shouts of joy.*] No sooner
ends the spring than the golden orange of summer,
launched across the sky to crown the season of the
year, bursts above Spain in a shower of honey,
while all the fruits of all the summers of the world
—butter-yellow melons, luscious grapes, figs oozing
blood, and apricots aflame—pour down in torrents
on our market-stalls. [*Shouts of joy.*] Here ends
their long, swift course in baskets from the countryside where they drank deep of sweetness and the
juices of the soil till they hung drooping over
meadows blue with heat amid innumerable springs
of living water which, drawn through roots and
stems, wound its way to their hearts, in a never-
failing honeyed flow, swelling them out and making
them heavier day by day.

Heavier, ever heavier! So heavy that in the end
they sank through the limpid air, set to trundling
over the lush grass, took ship on rivers or traveled
along roads from the four points of the compass,
acclaimed by joyful shouts and the clarion calls of
summer. [*Brief bugle-calls.*] So now they throng
the cities of men in testimony that the fathering
sky has kept its tryst with fertile mother earth.
[*All join in a shout of triumph.*] No, we have
nothing to fear. Summer has come again, bringing
largess, not disaster. Winter and its hard fare lie far
ahead. Today we have cheeses scented with rosemary, and the gifts of smiling seas—mullets, dories,
fresh sardines, and lobsters. The goats' milk froths
like soapsuds, and on marble slabs the red meat
frilled with crisp white paper and redolent of clover
proffers for men's nourishment blood and sap and
sunlight. Here's to the flower of the year, the cycle
of the seasons ringing their changes! Let's drink
ourselves into oblivion, nothing will happen!
[*Cheering, shouts of joy, trumpet calls, music. At*

the corners of the market place little scenes are enacted.]

FIRST BEGGAR: Give alms, good man! Hey, grandmother, spare a penny!

SECOND BEGGAR: Better now than never!

THIRD BEGGAR: You see what we mean, eh?

FIRST BEGGAR: But of course nothing's happened, needless to say!

SECOND BEGGAR: But perhaps something's going to happen. [*Steals a watch from a passer-by.*]

THIRD BEGGAR: Prove your charity. It's better to be on the safe side.

[*At the fish stalls.*]

THE FISHERMAN: My John Dory's fresh as a daisy. A flower of the sea. What have you got against it, lady?

THE OLD WOMAN: That ain't no John Dory; it's a dogfish!

THE FISHERMAN: A dog-fish indeed! I'll swear no dogfish ever entered my shop—not unless you're one yourself, old witch!

THE OLD WOMAN: Shame on you, young scalawag! Look at my white hair.

THE FISHERMAN: Get out of here, you old comet!
[*Suddenly all stop moving, their fingers to their lips.* VICTORIA *is standing at her window, behind the bars,* DIEGO *facing her.*]

DIEGO: It's been ages since we were together.

VICTORIA: You foolish boy, we were together at eleven this morning.

DIEGO: Yes, but your father was there.

VICTORIA: My father said "Yes." And we were so sure he was going to make difficulties!

DIEGO: It shows how right I was to go and put it straight to him.

VICTORIA: Yes, Diego, you were right. While he was thinking it over I shut my eyes, and I seemed to hear a thudding of hoofs in the distance, coming nearer and nearer, louder and louder, till my whole body was shaken by the thunder of their onrush. But then I heard my father's voice. I heard him say "Yes." It was the first dawn of the world. And in a sort of waking dream I saw love's black horses, still quivering, but tamed forever. Waiting for us. Yes, it was for us that they had come.

DIEGO: I, too, was neither deaf nor blind. But all I heard then was the throbbing of my blood. Swiftly yet serenely joy welled up in my heart. City of light, my city, now you are mine for life—until the hour when the earth folds us in her embrace. Tomorrow we shall ride away together, you and I, on the same saddle.

VICTORIA: Yes—speak our language, even though to others it may sound crazy. Tomorrow you will kiss my mouth. I look at yours, and my cheeks burn. Tell me, is it the south wind?

DIEGO: It is the wind of the south, and it burns me, too. Where is the fountain that will cool its flame? [*Goes up to the windows, and, thrusting his arms between the bars, grips her shoulders.*]

VICTORIA: Ah, it hurts, loving you so much, so fiercely much! Come nearer!

DIEGO: How lovely you are!

VICTORIA: How strong you are, Diego!

DIEGO: With what do you wash your cheeks, to make them white as new-peeled almonds?

VICTORIA: With pure water, but love adds its balm.

DIEGO: Your hair is cool as the night.

VICTORIA: That's because every night I wait for you at my window.

DIEGO: Is it, then, clear water and the night that have given you the fragrance of a lemon tree in flower?

VICTORIA: No, it is the soft wind of your love that has covered me with flowers in a single day.

DIEGO: The flowers will fall.

VICTORIA: But then the fruit will ripen.

DIEGO: Winter will come.

VICTORIA: But winter shared with you. Do you remember that little song you sang me once—what
ages ago it seems! Isn't it true as ever?

DIEGO:

> *When I am lying in the grave* ..
> *And many a century has rolled past,*
> *Were mother earth to ask me,*
> *"Have you forgotten her at last?"*
> *"Not yet," I would reply.*

[*A short silence.*]

But you're silent, dear. What is it?

VICTORIA: I'm too happy to speak. Drowned in happiness!

[*In the* ASTROLOGER'S *booth.*]

THE ASTROLOGER [*to a* WOMAN]:   The sun, dear lady,
was entering the sign of the Balance at the hour of
your birth. This means that you are under the influence of Venus, the sign in the ascendant being
the Bull which, as we all know, is ruled by Venus.
Thus you are naturally affectionate, amiable, and
impulsive. You should be gratified by this conjunction, though I am bound to warn you that the Bull
discountenances marriage and so your charming
qualities well may run to waste. Also I see a conjunction of Venus and Saturn which likewise dis-
favors marriage and children. What's more, this
conjunction augurs queer tastes and may point to
stomach trouble later on. But you needn't feel
alarmed. All that's needed is to be out in the sun as
much as possible. Sunlight not only stimulates the
mind and morals but is also a sovereign cure for
diarrhea. So, my dear young person, be sure to
choose your friends among the bulls, and don't for-

get your disposition is a lucky one, and the coming years have plenty of good things in store for you; in fact, you may look forward to a happy life. . . . My charge is six pesetas. [*Pockets the money.*]

THE WOMAN: I'm much obliged to you, sir. You're quite sure about what you've just been telling me, aren't you?

THE ASTROLOGER: Quite sure, you can depend on me. But there's just one thing I ought to add. Nothing happened this morning, that we're all agreed on. None the less, what has not happened may throw out my horoscope. I'm not responsible for what hasn't happened. [*The* WOMAN *goes away.*] Ladies and gentlemen, let me cast your horoscopes. The past, present, and the future guaranteed by the fixed stars. The *fixed* stars, mind you! [*Aside.*] For if comets take a hand in it, I'll have to look round for another job. I might try for the post of Governor.

A GROUP OF MALE GYPSIES [*speaking together*]: A friend who wishes you well. . . . A dark lady smelling of orange blossom. . . . A holiday in Madrid. . . . A legacy from an uncle in America. . . .

A GYPSY [*by himself*]: After your fair boy friend dies, lady, you'll be getting a dark letter . . .

[*On a mountebanks' makeshift stage in the background, a roll of drums.*]

AN ACTOR: Open your pretty eyes, sweet ladies, and you, my noble lords, lend ear. You have before you the most renowned actors of the whole kingdom of Spain. I have induced them, not without great pains, to leave the Court and come to your market place, where they now will play for your good pleasure that famous one-act piece *The Phantoms* by our immortal bard Pedro de Lariba. I warrant it will take your breath away, good people. Such is the genius of our bard that at its first performance this play was ranked among the greatest masterpieces. And so much did His Majesty the King delight in it that he insisted on having it played before him twice a day, and indeed would be watching it at this very moment, had I not convinced my friends here of the desirability of performing it in this market place and making it known to the public of Cadiz, the most enlightened public of all the Spains.

So step forward, ladies and gentlemen; the show is going to begin.

[*The performance begins as announced, but the actors' voices are drowned by the hubbub of the market.*]

Fresh fruit! Fresh fruit!

Come and see the lobster-girl—half lobster, half woman!

Try out hot sardines! Straight from the frying-pan!

Come and see the king of jail-breakers! No prison bars can hold him.

Laces and wedding trousseaux. Fit for queens.

Buy my tomatoes, lady. They're sweet and tender as your heart.

Painless extractions. Your teeth out in a jiffy, without a twinge. Come to Pedro, the wizard dentist!

NADA [*staggering from the tavern*]: Smash everything! Make a stew of the tomatoes and the lady's heart! Lock up the king of prison-breakers and let's extract the wizard dentist's teeth! Lynch the astrologer, who can't predict what's coming to us! Let's roast the lobster-girl and eat her, and to hell with everything—except what you can drink!

[*A richly clad foreign* MERCHANT *enters the market, followed by a bevy of girls.*]

THE MERCHANT: Come and buy my ribbons, guaranteed the genuine Comet brand.

VOICES IN THE CROWD: Ssh! Ssh! You mustn't use that word.

[*Someone whispers the explanation in his ear.*]

THE MERCHANT: Come and buy my pretty ribbons, guaranteed the genuine—Constellation brand.

[*Customers crowd round him. The* GOVERNOR *and his staff enter the market place and take their stand facing the populace.*]

THE GOVERNOR: Worthy townsfolk, your Governor wishes you good day. He is pleased to see you gathered here as usual and carrying on with the activities that ensure the peace and prosperity of Cadiz. I am glad to see that nothing's changed, for that is as it should be. I like my habits, and change is the one thing I detest.

A MAN IN THE CROWD: No, Governor, nothing has changed; as we poor people can assure you. We live on olives, bread, and onions, and, as usual, haven't a penny in our pockets at the end of the month. As for boiled fowl, we have the consolation that others eat it every Sunday; it never comes *our* way. This morning there was quite a to-do in the town and overhead. There's no denying we were scared. It almost looked as if a change was coming and all of a sudden we would be forced to live on chocolate creams. No wonder we were startled! But thanks to your kindness, Governor, we know now that nothing has happened, and our ears misled us. So, like you, we feel at ease again.

THE GOVERNOR: Your Governor is pleased to hear it. Nothing new is good.

THE ALCALDES: How right the Governor is! Yes, nothing new is good. We, the Alcaldes of Cadiz, possess the wisdom of age and long experience, and we prefer to think the poor of our city were not

indulging in irony when they spoke just now. For
irony is destructive of virtue; a good Governor
prefers constructive vices.

THE GOVERNOR: Meanwhile, let nothing move! I stand
for immobility.

THE DRUNKARDS FROM THE TAVERN [*grouped round*
NADA]: Yes, yes, yes. No, no, no. Let nothing
move, good Governor. Right now everything is
spinning around us, and that's exceedingly un-
pleasant. We, too, would much prefer immobility.
So let all movement cease. Let everything come to a
stop—except wine and folly.

CHORUS: Nothing's changed. Nothing's happening.
Nothing has happened. The seasons wheel sedately
on their axis and, up above, the tranquil stars are
following their appointed courses. Geometry in its
wisdom condemns those mad, erratic stars that burn
the prairies of the sky with their fiery tresses,
disturb the gentle music of the spheres with squeals,
and the eternal laws of gravity with the wind of
their speed; which make the constellations creak on
their hinges and drive stars into collision on the
highways of the firmament. Yes, thank heaven, all
is as it should be, the world has kept its balance.
This is the high noon of the year, the season of
stability. Summer is here; happiness is ours. Nothing
else counts, for we stake all on happiness.

THE ALCALDES: Since the universe has habits, all the
more thanks to our Governor for being the champion of habit. He, too, disapproves of runaway
horses. His realm is trim and tidy everywhere.

CHORUS: We shall behave well, never fear, since
nothing changes or will change. What foolish figures
we should cut with our hair streaming in the wind,
bloodshot eyes, and screaming mouths!

THE DRUNKARDS [*grouped round* NADA]: Damn all
movement, say we! Keep it down and under, and

let's stay put forever. This happy realm will have no history if we let the hours glide by without a jolt. Summer, dear sleepy summer, is the season nearest to our hearts, because it is the hottest—and the thirstiest!

[*The siren theme of the overture, which has been droning in the background for some minutes, suddenly rises to an ear-splitting stridence, and there are two ponderous thuds. One of the actors on the raised platform, while moving to the front and gesturing, staggers and topples over the edge among the crowd, which surges in on the fallen body. Complete silence follows; no one moves or speaks.*

A sudden commotion; DIEGO *is thrusting his way through the crowd, which slowly draws apart, revealing the prostrate man. Two doctors come up, examine the body, then, moving aside, confabulate excitedly.*

A young man accosts one of the doctors, and in pantomime, asks for an explanation; the doctor makes a gesture of refusal. But the young man is persistent, and seconded by the bystanders, presses him to answer, grips his shoulders, shakes him, and finally grapples with him until their faces are quite close, their lips almost touching. A gasp, a quick intake of breath is heard—as though the young man were snatching a word from the doctor's mouth. Then he moves away and after great efforts, as if the word were too big to be got out, ejaculates:
  "Plague!"

Everyone sags at the knees and totters. Meanwhile the word travels from mouth to mouth, louder and louder, faster and faster, while all take to their heels and circle wildly round the dais on which the GOVERNOR *has taken his stand again. The movement quickens, becomes a frantic swirl of agitated bodies: then abruptly all form into groups and remain quite still, while an old* PRIEST *speaks.*]

THE PRIEST: To church, all of you! Know that the
hour of reckoning has come and the ancient doom
has fallen on our city. It is the penalty with which
God has ever visited cities that have grown corrupt;
thus it is He punishes them for their mortal sin.
Your screams will be crushed down within your
lying mouths and a burning seal set on your guilty
hearts. Pray the God of justice to have mercy and
forgive your sins. Get you to the church, and pray.
[*Some hasten to the church. Others keep moving,
like wound-up toys, in circles, while a passing bell
is tolled. Upstage, the* ASTROLOGER *begins speaking
in a matter-of-fact tone, as if he were making a report to the* GOVERNOR.]

THE ASTROLOGER: An ominous conjunction of hostile
planets is taking form in the houses of the sky. It
forbodes famine, drought, and pestilence for all
and sundry. . . .
[*His voice is drowned by the shrill chatter of a
group of* WOMEN.]

THE WOMEN [*speaking in turn*]:   Didn't you see?
There was a huge beast fastened on his throat,
sucking his blood with a noise like a stomach-pump.
It was a spider, a big black spider.
No, it was a little green spider.
No, it was a sea-lizard.
You didn't see properly. It was an octopus, big as
a baby.
Diego! Where's Diego?
There'll be so many dead there won't be enough
living to bury them.
Oh, it's too horrible! If only I could get away!
That's it. For heaven's sake let's go away!

VICTORIA: Diego! Where's Diego?
[*Throughout this scene the sky teems with signs
and wonders, while the siren theme swells and rises,*

adding to the general alarm. A man runs out of a house, screaming: "The end of the world is coming! In forty days the Last Trumpet will sound!" *Another wave of panic sets the crowd gyrating, crying after him*: "The end of the world! The end of the world in forty days!" *While constables of the Watch arrest the prophet, a* SORCERESS *steps forward, crying herbal remedies.*]

THE SORCERESS: Here's mint and sage, here's balm and rosemary, saffron, lemon peel, almond paste. Mark my words, these remedies have never been known to fail. [*A cool wind rises as the sun begins to set; all raise their heads and gaze up at the sky.*] The wind! The wind is rising. No plague can stand up to wind. So the worst is over, take my word for it.

[*But, no sooner has she finished speaking than the wind drops, the wail of the siren rises to its shrillest, and two thuds, somewhat nearer and much louder than before, shake the air. Two men in the crowd fall down. Those near them totter, then begin to back away from the bodies. Only the* SORCERESS *remains, with the two men at her feet; each has the plague marks on his groin and neck. They writhe convulsively, move their arms feebly, and die, while darkness slowly falls on the crowd, which gradually disperses, leaving the corpses lying in the center of the stage.*

Complete darkness.

Lights come on in the church and in the Judge's house, while a spotlight plays on the Governor's palace. The action shifts from one place to another, beginning at the palace.]

AT THE PALACE

FIRST ALCALDE: Your Honor, the epidemic is developing so rapidly that we have no hope of fighting it. The contamination is far more widespread than

people realize; but I venture to suggest it would be
wiser to keep them in ignorance. In any case, it is
the outlying districts that are most affected; these
are congested areas and inhabited by the poorer
classes. Tragic as is the present state of things, this
is something to be thankful for.

[*Murmurs of approval.*]

AT THE CHURCH

THE PRIEST: Approach, and let each one confess in
public the worst thing he has done. Open your
hearts, you who are damned! Tell each other the
evil you have done and thought of doing, or else
the poison of sin will stifle you and will lead you
into hell as surely as the tentacles of the plague.
. . . I accuse myself, for my part, of having often
lacked in charity.

AT THE PALACE

[*Three pantomimed confessions occur during the
following dialogue.*]

THE GOVERNOR: All will be well. The annoying thing
is that I was to go hunting. These things always
happen when one has important business. What
shall I do?

FIRST ALCALDE: Do not by any means miss the hunt
—if only to set an example. The city must see what
a serene brow you can show in adversity.

AT THE CHURCH

THE CONGREGATION: We have left undone those things
which we ought to have done and done those things
which we ought not to have done. But thou, O
Lord, have mercy upon us.

IN THE JUDGE'S HOUSE

THE JUDGE [*surrounded by his family, reading
from the Psalms*]:   "I will say of the Lord, He is
my refuge and my fortress: my God; in him will I
trust. Surely he shall deliver thee from the snare of
the fowler, and from the noisome pestilence."

THE JUDGE'S WIFE: Casado, cannot we go out?

THE JUDGE: No, woman. You have gone out far too much in your life. And that has not brought us happiness.

THE JUDGE'S WIFE: Victoria has not come home, and I can't help fearing that some evil thing has happened to her.

THE JUDGE: You showed no fear of evil where you yourself were concerned. And thus you betrayed your honor. No, you must stay here; this house will be an oasis of calm while the storm rages all around. We shall remain behind locked doors so long as the plague lasts, and if God is willing, we shall escape the worst.

THE JUDGE'S WIFE: You are right, Casado. But we are not alone in the world, others are out in the storm. Victoria may be in danger.

THE JUDGE: Let them be, and think of the household. Of your son, for instance. Get in all the stores you can lay hands on, and never mind the price. The time has come for hoarding. Make your hoard! [*Continues reading*] "He is my refuge and my fortress . . ."

AT THE CHURCH

THE CHOIR [*intoning*]:   "Thou shalt not be afraid for the terror by night; nor for the arrow that flieth by day;

Nor for the pestilence that walketh in darkness; nor for the destruction that wasteth at noonday."

A VOICE: O great and terrible God!

[*The market place is illuminated. People are moving, swaying, to the rhythm of a* copla.]

THE CHOIR:

> *Thou hast signed in the sand,*
> *Thou hast written in the sea:*
> *Nothing endures but misery.*

[*Enter* VICTORIA. *A spotlight plays on the scene that follows.*]

VICTORIA: Diego! Where's Diego?

A WOMAN: Busy with the sick. He's doctoring all who ask his aid.

[*Moving across the stage,* VICTORIA *runs into* DIEGO, *who is wearing the plague-doctors' mask. She swerves aside with a little cry of fear.*]

DIEGO: Do I scare you so much Victoria?

VICTORIA [*joyfully*]:   Oh, it's you Diego! At last I've found you! Take off that ugly mask and clasp me in your arms. Hold me tightly, as tightly as you can, and then I shall feel safe from everything. [*He does not move.*] What is it, darling? Has something changed between us? For hours and hours I've been hunting for you everywhere; I was so horribly afraid you might have caught it. And now I've found you, you are wearing that mask, that ghastly reminder of the disease. Do please take it off and hold me in your arms. [*He takes off the mask.*] When I see your hands, my mouth is parched—kiss me! [*He does not move. She continues in a lower voice.*] Oh, kiss me, Diego; I'm dying of thirst. Have you forgotten that only yesterday we pledged our vows? All night I lay awake, waiting for this day to come, the day when you were going to kiss me with all your might. Please, Diego . . .

DIEGO: I am torn with pity for these poor people, Victoria.

VICTORIA: So am I. But I have pity for us, too. That's why I've been searching for you, calling out your name in all the streets, and stretching my arms out, longing for your embrace. [*Moves closer to him.*]

DIEGO: No, don't touch me!

VICTORIA: Why not?

DIEGO: I feel like another man, a stranger to myself. Never have I been afraid of any human being—but what's happening now is too big for me. Even honor is no help; I'm losing grip of everything I clung to. [*She comes toward him again.*] No, please keep away. For all I know I have the infection already and might pass it on to you. Wait a little, give me time to get my breath; all this horror is stifling me. Why, I've even lost the knack of laying hold of men so as to turn them over on their beds. My hands shake too much and I'm half blinded by my pity. [*Groans and cries in the distance.*] You hear? They're calling for me. I must go to help them. . . . All I ask, Victoria, is that you take great care of yourself—for the sake of both of us. We shall see it through, I'm certain.

VICTORIA: Do not leave me.

DIEGO: All this will end, like a bad dream. It *must!* I am too young, and I love you too much. I loathe the very thought of death.

VICTORIA [*with a quick, impulsive movement toward him*]:   But *I*, Diego—I am living.

DIEGO [*shrinking from her*]:   How shameful, Victoria! The disgrace of it!

VICTORIA: What do you mean? What's there to be ashamed of?

DIEGO: I believe that I'm afraid.

[*Again a sound of groans. He hurries away in their direction. The townsfolk are seen again, moving to the rhythm of a* copla.]

CHORUS:

> *Who is wrong and who is right?*
> *Truth is but surmise.*
> *Death and death alone is sure,*
> *All the rest is lies!*

[*Spotlights on the church and the Governor's palace. Psalms and prayers in the church. From the Palace the* FIRST ALCALDE *harangues the populace.*]

FIRST ALCALDE: These are the Governor's orders. As a sign of penitence regarding the calamity that has befallen us and for the prevention of contagion, all public gatherings and entertainments are forbidden from now on. Also . . .

[*A* WOMAN *in the crowd starts screaming.*]

THE WOMAN: There! Look there! Those people are hiding a corpse. It shouldn't be allowed. We'll all catch the infection. Why don't they go and bury it? [*General confusion. Two men step forward and lead away the* WOMAN.]

THE ALCALDE: I am instructed also to let you know that the Governor has taken the best medical advice and is now in a position to reassure our townsfolk as to the probable course of this epidemic that has broken out so unexpectedly. The doctors agree that all that is needed is for a sea wind to rise, and it will sweep away the plague. So, with God's help . . .

[*Two tremendous thuds cut him short, followed a moment later by two more; meanwhile the death knell tolls incessantly and a sound of prayers issues from the church. Then all sounds cease abruptly, and in a startled hush, all eyes turn toward two approaching figures, strangers to the town, a man and a woman. The* MAN *is fat, bare-headed, and wears a sort of uniform on which hangs a medal. The* WOMAN, *too, is in uniform, with white cuffs and collar. She is carrying a notebook. They walk forward to the palace and salute the* GOVERNOR.]

GOVERNOR: What do you want of me, strangers?

THE MAN [*in a courteous tone*]:   Your post.

VOICES: What's that? What did he say?

GOVERNOR: This pleasantry is ill-timed, my man, and your impertinence may cost you dear. . . . But probably we misunderstood your words. Who are you?

THE MAN: Ah, that you'd never guess!

FIRST ALCALDE: I don't know who you are, stranger, but I do know where you will end up.

THE MAN [*quite calmly*]: You fill me with alarm. . . . [*Turns to his companion.*] What do you think, my dear? Must we really tell them who I am?

THE SECRETARY: Well, as a rule we break it to them more gradually, of course.

THE MAN: Still these gentlemen seem in a great hurry to know.

THE SECRETARY: No doubt they have their reasons. After all, we are visitors here and it's up to us to conform to the customs of the country.

THE MAN: Very true. But mightn't it trouble the minds of these good people, if we declare ourselves?

THE SECRETARY: Better a little trouble than a discourteous act.

THE MAN: Neatly put. Still, I must say I feel scruples. . . .

THE SECRETARY: You have the choice of two alternatives.

THE MAN: I'm listening.

THE SECRETARY: Either you speak out, or you don't. If you do so, they will know at once. If you don't, they will find out later.

THE MAN: Nothing could be clearer.

THE GOVERNOR: That's enough of it! However, before proceeding to extreme measures, I call on you, for the last time, to tell me who you are and what you want.

THE MAN [*still in a matter-of-fact voice*]: I am . . . the Plague—if you really must know.

THE GOVERNOR: What's that you said? The Plague?

THE MAN: Yes, and I must ask you to hand over your post to me. I hate having to rush you like this, please take my word for it; but I shall have a lot to do here. Suppose I give you two hours to transfer your functions to me? Do you think that would be enough?

THE GOVERNOR: This time you have gone too far, and you will be punished for this outrageous conduct. Officers of the Watch!

THE MAN: Wait! I should dislike having to use coercion. Indeed it's a principle with me always to behave in a gentlemanly way. I quite understand that my conduct may surprise you and of course you don't know me—yet. But, quite sincerely, I hope you will transfer your functions to me without forcing me to show of what I am capable. Can't you take my word for it?

THE GOVERNOR: I have no time to waste, and this tomfoolery has lasted long enough. Arrest that man!

THE MAN: I suppose there's no alternative. Still I must say it goes against the grain. My dear, would you proceed to an elimination?
[*He points to an* OFFICER *of the Watch. The* SECRETARY *briskly crosses out an entry on her notebook. A dull thud. The* OFFICER *of the Watch falls. The* SECRETARY *scrutinizes him.*]

THE SECRETARY: All correct, Your Honor. The three marks are there. [*To the others, amiably*] One mark, and you're under suspicion. Two, and you're infected. Three, and the elimination takes effect. Nothing could be simpler.

THE MAN: Ah, I was forgetting to introduce my secretary to you. As a matter of fact, you know her, though perhaps her sex misleads you. And of course one meets so many people, doesn't one . . . ?

THE SECRETARY: Oh, I wouldn't blame them for that; they always recognize me in the end.

THE MAN: A sunny temperament, as you see. Always smiling, punctual, trim, and tidy.

THE SECRETARY: That's nothing to my credit. The work's so much easier when one's surrounded by fresh flowers and smiles.

THE MAN: How true! But let's return to our immediate business. [*To the* GOVERNOR] Have I made it sufficiently clear that you'd do well to take me seriously? You don't reply? Well, I can understand your feelings; I startled you just now. But I can assure you it was most distasteful, having to take that line. I'd have much preferred a friendly arrangement, based on comprehension on both sides and guaranteed by your word and mine—a gentleman's agreement, as they call it. Indeed even now it's not too late for that. Would two hours suffice for the formalities of handing over? [*The* GOVERNOR *shakes his head. The* MAN *turns to his* SECRETARY.] How tiresome all this is!

THE SECRETARY [*tossing her head*]: Yes, obviously he's one of those obstinate men. What a nuisance!

THE MAN [*to the* GOVERNOR]: Still, I particularly want to get your consent. In fact it would run counter to my principles if I took any steps before securing your approval. My charming secretary will proceed to make as many eliminations as are needed to persuade you to co-operate—of your own free will, of course—in the small reforms I have in mind. . . . Are you ready, my dear?

THE SECRETARY: My pencil's blunt. Just give me time to sharpen it and all will be for the best in the best of all possible worlds.

THE MAN [*sighing*]: How I'd loathe my job, if it wasn't for your cheerfulness!

THE SECRETARY [*sharpening her pencil*]: The perfect secretary is sure that everything can always be put right; that there's no muddle in the accounts that can't be straightened up in time, and no missed appointment that can't be made again. No cloud but has a silver lining, as they say. Even war has its advantages and even cemeteries can turn out to be paying propositions if the grants in perpetuity are canceled every ten years or so.

THE MAN: How right you are! Well? Is your pencil sharp enough?

SECRETARY: Yes. Now we can set to work.

THE MAN: Fire away, then!

[*He points to* NADA, *who has just come forward;* NADA *lets out a drunken guffaw.*]

THE SECRETARY: Might I point out, sir, that this fellow is the sort that doesn't believe in anything, in other words the sort of man who can be very useful to us?

THE MAN: Very true. In that case let's choose one of the Alcaldes.

THE GOVERNER: Stop! [*Panic among the* ALCALDES.]

THE SECRETARY: Ah! A good sign, Your Honor!

THE MAN [*courteously*]: Can I do anything to oblige you, Governor?

THE GOVERNOR: Suppose I let you take my place, will the lives of my family and the Alcaldes be spared?

THE MAN: Why, of course. That, as you should know, is customary.

[*The* GOVERNOR *confers with the* ALCALDES, *then turns to the populace.*]

THE GOVERNOR: Citizens of Cadiz, I feel sure you understand that a great change has come into our civic life. In your own interests it may be best that I should entrust the city to this new authority that has sprung up in our midst. Indeed I have no doubt that by coming to an arrangement with this gentleman I shall be sparing you the worst; and, more-

over, you will have the satisfaction of knowing that
a government exists outside your walls which may
be of service to you in the future. Need I tell you
that, in speaking thus, I am not thinking of my
personal safety, but . . .

THE MAN: Excuse my interrupting. But I should be
grateful if you would make a public declaration
that you are entering into this excellent arrangement of your own free will, and that there is no
question of any sort of compulsion.

[*The* GOVERNOR *looks at the* MAN; *the* SECRETARY
raises her pencil to her lips.]

THE GOVERNOR [*obviously flustered*]: Yes, yes, that's
understood, of course. I am making this agreement of my own free will. [*Edges away, then
frankly takes to his heels. A general move begins.*]

THE MAN [*to the* FIRST ALCALDE]: Be good enough
to stay. I need someone who has the confidence
of the citizens and will act as my mouthpiece for
making known my wishes. [*The* FIRST ALCALDE
hesitates.] You agree, I take it? [*To the* SECRE-
TARY] My dear . . .

FIRST ALCALDE: But of course I agree, and I feel it
a great honor. . . .

THE MAN: Excellent. Now that's settled, will you
be kind enough, my dear, to make known to the
Alcalde the rules and regulations he is to promulgate to these good people, so that they may start
living under state control.

THE SECRETARY: Regulation Number One, drawn
up and promulgated by the First Alcalde and his
Committee.

FIRST ALCALDE: But I haven't drawn up anything yet!

THE SECRETARY: We're saving you the trouble. And
it seems to me you should feel flattered at the
trouble our department is taking to frame these
regulations that you will have the honor of signing.

FIRST ALCALDE: Quite so. All the same . . .

THE SECRETARY: This regulation shall carry the force of an edict issued and validated in pursuance of the will of our beloved sovereign, for the control and charitable succor of all citizens infected with disease, and for the issuance of by-laws and the guidance of all personnel appointed under the said edict, such as overseers, attendants, guards, and gravediggers, who will be bound by oath strictly and punctually to carry out all such orders as may be given them.

FIRST ALCALDE: Might I know the point of all this rigmarole?

THE SECRETARY: It's intended to get them used to that touch of obscurity which gives all government regulations their peculiar charm and efficacy. The less these people understand, the better they'll behave. You get my point? Good. Here are the regulations that I'll ask you to have proclaimed by the town criers in every district, so that they may be mentally digested by your townsfolk, even by those whose mental digestions are most sluggish. Ah, here they come, the town criers. Their pleasant appearance will help to fix the memory of what they say in the minds of their hearers.

[*The town criers line up.*]

VOICES IN THE CROWD: The Governor's going away! The Governor's leaving us!

NADA: And he has every right to do so, remember that, good people. He is the government and governments must be protected.

VOICES IN THE CROWD: He *was* the government, and now he's nothing! The Plague has stepped into his shoes.

NADA: What can that matter to you? Plague or Governor, the government goes on.

FIRST TOWN CRIER: All infected houses are to be marked on their front doors with the plague sign—

a black star with rays a foot long, and headed by this inscription: "We all are brothers." The star is to remain in place until the house is reopened. Any breach of this regulation will be punished with the utmost rigor of the law. [*Withdraws.*]

A VOICE: What law?

ANOTHER VOICE: The new one, of course.

CHORUS: Our masters used to say they would protect us, but now we are forsaken. Hideous fogs are gathering at the four corners of the town, swamping the fragrance of the fruit and the roses, tarnishing the luster of the season, deadening the joys of summer. Alas, poor Cadiz, city of the sea! Only yesterday the south wind, desert-born and wafting to us perfumes of the gardens of Africa, was sweeping across the Straits, breathing its warm languors into our maidens' hearts. But now the wind has dropped, and nothing else could purify our city. Our masters used to assure us that nothing would ever happen, but that man was right; something *is* happening and we are in the thick of it, we must escape while there yet is time, before the gates are closed on our calamity.

SECOND TOWN CRIER: As from today all essential foodstuffs must be placed at the disposal of the community—that is to say, they will be doled out in equal and exiguous shares to all who can prove their adhesion to the new social order.

[*The First Gate closes.*]

THIRD TOWN CRIER: All lights must be extinguished at nine p.m. and no one is permitted to remain in any public place after that hour, or to leave his home without an official permit in due form, which will be accorded only in very special cases and at our good pleasure. Any breach of this regulation will be punished with the utmost rigor of the law.

VOICES [*crescendo*]: They are going to close the gates. The gates are closed.

No, some are open still.

CHORUS: Ah, let us make haste to those that still are open. We are the sons of the sea. Away, away! The sea is calling us to happy places without walls or gates, to shores whose virgin sands are cool as maidens' lips, and where our eyes grow dazzled gazing seaward. Let us go forth to meet the wind. Away! Away to the sea! To the untrammeled waves, to clean, bright water, the shining winds of freedom!

VOICES: To the sea! To the sea!

FOURTH TOWN CRIER: It is strictly forbidden to give help to any person stricken with the disease, except by reporting the case to the authorities, who then will take the necessary steps. A favorable view is taken of reports made by any member of a family as regards any other member or members of the said family, and such reports will entitle their makers to the double food ration, known as the Good Citizenship Ration.

[*The Second Gate closes.*]

CHORUS: The sea, the sea! The sea will save us. What cares the sea for wars and pestilences? Governments come and go, but the sea endures; how many governments has it engulfed! And how simple are its gifts! Red mornings and green sunsets, and from dusk to dawn the murmur of innumerable waves under the dome of night fretted with myriads of stars.

O vast sea-spaces, shining solitude, baptism of brine! Ah, to be alone beside the sea, facing the blue expanse, fanned by the wind and free at last of this city sealed like a tomb, and these all-too-human faces clamped by fear! Away! Away! Who will deliver me from man and the terrors that infest him? How happy I was but a little while ago at the summit of the year, taking my ease among the fruits; when nature was kind and smiled on me. I loved the world, Spain and I were at one. But no longer can I hear the sound of the waves. All around are panic, insults, cowardice; my brothers are sodden with fear and sweat, and my arms are too weak to succor them. Who will give back to me the waters of forgetting, the slumbrous smoothness of the open sea, its liquid pathways, long furrows that form and fold upon themselves? To the sea! To the sea, before the gates are shut!

A VOICE: Take care! Keep clear of that man who was just beside the corpse.

A VOICE: Yes, he has the marks.

A VOICE: Keep away! Don't come near me!

[*They drive the man away with blows. The Third Gate closes.*]

A VOICE: O great and terrible God!

A VOICE: Quick! Get what's needed, the mattress and the bird cage. Oh, and don't forget the dog's collar. And the pot of mint as well. We can munch it on our way to the sea.

A VOICE: Stop thief! He's stolen our damask tablecloth, the one we used at my wedding.

[*The man is pursued, caught, belabored. The Fourth Gate closes.*]

A VOICE: Be careful, don't let people see our food.

A VOICE: I haven't anything to eat on the way; spare me a loaf of bread, brother. I'll give you my guitar, the one with the mother-of-pearl studs.

A VOICE: This bread is for my children, not for those who call themselves my brothers when they want something off me!

A VOICE: Just one loaf! I'll give all the money in my pocket for a loaf of bread, just one!

[*The Fifth Gate closes.*]

CHORUS: Quick! Only one gate is left. The Plague moves faster than we. He hates the sea and wants to cut us off from it. Out there the nights are calm, stars glide above the masthead, mirrored in the blue. What's the Plague after in this city? He wants to keep us in his clutches, for he loves us in his fashion. He wants us to be happy, not in the way we like, but in the way that he approves of. Penitential pleasures, cold comfort, convict happiness. Everything is turning hard and dry, no longer do we feel the cool kiss of the wind upon our lips.

A VOICE: Do not leave me, priest; I am one of the poor men of your flock. [*The* PRIEST *begins to walk away.*] Look! He's going. . . . No, stand by me, it's your duty to look after me, and if I lose you, then I've lost all. [*The* PRIEST *quickens his steps. The poor man falls to the ground with a great cry.*] Christians of Spain, you are forsaken!

FIFTH TOWN CRIER [*emphasizing each word*]:   Lastly, and this will be the summing-up. [*Standing in front of the* FIRST ALCALDE, *the* PLAGUE *and the* SECRETARY *exchange smiles and looks of self-satisfaction.*] So as to avoid contagion through the air you breathe and since words are carriers of infection, each of you is ordered to keep permanently in his mouth a pad soaked in vinegar. This will not only protect you from the disease but teach you discretion and the art of silence.

[*From now on everyone has a handkerchief in his mouth and the number of voices steadily diminishes, as does the volume of the background music. Beginning with several voices, the* CHORUS *ends with that of a single speaker, and finally there is a pantomime, during which the lips of all are puffed out and firmly closed. The Last Gate is slammed to.*]

CHORUS: Alas! Alas! The last gate is shut and we are

locked up together, we and the Plague. We can
hear nothing any more and henceforth the sea is out
of reach. Sorrow is our companion, we can only turn
in dreary circles within this beleaguered city, cut off
from the sounds of leaves and waters, prisoned behind tall, smooth gates. So now, beset with howling
crowds, Cadiz will become a huge, red-and-black
arena in which ritual murders are to be enacted.
Brothers, our plight is surely greater than our sin;
we did not deserve this imprisonment. True, our
hearts were not innocent, still we greatly loved the
world of nature and its summers—surely that might
have saved us from this doom. The winds have
failed, the sky is empty, for a long while we shall
be silent. But for the last time, the last, before fear
gags our mouths for many a long day, let us lift
our voices in the desert.

[*Groans, then silence. All the instruments in the orchestra have ceased playing, except the bells. The
buzzing of the comet starts again, very softly. The
PLAGUE and the SECRETARY are seen in the Governor's palace. The SECRETARY steps forward, crossing
out a name at every step, while the percussion
instruments in the orchestra punctuate each gesture
that she makes. The death-cart creaks by. NADA
grins.*

*The PLAGUE has taken his stand on the highest
point of the palace and makes a sign. All sounds
and movement cease.*]

THE PLAGUE: I am the ruler here; this is a fact,
therefore it is a right. A right that admits of no discussion; a fact you must accept.

In any case, make no mistake; when I say I rule
you, I rule in a rather special way—it would be
more correct to say I function. You Spaniards always have a tendency to be romantic, and I'm sure
you'd like to see me as a sort of black king or some

monstrous, gaudy insect. That would satisfy your
dramatic instincts, of which we've heard so much.
Well, they won't be satisfied this time. I don't wield
a scepter or anything like that; in fact I prefer to
look like a quite ordinary person, let's say a sergeant
or a corporal. That's one of my ways of vexing you,
and being vexed will do you good; you still have
much to learn. So now your king has black nails
and a drab uniform. He doesn't sit on a throne,
but in an office chair. His palace is a barracks and
his hunting-lodge a courthouse. You are living in a
stage of siege.

That is why when I step in all sentiment goes by
the board. So take good notice, sentiment is banned,
and so are other imbecilities, such as the fuss you
make about your precious happiness, the maudlin
look on lovers' faces, your selfish habit of contem-
plating landscapes, and the crime of irony. Instead
of these I give you organization. That will worry
you a bit to start with, but very soon you'll realize
that good organization is better than cheap emotion.
By way of illustration of this excellent precept I
shall begin by segregating the men from the women.
This order will have the force of law. [*The Guards
promptly carry out the order.*]

Your monkey-tricks have had their day; the time
has come for realizing that life is earnest.

I take it you have grasped my meaning. As from
today you are going to learn to die in an orderly
manner. Until now you died in the Spanish manner,
haphazard—when you felt like it, so to say. You
died because the weather suddenly turned cold, or
a mule stumbled; because the skyline of the Pyre-
nees was blue and the river Guadalquivir has a
fascination for the lonely man in springtime. Or
else it was because there are always brawling fools
ready to kill for money or for honor—when it's

so much more elegant to kill for the delight of being logical. Yes, you muffed your deaths. A dead
man here, a dead man there, one in his bed, another
in the bull ring—what could be more slovenly?
But, happily for you, I shall impose order on all
that. There will be no more dying as the fancy
takes you. Lists will be kept up—what admirable
things lists are!—and we shall fix the order of your
going. Fate has learned wisdom and will keep its
records. You will figure in statistics, so at last you'll
serve some purpose. For, I was forgetting to tell
you, you will die, that goes without saying, but
then—if not before—you will be packed off to the
incinerator. Nothing could be more hygienic and
efficient, and it fits in with our program. Spain first!

So line up for a decent death, that's your first
duty. On these terms you will enjoy my favor. But
take care that you don't indulge in nonsensical ideas,
or righteous indignation, or in any of those little
gusts of petulance which lead to big revolts. I have
suppressed these mental luxuries and put logic in
their stead, for I can't bear untidiness and irrational-
ity. So from this day on you are going to be rational
and tidy; the wearing of badges will be compulsory.
Besides the mark on your groins you will have the
plague star under your armpits, for all to see—meaning that you are marked down for elimination. So
the others, people who think these marks are no
concern of theirs and line up cheerfully for the
bullfight every Sunday, will treat you as suspects
and edge away from you. But you need not feel
aggrieved; these marks concern them also, they're
all down on our lists and nobody is overlooked. In
fact all are suspects—that's the long and the short
of it.

Don't take all this to mean I haven't any feelings.
As a matter of fact I like birds, the first violets of

the year, the cool lips of girls. Once in a while it's
refreshing, that sort of thing. Also, I'm an idealist.
My heart. . . . No, I fear I am getting sentimental
—that's enough for today. Just a word more, by
way of summing up. I bring you order, silence,
total justice. I don't ask you to thank me for this;
it's only natural, what I am doing here for you.
Only, I must insist on your collaboration. My administration has begun.

C U R T A I N

SECOND PART

*A public square in Cadiz. Stage-left: the cemetery en-
trance and keeper's office; stage-right: a wharf, near
which is the Judge's residence.*

*When the curtain rises gravediggers in convict uni-
form are collecting dead bodies. The creaking of the
death-cart is heard off stage; presently it comes into
view and halts in the center of the stage. The convicts
load the bodies onto it; then it creaks off toward the
cemetery. As it halts at the entrance a military band
starts playing and one wall of the cemetery office slides
open, enabling the audience to see the interior: a large,
roofed-in vestibule resembling the covered playground
of a school. The SECRETARY is sitting there, presiding,
while at a lower level are aligned some tables like those
in food offices where ration cards are distributed. At
one of the tables the white-mustached FIRST ALCALDE is
seated with some other members of the staff. On the
other side of the stage Plague Guards are rounding up
the crowd and herding them toward the food office,
men and women being kept apart.*

*A light plays on the center and the PLAGUE is seen
on the summit of his palace, directing a gang of workers for the most part concealed from view, though we
have occasional glimpses of their activities on the out-
skirts.*

THE PLAGUE: Now then! Don't dawdle! It's really
scandalous how slowly things move in this town, I
never saw such a pack of idlers. Leisure is what
you like, that's evident. Well, I don't stand for

inactivity—except in barracks and in bread lines. That sort of leisure suits my book; it drains the energy from heart and limbs, and serves no purpose. Get a move on! Finish building my observation tower, and put a hedge of barbed wire around the town. Everyone has the spring flowers he prefers; mine are iron roses. Stoke up the death-ovens, they're our stand-bys. Guards, affix our stars to the houses where I'm going to get busy. And you, my dear, start compiling our lists and drawing up our certificates of existence. [*Exit the* PLAGUE.]

THE FISHERMAN [*acting as spokesman*]: A certificate of existence, he said? What's the big idea?

THE SECRETARY: What's the idea, you say? Why, how could you live without a certificate of existence?

THE FISHERMAN: We used to get along quite well without one.

THE SECRETARY: That's because you weren't governed. Now you are. And the whole point of our government is that you always need a permit to do anything whatever. You can dispense with bread and with a wife, but a properly drawn-up certificate, no matter what it says, is something you can't possibly dispense with.

THE FISHERMAN: For three generations we've been fishing folk in my family, we have lived by casting our nets into the sea, and we have always given satisfaction to our customers—and there never was no question of a certificate, that's the gospel truth, young lady.

A VOICE: For years and years, from father to son, we have been butchers, and we never needed a certificate for slaughtering sheep.

THE SECRETARY: You were living in a state of anarchy, that's all. Mind you, we have nothing against slaughterhouses—quite the contrary. Only, we apply to them the latest methods of accounting, we've brought them up to date, in short. There was some mention of casting nets just now; well, you'll discover that we, too, are experts in that line.

Now, Mr. First Alcalde, have you the forms ready?

FIRST ALCALDE: Quite ready.

THE SECRETARY: Officers, will you help the gentleman to come forward.

[*The* FISHERMAN *is led up to the table.*]

FIRST ALCALDE [*reading*]:   Family name, Christian names, occupation?

THE SECRETARY: Let that be. He can fill in the blanks himself.

FIRST ALCALDE: Your *curriculum vitæ?*

THE FISHERMAN: My what? I didn't catch it.

THE SECRETARY: You are to record on the dotted line the chief events of your life. It's our way of becoming acquainted with you.

THE FISHERMAN: My life's my private concern, and nobody else's business.

THE SECRETARY: Your private concern, you say? Those words don't mean anything to us. What interests us is your public life, and that as a matter of fact is the only life you are allowed by us to have. Well, Mr. Alcalde, let's get down to details.

FIRST ALCALDE: Married?

THE FISHERMAN: Yes. I married in '31.

FIRST ALCALDE: Your reasons for the marriage?

THE FISHERMAN: Reasons indeed! God! It's enough to make one's blood boil.

THE SECRETARY: It's in the rules. And it's an excellent way of making public what has got to cease being private.

THE FISHERMAN: Well, if you *must* know, I got married because that's a thing one usually does when one's a man.

FIRST ALCALDE: Divorced?

THE FISHERMAN: No, a widower.

FIRST ALCALDE: Remarried?

THE FISHERMAN: No.

THE SECRETARY: Why not?

THE FISHERMAN [*furiously*]:   Damn it, I loved my wife!

THE SECRETARY: How quaint! May we know why?

THE FISHERMAN: Can one account for everything one does?

THE SECRETARY: Yes, in a well-organized community.

THE ALCALDE: Your record?

THE FISHERMAN: Meaning what?

THE SECRETARY: Have you been convicted of robbery, perjury, or rape?

THE FISHERMAN: Certainly not.

THE SECRETARY: An upright man—I suspected as much. Mr. First Alcalde, please add a footnote: "To be watched."

FIRST ALCALDE: Civic feelings?

THE FISHERMAN: I've always dealt fairly by my fellow citizens, if that's what you mean. What's more, I never let a poor man leave my fish-stall empty-handed.

THE SECRETARY: That's not a proper answer to the question.

FIRST ALCALDE: Oh, that anyhow I can explain. What we call civic feelings, needless to say, are in my line. We want to know, my good fellow, if you are one of those who respect the existing order for the sole reason that it exists.

THE FISHERMAN: Certainly, if it's just and reasonable.

THE SECRETARY: Doubtful. Write that his civic feelings are doubtful. And now read the last question.

FIRST ALCALDE [*deciphering the words with difficulty*]:   Reasons for existing?

THE FISHERMAN: Well, let my mother be bitten at the place where it hurts most, if I can understand a word of this rigmarole!

THE SECRETARY: It's quite simple, surely. You must state your reasons for being alive.

THE FISHERMAN: My reasons for being alive! But what the devil do you expect me to say?

THE SECRETARY: Aha! Make a note, Mr. First Alcalde, that the undersigned admits that his existence is unjustifiable. That will simplify matters when the time comes for us to deal with him. Also, that will bring it home to you, the undersigned, that the certificate of existence granted you is temporary and of short duration.

THE FISHERMAN: Temporary or not, let me have it. They're waiting for me at home and I want to get away.

THE SECRETARY: By all means. Only you must begin by submitting to us a certificate of health. You can procure this, after complying with some formalities, on the first floor, Department of Current Affairs, Bureau of Pending Cases, Auxiliary Division. [*The* FISHERMAN *goes away. Meanwhile the death-cart has reached the cemetery gate and is being unloaded. Suddenly* NADA *jumps down from the cart, staggering and bawling.*]

NADA: But, damn it all, I tell you I'm not dead! [*They try to replace him on the cart, but he breaks loose and runs into the food office.*] Did you ever hear the like! Telling me I'm dead when I'm alive and kicking! Oh, pardon . . . !

THE SECRETARY: Don't mention it. Come.

NADA: They loaded me onto the cart. But I wasn't dead—only dead drunk. It's my way of suppressing.

THE SECRETARY: Suppressing what?

NADA: Why, everything, my dear young lady. The more one suppresses, the better things are. Ah, if only one could suppress everything and everyone, wouldn't it be fine! Lovers, for instance—there's nothing I loathe more. When I see a loving couple in front of me I spit at them. On their backs, of course; some of them might turn nasty. And children, filthy little brats! And flowers that goggle at you like half-wits, and rivers that have only one idea. So let's annihilate everything, I say. That's my philosophy. God denies the world, and I deny God. Long live nothing, for it's the only thing that exists.

THE SECRETARY: And how do you propose to suppress all that?

NADA: By drinking, drinking till I'm blind to the whole damned world.

THE SECRETARY: A clumsy way of going about it. We have a better one. What's your name?

NADA: Nothing.

THE SECRETARY: What?

NADA: Nothing.

THE SECRETARY: I asked you to tell me your name.

NADA: That *is* my name.

THE SECRETARY: Fine! With a name like that, we should get on well together. Come this way. We'll find you a job in our administration. [*The* FISHERMAN *comes back*.] Mr. Alcalde, would you please instruct our friend Nothing in his duties? Meanwhile you, the Guards, get busy selling our badges. [*She goes toward* DIEGO.] Good day. Would you like to buy a badge?

DIEGO: What badge?

THE SECRETARY: Why, the plague badge, of course. [*Pauses*.] You are free to refuse it, of course. It's not compulsory.

DIEGO: In that case, I refuse.

THE SECRETARY: Very good. [*Turning to* VICTORIA] And you?

VICTORIA: I don't know you.

THE SECRETARY: Quite so. But I feel I should inform you that those who refuse to wear that badge are obliged to wear another.

VICTORIA: And what is that?

THE SECRETARY: Why, the badge of those who refuse to wear the badge, obviously. That way we see at once with whom we have to deal.

THE FISHERMAN: I beg your pardon, miss. . . .

THE SECRETARY [*to* DIEGO *and* VICTORIA]: Good-by then, for the present. [*To the* FISHERMAN] Well, what is it *now?*

THE FISHERMAN [*with rising exasperation*]: I've been up to the office on the first floor and they told me to come back here. It seems I have to get a certificate of existence before I can get a certificate of health.

THE SECRETARY: That goes without saying.

THE FISHERMAN: "Goes without saying!" What do you mean by that?

THE SECRETARY: Why, it proves that this city is beginning to reap the benefits of a strong administration. We start with the premises that you are guilty. But that's not enough; you must learn to feel, yourselves, that you are guilty. And you won't feel guilty until you feel tired. So we weary you out; that's all. Once you are really tired, tired to death in fact, everything will run quite smoothly.

THE FISHERMAN: Anyhow, is there some way of getting this damned certificate of existence?

THE SECRETARY: Well, it really looks as if you couldn't. You see, you need to get a certificate of health first, before you are given a certificate of existence. It's a sort of deadlock, isn't it?

THE FISHERMAN: Then—what?

THE SECRETARY: Then you have to fall back on our good will. But like most sorts of good will ours is of limited duration. Thus we may grant you this certificate as a special favor. Only I warn you it will be valid for one week only. After that, we'll see. . . .

THE FISHERMAN: See what?

THE SECRETARY: See if there are reasons for renewing it for you.

THE FISHERMAN: And supposing it's not renewed?

THE SECRETARY: Since there is then no proof of your existence we may have to take steps for your elimination. Alcalde, would you draw up the certificate? Thirteen copies, please.

FIRST ALCALDE: Thirteen?

THE SECRETARY: Yes. One for the applicant and twelve for our files.

[*Light on the center of the stage.*]

THE PLAGUE: Now we can get started on the great useless public works. And you, my dear, get busy with the record of deportations and concentrations. We must speed up the transformation of innocent into guilty parties; that's the only way of making sure of our labor supply. Just now it looks as if our man power might run short. How far have you got with the census?

THE SECRETARY: It's under way, all is for the best, and I think these good people are getting to understand me.

THE PLAGUE: Really, my dear, you shock me. Fancy wanting to be understood. That's a sentimental fancy; in our profession we have no right to indulge in sentiment. Of course these good people, as you call them, haven't understood a thing—but that has no importance. What we want of them isn't comprehension but execution of their duties. Not a bad expression. Singularly apt under the circumstances, you'll agree?

THE SECRETARY: An excellent slogan, yes.

THE PLAGUE: It covers everything. Execution—that puts it in a nutshell. And the man who is to die is expected to collaborate in his own execution—

which is the aim and the bedrock, too, of all good government. [*Noises in the background.*] What's that?

[*The* CHORUS OF WOMEN *is showing signs of excitement.*]

THE SECRETARY: It's the women making a demonstration.

CHORUS OF WOMEN: This lady has something to say.

THE PLAGUE: Let her step forward.

A WOMAN [*coming forward*]: Where's my husband?

THE PLAGUE: There now! Your heart's in the right place, my good woman, I can see. And what has happened to this husband of yours?

THE WOMAN: He didn't come home last night.

THE PLAGUE: What's remarkable about that? He found another bed to sleep in, most likely. Try to take it in your stride.

THE WOMAN: But my husband isn't that sort of man; he respects himself.

THE PLAGUE: Ah, I see: a model husband. [*To the* SECRETARY] You'd better look into this, my dear.

THE SECRETARY: Surname and Christian name?

THE WOMAN: Galvez, Antonio.

[*The* SECRETARY *inspects her writing-pad and whispers in the* PLAGUE's *ear.*]

THE SECRETARY: Well, you may congratulate yourself. He's alive and well looked after.

THE WOMAN: Where is he?

THE SECRETARY: In a palatial residence, where the company's select.

THE PLAGUE: Yes, I deported him along with some others who were giving trouble but whose lives I wished to spare.

THE WOMAN [*shrinking away*]: What have you done to them?

THE PLAGUE [*his voice shrill with fury*]: What have I done to them? I have concentrated them. They

had been living at a loose end, frittering their time
away, dispersing their energies. Now they've been
pulled together, they are *concentrated.*

THE WOMAN [*running to the* CHORUS, *whose ranks
open to make way for her*]:   Pity! Pity on me!

CHORUS OF WOMEN: Pity on us all!

THE PLAGUE: Silence! Don't idle about! *Do* something! Get busy! [*Pensively murmurs to himself*]
Execution, occupation, concentration. Ah, how useful those long words are! We couldn't do without
them.

[*Light is flashed on the food office, showing* NADA
seated beside the ALCALDE, *with batches of petition-
ers lined up before them.*]

A MAN: The cost of living has gone up and our
wages aren't enough to live on.

NADA: We are aware of that, and we have a new wage
scale all ready. It has just been drawn up.

THE MAN: Good! What sort of raise can we expect?

NADA: I'll read it out to you. It's quite easy to follow
if you listen carefully. [*Reads*] "Wage Scale Number 108. This reassessment of the wage-earner's
emoluments and all remunerations thereto assimilated involves the suppression of the basic living
wage and entire decontrol of the sliding scales hith-
erto in force, which now are free to reach the level
of a maximum wage whose monetary value is to be
determined subsequently. Nevertheless, the sliding
scale, after deduction of the increases nominally
accorded under Wage Scale Number 107 shall
continue being assessed, irrespective of the terms
and conditions of the above-mentioned reassessment,
in terms of the basic living wage suppressed by the
first clause of this regulation."

THE MAN: That sounds fine! But what raise exactly
can we count on?

NADA: The raise will come later; meanwhile you have
   our new wage scale to go on with. We are increasing
   your pay by a wage scale; that's what it amounts to.

THE MAN: But what the hell can we do with your
   new wage scale?

NADA [*shrilly*]:   Eat it! Put it in your pipes and
   smoke it! Next. [*Another man steps forward.*] Ah,
   you want to open a shop, do you? Now that's a
   really bright idea. Well, the first thing is to fill up
   this form. Dip your fingers in the ink. Then press
   them here. Right.

THE MAN: Where can I wipe my hand?

NADA: Where can you wipe your hand? Let's see.
   [*Flips the pages of a file in front of him.*] Nowhere.
   It's not provided for in the regulations.

THE MAN: But I can't stay like this!

NADA: Why not? Anyhow what does a little ink on
   your fingers matter, seeing that you're not permitted
   to touch your wife. What's more, it's good for
   your morals.

THE MAN: Good? In what way?

NADA: It humiliates you; that's why. But let's get
   back to this shop you want to open. Would you
   rather have the benefits of Article 208 of Chapter
   62 of the sixteenth supplement to the fifth issue of
   the Trading Regulations, or would you rather come
   under Clause 27 of Article 207, Circular Number
   15, concerning special cases?

THE MAN: But I don't know the first thing about
   either of them!

NADA: Naturally, my man, you wouldn't know it.
   Nor do I, for that matter. Still, as things have to
   be settled one way or another, we shall let you have
   the benefits of both articles at once.

THE MAN: That's really kind of you, Nada. I'm much
   obliged.

NADA: Don't mention it! As a matter of fact I rather

think that one of these bylaws gives you the right to open your shop, while the other forbids your selling anything in it.

THE MAN: But—what's the idea, then?

NADA: Discipline, my friend; discipline. [*A woman runs up in a state of great agitation.*] Well, what is it, my good woman?

THE WOMAN: They've requisitioned my house.

NADA: Good.

THE WOMAN: And a government office has been installed in it.

NADA: Naturally.

THE WOMAN: But I haven't anywhere to live, though they promised to find me a new house.

NADA: Well, doesn't that show how considerate they are?

THE WOMAN: Yes—but I've been told to submit an application through the usual channels. And, meanwhile, my children haven't a roof over their heads.

NADA: All the more reason to put in your application right away. Fill in this form.

THE WOMAN [*taking the form*]:   But will it go through quickly?

NADA: Yes, provided you claim priority and support your claim with the necessary documents.

THE WOMAN: What exactly is needed?

NADA: A duly authenticated certificate declaring that it's a matter of urgency for you to be given accommodation.

THE WOMAN: My children haven't anywhere to sleep. Surely that's urgent enough for anyone?

NADA: You will not be given accommodation because your children are homeless. You will be given it if you supply a certificate. Which is not the same thing.

THE WOMAN: I never heard such talk! The devil may know what it can mean—*I* don't!

NADA: Precisely! That, my good woman, is part of

our program. We want to fix things up in such a way that nobody understands a word of what his neighbor says. And, let me tell you, we are steadily nearing that perfect moment when nothing anybody says will rouse the least echo in another's mind; when the two languages that are fighting it out here will exterminate each other so thoroughly that we shall be well on the way to that ideal consummation —the triumph of death and silence.

THE WOMAN: Justice means that children have enough to eat and are sheltered from the cold. That my little ones can live. When I brought them into the world the good earth was their birthright. And the sea gave the water for their baptism. That's all the wealth they need. I ask nothing more for them than their daily bread and poor people's right to sleep nights. Little enough indeed—but you deny it to them. And if you deny the poor their daily bread, no luxury, no fine speeches, no wonderful promises you make can ever earn you our forgiveness.

NADA [*speaking at the same time as the woman*]: Choose to live on your knees rather than to die standing; thus and thus only will the world acquire that neat, nicely ordered layout whose template is the gibbet, and be shared between well-drilled ants and the placid dead: a puritan paradise without food, fields, or flowers, in which angel police float around on pinions of red tape among beatific citizens nourished on rules and regulations and groveling before this decorated God, whose delight it is to destroy and doggedly to dissipate the dear delusions of a too delicious age.

NADA [*speaking alone*]: Down with everything! Nobody knows what anybody means—the golden age has come.

[*Light on the center of the stage, showing up huts,*

*barbed-wire fences, observation towers, and other
forbidding structures.* DIEGO *enters; he is still wearing the mask and he has the bearing of a hunted
man. He gazes at the scene before him, the townsfolk, and the* PLAGUE.]

DIEGO [*to the* CHORUS]:   Where is Spain? Where's
Cadiz? This scene does not belong to any known
country. We are on another planet, a planet where
man is out of place. Why are you silent?

CHORUS: We are afraid. Ah, if only the wind would
rise . . . !

DIEGO: I, too, am afraid. But it does good to cry one's
fear aloud. Cry, and the wind will answer.

CHORUS: Once we were a people and now we are a
herd. Once we were invited, now we are summoned.
Once we could buy and sell our milk and bread;
now we are rationed. We queue up and wait our
turns. We toe the line, for no one can do anything
for his neighbor, we can only wait in the line, at
the place assigned us. What is the use of crying out?
No longer have our women those flowerlike faces
that set our hearts aflame with desire, and Spain is
Spain no longer. Line up! Line up! Keep your
places! No joy is left in life. We are stifling, stifling
to death, in this prison house that was once a city.
Ah, if only the wind would rise . . . !

THE PLAGUE: They have learned wisdom. Come,
Diego, now that you have understood.

[*Sounds of "eliminations" in the upper air.*]

DIEGO: We are innocent. [*The* PLAGUE *guffaws.*] Innocence, you murderer—do you know what's meant
by innocence?

THE PLAGUE: Innocence? That's a new one on me!

DIEGO: Then let's have it out, you and I. The stronger
of us two will kill the other.

THE PLAGUE: *I* am the stronger, you poor innocent.

Look! [*Beckons to his Guards. They step toward*
DIEGO, *who takes to flight.*] Run after him! Don't
let him escape. A man who runs away is ours. Put
the marks on him!

[*The hunt is on. The Guards pursue* DIEGO *through
windows, doors, etc., in and out. Whistles, sirens.*]

CHORUS: He is running away. He is afraid, and admits it. He has lost all self-control, he's crazy. But
we know better, we have come to our senses. We
are ruled and the state looks after us. And yet—in
the dusty silence of their offices sometimes we hear
a long, restrained cry, the cry of hearts that are
separated, and it tells of sunlit seas at noon, the
fragrance of reeds at nightfall, the sweet embraces
of our women. Our faces are sealed up, our steps
counted, our hours fixed—and yet our hearts reject
this silence of the grave. They reject the never-ending forms to be filled out; the miles and miles of
walls; barred windows; and daybreaks bristling with
guns. They reject these things as does he who is
fleeing from this setting of shadows and numbers,
seeking a house for refuge. But the only refuge is
the sea, and the walls cut us off from it. Let the sea
wind but rise, and at last we shall breathe freely.

[DIEGO *has fled into a house. The Guards halt at
the door and post sentries outside.*]

THE PLAGUE [*shrilly*]: Brand them! Brand them all!
Even what they do not say makes itself heard.
They can no longer raise their voices in protest, but
their silence grates on our ears. Smash their mouths,
gag them, din our slogans into them, until they, too,
are saying the same thing over and over again—
until they become good citizens of the kind we need.

[*A cataract of slogans, raucous as if they issued from
loud-speakers, pours down from the flies, growing
louder and louder with each reiteration until it*

drowns the muttering of the CHORUS. *Abruptly silence falls.*] One plague, one people! Concentrate, execute orders, keep busy! One good plague is worth two freedoms. Deport and torture, there'll always be something left!

[*Lights go on in the Judge's house.*]

VICTORIA: No, father. You can't hand over our old servant just because they say she's infected. Have you forgotten how good she was to me when I was a child and how loyally she's served you all her life?

JUDGE CASADO: I have made my decision and it's not for you or anyone else to question it.

VICTORIA: You cannot have the last word always; grief, too, should have a hearing.

JUDGE CASADO: My duty is to watch over this house and to see that the disease is not allowed to enter it. [DIEGO *enters abruptly.*] Who gave you leave to enter?

DIEGO: It's fear that has driven me to ask shelter here. I am running away from the Plague.

JUDGE CASADO: Running away? No, you have it with you. [*He points to the mark on* DIEGO's *armpit. A short silence. Then police whistles are heard in the distance.*] Leave this house.

DIEGO: Let me stay, I beg you. If you turn me out they'll get me, and I shall be shut up with all those other wretched people in the death-house.

JUDGE CASADO: I cannot permit you to remain here. As judge, I am a servant of the law and must obey it.

DIEGO: The old law, yes. But these new laws are no concern of yours.

JUDGE CASADO: I do not serve the law because of what it says but because it is the law.

DIEGO: And suppose the law's identical with crime?

JUDGE CASADO: If crime becomes the law, it ceases being crime.

DIEGO: And then it's virtue you must punish!

JUDGE CASADO: As you say, virtue must be punished if it is so presumptuous as to break the law.

VICTORIA: Casado, it's not the law that's making you behave like this; it's fear.

JUDGE CASADO: Isn't that man, too, afraid?

VICTORIA: But he has not yet played the traitor.

JUDGE CASADO: He will. Fear always leads to betrayal, and everyone feels fear because nobody is pure.

VICTORIA: Father, I belong to this man; you have given your consent to it. You cannot rob me of him today after having given him to me yesterday.

JUDGE CASADO: I never consented to your marriage. I consented to your leaving us.

VICTORIA: Yes, I always knew you didn't love me.

JUDGE CASADO [*looking intently at her*]:   All women disgust me. [*Loud knocks at the door.*] What is it?

A GUARD [*outside*]:   This house is put in quarantine, as harboring a suspect, and all its occupants are under close surveillance.

DIEGO [*laughing loudly*]:   And the law's infallible, as you pointed out just now. Only, as this one is a trifle new, you weren't quite at home in it. Well, now you know, and so here we are, all in the same boat—judge, accused, and witnesses. Brothers all! [*The* JUDGE's WIFE *enters, with her little son and younger daughter.*]

THE JUDGE's WIFE: They've boarded up the door.

VICTORIA: Yes, we're in quarantine.

JUDGE CASADO: That's *his* fault. Anyhow I shall report him to the authorities. Then they will open the house.

VICTORIA: Father, you can't do that. Your honor forbids you.

JUDGE CASADO: Honor is practiced between men, and there are no men left in this city.

[*Whistles outside, and sounds of running feet near-*

ing the house. DIEGO *listens, gazes frantically around him, then suddenly picks up the little boy.*]

DIEGO: Look, servant of the law! If you stir a finger or utter a sound I shall press your son's lips to the plague mark.

VICTORIA: Diego, that's cowardly.

DIEGO: Nothing is cowardly in this city of cowards.

THE JUDGE'S WIFE [*rushing toward her husband*]: Promise, Casado! Promise this madman that you'll do what he wants.

THE JUDGE'S DAUGHTER: No, father, don't do anything of the sort. It's no concern of ours.

THE JUDGE'S WIFE: Don't listen to her. You know quite well she hates her brother.

JUDGE CASADO: She is right; it's no concern of ours.

THE JUDGE'S WIFE: And you, too, hate my son.

JUDGE CASADO: *Your* son, as you rightly say.

THE JUDGE'S WIFE: Oh, how vile of you to rake up something that was forgiven years ago!

JUDGE CASADO: I did *not* forgive. I complied with the law and in the eyes of the law that boy is my son.

VICTORIA: Is this true, mother?

THE JUDGE'S WIFE: So you, too, despise me?

VICTORIA: No, only it's as if the bottom had dropped out of the world I knew, and everything were falling in ruins. My mind is reeling.

[*The* JUDGE *takes a step toward the door.*]

DIEGO: The mind may reel, but the law keeps us on our feet—isn't that so, Judge? As we all are brothers [*holding the little boy in front of him*], I'm going to give you a nice brotherly kiss, my little man!

THE JUDGE'S WIFE: Oh, please, Diego, don't act hastily! Don't behave like one whose heart has turned to stone! Only wait, and it will soften. Wait, I beg you! [*Runs to the door and bars the way to the* JUDGE.] You'll do as Diego wishes, won't you?

THE JUDGE'S DAUGHTER: Why should my father truckle to Diego? What interest has he in this bastard, this interloper in our family?

THE JUDGE'S WIFE: Keep silent! It is your envy speaking, from the black pit of your heart. [*To the* JUDGE] But you at least—you whose life is drawing to a close—surely you have learned that nothing on this sad earth is enviable but tranquillity and sleep. And you will sleep badly in your solitary bed if you let this monstrous thing be done.

JUDGE CASADO: I have the law on my side. And the law will ensure my rest.

THE JUDGE'S WIFE: I spit on your law! I have on my side the right of lovers not to be parted, the right of the criminal to be forgiven, the right of every penitent to recover his good name. Yes, I spit on your law and all its works! Had you the law on your side when you made those cowardly excuses to the captain who challenged you to a duel, after you'd made a false declaration so as to escape your military service? Was the law on your side when you asked that girl who was suing a dishonest employer to sleep with you?

JUDGE CASADO: Keep silent, woman!

VICTORIA: Yes, mother, please, please stop.

THE JUDGE'S WIFE: No, Victoria, I must have my say. I have kept silence all these years—for the sake of my honor and for the love of God. But honor has left the world. And a single hair of that child's head is dearer to me than heaven itself. I shall not hold my peace. And I will say to this man, my husband, that he has never had justice on his side; for justice—do you hear, Casado?—is on the side of the sufferers, the afflicted, those who live by hope alone. It is not and can never be with those who count their pennies and cling to their miserable hoard.

[DIEGO *has put the child down.*]

THE JUDGE'S DAUGHTER: The right you champion is
   the right to adultery.

THE JUDGE'S WIFE [*her voice rising to a scream*]:   I
   have no wish to hide my sin. No, no, I'll cry it on
   the housetops. But, abject as I am, this much I
   know: that, if the flesh has its lapses, the heart has
   its crimes. And what is done in the heat of passion
   should meet with pity.

THE JUDGE'S DAUGHTER: Pity for the bitches!

THE JUDGE'S WIFE: Why not? Bitches, too, have a
   belly for their pleasure and their parturition.

JUDGE CASADO: Woman, your arguments are worth-
   less. I shall denounce the young man who has
   brought all this trouble upon us. And I shall do it
   with the greater satisfaction since I shall be not only
   carrying out the law, but also giving vent to my
   hatred.

VICTORIA: Ah, so at last the truth is out, more shame
   to you! Always you have judged in terms of hatred,
   though you masked it with the name of law. Thus
   even the best laws took on a bad taste in your
   mouth—the sour mouth of those who have never
   loved anything in their lives. Oh, I'm suffocating
   with disgust. Come, Diego, take me in your arms
   and let's rot together. But let that man live; life
   is punishment enough for him.

DIEGO: Let me be! Oh, I'm sick with shame when I
   see what we have come to!

VICTORIA: I feel as you do. I could die of shame.
   [DIEGO *makes a dash to the window and jumps out.*
   The JUDGE *runs also.* VICTORIA *slips out by a con-*
   cealed door.]

THE JUDGE'S WIFE: The time has come when the
   buboes have got to burst, and we are not the only
   ones. The whole city is in the grip of the same
   fever.

JUDGE CASADO: You bitch!

THE JUDGE'S WIFE: You—judge!

[*The light leaves the Judge's house, then settles on the food office, where* NADA *and the* ALCALDE *are preparing to leave.*]

NADA: Orders have been given to the district wardens to see to it that all the citizens under their charge vote for the new government.

FIRST ALCALDE: That won't be too easy. Quite likely some will vote against it.

NADA: No, not if we use the right method.

FIRST ALCALDE: The right method?

NADA: The right method is to declare that the voting's free. Which means that votes cast in favor of the government are freely given. As for the others, account must be taken of the pressure brought to bear on voters to prevent their voting of their own free will. Thus votes of this kind will be counted in accordance with the preferential method; that is to say, votes on the same ticket for candidates belonging to different parties will be assimilated to the quota of the uncast votes in the ratio of one third of the votes eliminated. Is that quite clear?

FIRST ALCALDE: Quite clear? Well. . . . Still I think I have an inkling of what you mean.

NADA: In that case I congratulate you, Alcalde. Anyhow, whether you understand or not, don't forget that the practical effect of this admirable use of applied mathematics is to cancel out all votes unfavorable to the government.

FIRST ALCALDE: But didn't you say the voting was free?

NADA: And so it is. Only we base our system on the principle that a vote against us isn't a free vote. It's a mere romantic gesture, conditioned by prejudice and passion.

FIRST ALCALDE: Well, well! I'd never have thought of
that!

NADA: That's because you've never really grasped
what freedom means.

[*Light on the center.* DIEGO *and* VICTORIA *enter,
running, and halt in the front of the stage.*]

DIEGO: Victoria, I'd like to run away from all this.
I've lost my bearings and I no longer know where
my duty lies.

VICTORIA: Do not leave me. A man's duty is to stand
by those he loves. We will see this through together.

DIEGO: But I'm too proud to love you if I can no
longer respect myself.

VICTORIA: What's there to prevent your respecting
yourself?

DIEGO: You, Victoria—when I see how brave you
are.

VICTORIA: For heaven's sake, for our love's sake,
Diego, don't talk like that or I'll let you see the ugly
truth—the coward that I really am! For you're
mistaken. I'm not so brave as you think. All my
courage wilts when I think of the time when I
could feel I was yours, body and soul. How far
away it seems, that time—when I felt love welling
up in my heart, like a tempestuous flood, whenever anybody spoke your name! And when I had a
thrill of happy triumph, like a sailor who has made
his landfall, whenever I saw you coming toward
me! Yes, I'm losing grip, I feel like sinking to the
ground, all my courage is dying of a cowardly
regret. If somehow I still keep on my feet, it's the
momentum of my love carrying me blindly on.
But if you were to go out of my life, I'd stop dead,
I'd fall and never rise again.

DIEGO: Ah, if only I could tie myself to you and we
two, bound limb to limb, could drown together in
a sleep that has no end!

VICTORIA: Come!

[*Slowly they move toward each other, each gazing into the other's eyes. But before they can embrace, the* SECRETARY *suddenly comes forward and thrusts herself between them.*]

THE SECRETARY: What are you up to, you two?

VICTORIA [*shrilly*]: Can't you see? We're making love!

[*A terrific crash in the air overhead.*]

THE SECRETARY: Ssh! Some words must not be spoken. You should have known that that one was forbidden. Look! [*Strikes* DIEGO *on the armpit, branding him for the second time.*] So far you were only under suspicion. Now you are infected. [*Gazes at him.*] A pity! Such a good-looking lad. [*To* VICTORIA] Sorry, but frankly I prefer men to women, I get on with them so much better. Good evening.

[DIEGO *stares with horror at the new mark under his arm; then, after gazing wildly round him, rushes toward* VICTORIA *and clasps her in his arms.*]

DIEGO: Oh, how I hate your beauty—now that I know it will survive me! No, I cannot bear to think that others will enjoy it after I am dead. [*Crushing her to his breast*] Good! Anyhow this way I shall not be alone. What do I care for your love if it doesn't rot along with me?

VICTORIA [*struggling*]: Stop! You're hurting me.

DIEGO: Ah! So you're afraid? [*Shakes her, laughing wildly.*] Those black horses of love, where are they now? So long as the weather's fair a woman's love continues, but let the storm break, and the black horses gallop away in panic. . . . At least you can die with me!

VICTORIA: *With* you, yes; but never *against* you! I loathe the look of fear and hatred you have now.

Let me go. Leave me free to discover in you the love that once was yours—and then, and then my heart will speak again.

DIEGO [*half releasing her*]: I can't bear the thought of dying. And now all that is dearest to me in the world is forsaking me, refusing to follow me to the grave.

VICTORIA [*flinging herself against him*]: But, Diego, I *will* follow you—to hell, if need be. Ah, my old Diego has come back. I feel my limbs quivering against yours. Kiss me, kiss me and crush back the cry that rises from the depths of my body, forcing its way up through my lips! . . . Ah!

[*He presses his lips to her mouth's kiss, then breaks free and leaves her trembling with emotion in the center of the stage.*]

DIEGO: Wait! . . . No, you are unscathed. There is no sign on you. This foolish act will have no consequences.

VICTORIA: Take me in your arms again. It's with cold that I am trembling now. A moment ago your breast was burning my hands and the blood ran like wildfire through my veins. But now . . .

DIEGO: No. Let me go my own way. I cannot stand aloof with all this suffering around me.

VICTORIA: Come back, Diego. All I want is to be consumed by the same fever, to die of the same wound, and to join my last cry with yours.

DIEGO: No. From now on I am with the others, all those wretched people who are marked as I am marked. Their agonies appall me; they fill me with the disgust that used to make me shrink from every contact. But now their calamity is mine, and they need me.

VICTORIA: If you must die, I'll envy even the earth that wraps your body.

DIEGO: You are on the other side of the barricade, the side of the living.

VICTORIA: I can still be with you, Diego, if only you keep your love for me.

DIEGO: Love? They have ruled love out. But, ah, how I hate the thought of losing you!

VICTORIA: No, Diego; do not talk of losing me. Oh, I've seen quite well what they are after; they do all they can to make love impossible. But I'll defeat them, for I am stronger than they.

DIEGO: Perhaps, but I am not. I know my weakness and I have no wish to share my defeat with you.

VICTORIA: There's no flaw in my armor; my love is all my life. I fear nothing now; even were the skies to fall, I should go down to death crying out my happiness, if only I still had your hand in mine.

[*Cries in the distance.*]

DIEGO: Others are crying, too.

VICTORIA: I'm deaf to their cries, my ears are sealed against them!

DIEGO: Look!

[*The death-cart rumbles past.*]

VICTORIA: My eyes see nothing. Love has dazzled them.

DIEGO: Don't you feel the very sky weighing down on us with its load of sorrows?

VICTORIA: When it's the utmost I can do to bear the weight of my love, how can you ask me to take on my shoulders the burden of the sorrows of the world as well? No, that's a man's idea of duty— one of those futile, preposterous crusades you men engage in as a pretext for evading the one struggle that is truly arduous, the one victory of which you could be rightly proud.

DIEGO: What else should I struggle against in this world of ours if not the injustice that is done us?

VICTORIA: The anguish that you have within yourself. Master that, and all the rest will follow.

DIEGO: I am alone. And that anguish is too great for
me to master.

VICTORIA: You are *not* alone. I stand beside you and
I am armed for the fight.

DIEGO: How beautiful you are, Victoria, and how
I'd love you—if only I were not afraid!

VICTORIA: How little you would fear, if only you'd
consent to love me!

DIEGO: I *do* love you. . . . But I don't know which
of us is in the right.

VICTORIA: The one who has no fear. And my heart
is fearless. It burns with a single, steady flame, a
pillar of fire, like those beacon fires with which our
mountaineers hail each other on midsummer's night.
And it, too, conveys a message, it is calling you.
This is our midsummer's night.

DIEGO: In a charnel house!

VICTORIA: Charnel house or mountaintop—how can
that affect my love? And my love, anyhow, is
benign, it does no harm to anyone. But who is
benefited by your crazy self-devotion? Not I, in
any case; each word you utter is a dagger in my
heart.

DIEGO: Don't cry, foolish one! . . . But, oh, the
cruelty of my predicament! Why should I be
singled out for this ordeal? I could have drunk
those tears and, with my lips seared by their bitterness, have strewn as many kisses on your face as an
olive tree has leaves!

VICTORIA: At last! At last you have come back to me
and that's *our* language you are speaking once
again. [*Stretches out her arms toward him.*] Let me
make sure that it is you, really *you*, come back.

[*But* DIEGO *steps quickly back, showing the plague*

marks on him. She moves her hands forward, then hesitates.]

DIEGO: So you, too, are afraid?

[*She places the palms of her hands firmly on the plague marks. Startled, he recoils from her, but she stretches out her arms again.*]

VICTORIA: Come! Let me take you in my arms. You have nothing to fear now. [*The groans and imprecations in the background grow louder.* DIEGO *gazes blankly around him like a madman, then abruptly hurries away.*] Diego! No, he has forsaken me. I am alone, alone!

CHORUS OF WOMEN: We are the guardians of the race. This ordeal is more than we can cope with, we can but wait for it to end. So let us hold our peace until winter comes, bringing the hour of liberation when these groans and curses cease and our men come back to us, clamoring for what they treasure in their memories and cannot do without: the freedom of the great sea spaces, empty skies of summer, love's undying fragrance. But meanwhile we are like autumn leaves drenched by the September gales, which hover for a while in air and then are dragged down by the weight of water on them. We, too, are drooping earthward with bent backs, and until the day when these battle cries have spent their force, we listen only to the slow tides of happiness murmuring deep down within us. When the bare boughs of the almond trees grow bright with frost flowers we shall straighten up a little, fanned by a rising wind of hope, and soon in that second springtime we shall hold our heads high once more. Then those we love will turn again to us and as they draw near, step by step, we shall be like those heavy boats that the tide lifts inch by inch from the mud flats—steeped in brine and reeking with the harsh tang of the sea—until at last

you see them dancing on the waves. Ah, if only the
wind would rise, if only the wind would rise . . . !
[*Darkness. Then light plays on the wharf.* DIEGO
*enters and hails a boat that he has seen approaching.
The male chorus is massed in the background.*]

DIEGO: Ahoy there! Ahoy!

A VOICE: Ahoy!

[*During the scene that follows the boat is invisible.
only the boatman's head appears above the level of
the wharf.*]

DIEGO: What are you up to?

THE BOATMAN: Carrying provisions.

DIEGO: For the city?

THE BOATMAN: No, that's the food controller's job.
He issues the ration cards to the people, and that's
all they get. I supply my customers with bread and
milk. You see, there's some ships at anchor out
there, with whole families aboard, people who've
gone there to escape contagion. I bring their letters
ashore and take back their food.

DIEGO: But that's forbidden by the authorities.

THE BOATMAN: So I've heard tell. But I was at sea
when the new laws were passed, and I've never
learned to read. So I can't be expected to know
their precious regulations, can I?

DIEGO: Take me with you.

THE BOATMAN: Where?

DIEGO: To one of those ships you spoke of.

THE BOATMAN: Nothing doing. It's forbidden.

DIEGO: But just now you said you didn't know anything about the regulations.

THE BOATMAN: I didn't mean forbidden by the
authorities here; it's the people on the ships who
don't allow it. You can't be trusted.

DIEGO: Can't be trusted? What do you mean?

THE BOATMAN: Why, you might bring 'em with you.

DIEGO: Bring what?

THE BOATMAN: Ssh! [*Looks round to make sure no one is listening.*] Why, germs, of course. You might bring the germs on board.

DIEGO: Look here! I'll pay you well.

THE BOATMAN: Don't tempt me, sir. I don't like saying No to a gentleman.

DIEGO: As I said, I won't haggle over the terms.

THE BOATMAN: And you'll take it on your conscience if it leads to trouble?

DIEGO: Yes.

THE BOATMAN: Then step on board, sir. The sea is like a lake tonight.

[DIEGO *is about to step down from the wharf when suddenly the* SECRETARY *appears behind him.*]

THE SECRETARY: No. You're not to go.

DIEGO: What the devil . . . ?

THE SECRETARY: It's a contingency that's not provided for. Also, I know you better, you won't desert your post.

DIEGO: Nothing will prevent me from going.

THE SECRETARY: That's where you're mistaken. If I wish you to stay you will stay. And in fact I *do* wish you to stay; I've some business to transact with you. . . . You know who I am, don't you?

[*She moves back some steps, as if to draw him away from the edge of the wharf.* DIEGO *follows her.*]

DIEGO: To die is nothing. But to die degraded . . .

THE SECRETARY: I understand. Mind you, I'm a mere executive. But by the same token I have been given a sort of jurisdiction over you. The right of veto, if I may put it so.

[*Consults her notebook.*]

DIEGO: The men of my blood belong to the earth, and to the earth alone.

THE SECRETARY: That's what I meant. You belong to me after a fashion. After a fashion only, mind you.

perhaps not in the way I'd like you to be mine . . .
when I look at you. (*Naïvely*) You know, I'm
rather taken by you, really. Unfortunately I have
my orders.

[*Toys with her notebook.*]

DIEGO: I prefer your hatred to your smiles. And I
despise you!

THE SECRETARY: Have it your own way! In any case
this talk we're having isn't quite in order. But I find
that tiredness often makes me sentimental, and with
all this never-ending bookkeeping, I sometimes find
myself losing grip a bit—especially on nights like
tonight. [*She is twiddling the notebook between
her fingers.* DIEGO *tries to snatch it from her.*] No,
darling, don't be naughty. What would you see in
it, anyhow, if you got it? Just lines and lines of
entries. It's a sort of memorandum book, you see, a
cross between a diary and a directory. [*Laughs*]
My little memory-jogger!

[*She stretches a hand toward* DIEGO *as if to fondle
him, but he moves hastily back to where the* BOAT-
MAN *was.*]

DIEGO: Ah! He's gone!

THE SECRETARY: So he has. Another simpleton who
thinks he's out of it, but whose name is in my book,
like everybody else's.

DIEGO: You're double-tongued, and that, as you
should know, is enough to put any man against
you. So, let's be done with it.

THE SECRETARY: I don't know what you mean by
"double-tongued." Really it's all quite simple and
aboveboard. Every town has its list. This is the
Cadiz list. Our organization's excellent, I can assure
you; nobody's left out.

DIEGO: Nobody's left out, yet all escape.

THE SECRETARY [*indignantly*]:   How can you talk
such nonsense! [*Ponders for a moment.*] Still, I

admit, there are exceptions. Now and then we overlook someone. But he always ends up by giving himself away, sooner or later. When a man reaches the age of a hundred he can't help bragging about it—fool that he is! Then it gets into the newspapers. It's only a question of time. When I read the morning papers I note their names—collate them, as we call it. Oh, never fear, we always get them in the end.

DIEGO: But for a hundred years, anyhow, they've snapped their fingers at you—just like all the people in this city.

THE SECRETARY: What's a hundred years? To you no doubt that sounds like a lot of time, because you see these things from too near. But I can take a longer and a broader view. In a list of three hundred and seventy-two thousand names, what does one man matter, I ask you—even if he is a centenarian? In any case, we make up for it by pulling in a certain number of teen-agers; that levels up our average. It only means eliminating a bit quicker. Like this. . . . [*She crosses out an entry in her notebook. There is a cry out at sea and the sound of a body falling into the water.*] Oh! That was the boatman you were talking to. I did it without thinking. It was just a fluke.

[DIEGO, *who has risen to his feet, is gazing at her with horror and repugnance.*]

DIEGO: You disgust me so much that I feel like vomiting.

THE SECRETARY: Oh, I know I have a beastly job. It's terribly exhausting, and then one has to be so meticulous. At the start I fumbled a bit, but now I've a steady hand. [*Approaches* DIEGO.]

DIEGO: Keep away from me!

THE SECRETARY: Really I shouldn't tell you; it's a secret. But soon there won't be any more mistakes.

We've invented a new system that will run like clockwork, once it gets going. Just wait and see. [*While speaking, she has been coming closer and closer, phrase by phrase, to* DIEGO. *Suddenly, trembling with rage, he grips her by the collar.*]

DIEGO: Stop this play acting, damn you! What are you waiting for? Get on with your job and don't try to play cat-and-mouse with me—I'm bigger than you, if you only knew it. So kill me; that's the only way of making good that wonderful system of yours, which leaves nothing to chance. But of course only masses count with you; it's only when you're dealing with a hundred thousand men or more that you condescend to feel some interest. Then you can compile statistics—and statistics are conveniently dumb. It's easier working on whole generations, at an office table, in silence and with a restful smell of ink. But a single man, that's another story; he can upset your applecart. He cries aloud his joys and griefs. And as long as I live I shall go on shattering your beautiful new order with the cries that rise to my lips. Yes, I resist you, I resist you with all the energy that's in me.

THE SECRETARY: My darling!

DIEGO: Keep silent! I am of a race that used to honor death as much as life. But then your masters came along, and now both living and dying are dishonorable.

THE SECRETARY: Well, it's true . . .

DIEGO: It's true that you are lying and that you will go on lying until the end of time. Yes, I've seen through your famous system. You have imposed on men the pangs of hunger and bereavement to keep their minds off any stirrings of revolt. You wear them down, you waste their time and strength so that they've neither the leisure nor the energy to vent their anger. So they just mark time—which is

what you want, isn't it? Great as are their numbers,
they are quite as much alone as I am. Each of us is
alone because of the cowardice of the others. Yet
though, like them, I am humiliated, trodden down,
I'd have you know that you are nothing, and that
this vast authority of yours, darkening the sky, is
no more than a passing shadow cast upon the earth,
a shadow that will vanish in a twinkling before a
great storm wind of revolt. You thought that everything could be expressed in terms of figures, for-
mulas. But when you were compiling your precious
registers, you quite forgot the wild roses in the
hedges, the signs in the sky, the smiles of summer,
the great voice of the sea, the moments when man
rises in his wrath and scatters all before him. [*She
laughs.*] Don't laugh! Don't laugh, you fool! You're
doomed, I tell you, you and your associates. Even
when you are flushed with victory, defeat is knocking at the door. For there is in man—look at me,
and learn—an innate power that you will never
vanquish, a gay madness born of mingled fear and
courage, unreasoning yet victorious through all
time. One day this power will surge up and you will
learn that all your glory is but dust before the
wind. [*She laughs again.*] No, don't laugh. There's
nothing to laugh about.

[*She goes on laughing. He slaps her face and at the
same moment the men in the chorus tear off their
gags and utter a great cry of joy. In his excitement
DIEGO has crushed out his plague mark; he touches
the place where it was, then gazes at it in amazement.*]

THE SECRETARY: Splendid! Simply splendid!

DIEGO: What do you mean?

THE SECRETARY: You're simply splendid when you
are angry. I like you even better.

DIEGO: But—what's happened?

THE SECRETARY: You can see for yourself. The mark is disappearing. Carry on; you're going about it the right way.

DIEGO: Does that mean I am cured?

THE SECRETARY: Now I'm going to tell you a little secret. Their system is excellent, as you have observed; still there's a defect in their machine.

DIEGO: I don't follow.

THE SECRETARY: It has a weak point, darling. As far back as I can remember the machine has always shown a tendency to break down when a man conquers his fear and stands up to them. I won't say it stops completely. But it creaks, and sometimes it actually begins to fold up.

[*A short silence.*]

DIEGO: Why do you tell me that?

THE SECRETARY: Oh, you know, even when one has to do what I do, one can't help having a soft spot. And you've discovered mine.

DIEGO: Would you have spared me if I hadn't struck you?

THE SECRETARY: No. I came here to finish you off according to the rules.

DIEGO: So I'm the stronger?

THE SECRETARY: Tell me, are you still afraid?

DIEGO: No.

THE SECRETARY: Then I can't do anything to harm you. That, too, is down in the regulations. But I don't mind telling you it's the first time I'm glad about that loophole in our code.

[*She moves slowly away.* DIEGO *runs his hand over his chest, glances at his hand again, then quickly swings round and gazes in the direction whence groans are coming. The scene that follows is in pantomime. He goes toward a man who is still gagged and lying on the ground, and undoes the gag. It is the* FISHERMAN. *The two men eye each other in silence for some moments.*]

THE FISHERMAN [*with an effort*]: Good evening, brother. It's quite a while since I spoke last. [DIEGO *smiles toward him. The man glances up at the sky.*] What's happening?

[*The sky has brightened. A light breeze has sprung up, a door is flapping, and some clothes are fluttering on a line. The populace gathers round the two men; they, too, have removed their gags and are gazing up at the sky.*]

DIEGO: Yes. The wind is rising. . . .

C U R T A I N

THIRD PART

The townsfolk of Cadiz are moving about in the public square, engaged in various tasks that DIEGO, *standing at a slightly higher level, supervises. A brilliant lighting brings out the artificiality of the stage properties set up by the* PLAGUE, *and thus renders them less impressive.*

DIEGO: Rub out the stars. [*The stars are obliterated.*] Open the windows. [*Windows are opened.*] Group the sick together. [*The crowd obeys.*] Make more space for them. Good. Now stop being frightened; that's the one condition of deliverance. Let all of you who can, rise to their feet. Why are you cowering like that? Hold up your heads; the hour of pride has struck. Throw away your gags and proclaim with me that you have stopped being afraid. [*Raising his arm.*] O spirit of revolt, glory of the people, and vital protest against death, give these gagged men and women the power of your voice!

CHORUS: Brother, we hear you, and wretched as is the plight of men like us who live on bread and olives, by whom a mule is reckoned as a fortune, and who touch wine but twice a year, on wedding days and birthdays, we, abject as we are, can feel hope stirring in our hearts. But the old fear has not left them. Olives and bread give life a savor, and little though we have, we are afraid of losing it and our lives.

DIEGO: You will lose your bread and olives and

your lives as well if you let things continue as they are. Even if all you want is to keep your daily bread, you must begin by fighting down your fear. Spirit of Spain, awake!

CHORUS: We are poor and ignorant. But we have been told that the plague follows the course of the seasons. It has its spring when it strikes root and buds, a summer when it bears its fruit. Perhaps when winter comes it dies. But tell us, brother, is winter here, has winter really set in? Is this breeze that has sprung up really blowing from the sea? Always we have paid for everything with a currency of toil and tears; must we now pay in the currency of blood?

CHORUS OF WOMEN: There they are again, the men, prating of the concerns of men! But we are here to remind you of moments that fall into your hands like sun-ripe fruit, of days fragrant with flowers and the black wool of ewes—the scents and sights of Spain. We are weak and you, with your big bones, can always master us. But, none the less, do not forget, in the dust and heat of your shadow-fights, our flowers of flesh.

DIEGO: It is the plague that is wearing us to the bone, parting lovers, withering the flowers of our days. And our first duty is to fight the plague.

CHORUS: Has winter really come? The oaks in our forests are still clad with tiny, gleaming acorns and wasps are buzzing round their trunks. No, winter has not yet begun.

DIEGO: The winter of your wrath—let that be your beginning.

CHORUS: Yes, but is hope waiting for us at the end of the road? Or must we die of despair upon the way?

DIEGO: Cease talking of despair! Despair is a gag. And today the thunder of hope and a lightning flash of happiness are shattering the silence of this beleaguered city. Stand up, I tell you, and act like men! Tear up your certificates, smash the windows of their offices, leave the ranks of fear, and shout your freedom to the four winds of heaven!

CHORUS: We are the dispossessed and hope is our only riches—how could we live without it? Yes, brother, we will fling away these gags. [*A great shout of deliverance.*] Ah, now the first rain is falling on the parched earth, sealing the cracks that the summer heat has made. Autumn is here with her mantle of green, and a cool wind is blowing from the sea. Hope buoys us up like a great wave. [DIEGO *moves away. The* PLAGUE, *enters, on the same level as* DIEGO, *but from the opposite side, followed by* NADA *and the* SECRETARY.]

THE SECRETARY: What's all this commotion about? Will you be good enough to replace your gags—*at once!*

[*Some of the crowd, in the center, put back their gags. But some men have followed* DIEGO *and are carrying out his instructions in an orderly manner.*]

THE PLAGUE: They're getting out of hand.

THE SECRETARY: As usual!

THE PLAGUE: Well, we must take severer measures.

THE SECRETARY: Yes, I suppose we must. [*She opens her notebook and starts turning over the pages with a certain listlessness.*]

NADA: Why, of course we must! We are on the right track, that's sure. To abide by the regulations or not to abide by them—there you have all philosophy and ethics in a nutshell. But in my opinion, if Your Honor will permit me to express it, we don't go far enough.

THE PLAGUE: You talk too much.

NADA: That's because I'm bubbling over with enthusiasm, and while I've been with you I have learned quite a lot. Suppression—that's always been my gospel. But until now I had no good arguments to back it up. Now I have the regulations on my side.

THE PLAGUE: But the regulations do not suppress everything. Watch your step, my man, you're not in line.

NADA: Mind you, there were rules and regulations before you came on the scene. But no one had had the idea of an all-embracing regulation, a sum total of all accounts, with the human race put on the index, all life replaced by a table of contents, the universe put out of action, heaven and earth at last devalued and debunked. . . .

THE PLAGUE: Go back to your work, you drunken sot. And you, my dear, get busy.

THE SECRETARY: How shall we start?

THE PLAGUE: Oh, at random. That way it's more impressive.

[*The* SECRETARY *strikes out two names. Two thuds in quick succession; two men fall. The crowd surges back; the workers stop work and gaze at the dead men with dismay. Plague Guards rush up, replace the stars on the doors, close windows, pile the corpses up on the side.*]

DIEGO [*at the back of the stage; quietly*]: Long live death! You no longer frighten us.

[*The crowd surges forward. The men start work again. The Guards retreat. Same action as before, but in reverse. The wind whistles each time the crowd moves forward, and dies away when the Guards return.*]

THE PLAGUE: Eliminate that man.

THE SECRETARY: Impossible.

THE PLAGUE: Why?

THE SECRETARY: He has ceased being afraid.

THE PLAGUE: You don't say so! Does he *know?*

THE SECRETARY: He has suspicions.
[*She strikes out some names. Dull thuds. The crowd surges back. Same action as before.*]

NADA: Splendid! They're dying like flies. Ah, if only we could blow up the whole world!

DIEGO [*calmly*]:   Go to the help of those who fall.
[*Some movements of the crowd, in reverse.*]

THE PLAGUE: That fellow is really going too far.

THE SECRETARY: As you say, he's going far.

THE PLAGUE: Why do you sound so sad about it? You haven't by any chance let him know how things stand, have you?

THE SECRETARY: No. He must have found that out for himself. A sort of clairvoyance.

THE PLAGUE: He may have clairvoyance, but I have the means of action. We shall have to try new tactics. I leave their choice to you.
[*Goes out.*]

CHORUS [*flinging off the gags*]:   Ah! [*A huge sigh of relief.*] This is the beginning of the end, the strangle hold is loosening, the sky is clearing, the air growing breathable. Listen! You can hear it again, the murmur of the streams that the black sun of the plague had dried up. Summer is passing, and soon we shall no longer have the grapes of the vine arbor, nor melons, green beans, and fresh salad. The water of hope is softening the hard earth and promising us the solaces of winter—roast chestnuts, corn with the grains still green, tender walnuts, milk simmering on the hearth.

CHORUS OF WOMEN: Ignorant as we are, this much we know—that too high a price should not be paid for these good things. Everywhere in the world, and whoever be the master, there will always be fresh fruit for the plucking, the poor man's cup of wine, a fire of vine twigs at which we can warm our hands, waiting for better times. . . .

[*The* JUDGE'S DAUGHTER *jumps out of a window in the Judge's house, runs across to the group of women and hides among them.*]

THE SECRETARY [*coming down toward the crowd*]: Really you'd think we were in the midst of a revolution. But that is not the case, as you are well aware. Anyhow, it's not the masses who launch revolutions nowadays, and it's no use trying to put the clock back. Modern revolutions don't need insurgents. The police attend to everything, even to the overthrow of the government in power. And, when you think of it, isn't that a great improvement? That way the common people can take it easy, while some kind souls do all the thinking for them and decide what modicum of welfare they can do with.

THE FISHERMAN: I've half a mind to knock that damned eel on the head and rip her guts out.

THE SECRETARY: So, my good friends, wouldn't you do best to let it go at that? Once a government has settled in, it always costs more than it's worth to change it. Even if the present system strikes you as intolerable, there's always the hope of getting some concessions.

A WOMAN: What concessions?

THE SECRETARY: How can I tell? But surely you women realize that every upheaval costs a lot of suffering, and a good appeasement often pays better than a ruinous victory?

[*The women approach. Some men, too, leave Diego's group.*]

DIEGO: Don't listen. All she said has been thought up in advance.

THE SECRETARY: What do you mean by "thought up"? I'm talking common sense, that's all.

A MAN: Just what concessions did you have in mind?

THE SECRETARY: Well it's difficult to answer that right

off. Still, to give an example, I don't see why we shouldn't join with you in appointing a committee to decide, by a majority of votes, what eliminations should be ordered. Then this notebook in which the eliminations are made would be kept in the possession of the committee. Mind you, I'm only saying this by way of illustration of an arrangement we might come to. [*She is dangling the notebook at arm's length. A man snatches it from her hand. She addresses him with feigned indignation*] Will you give me back that notebook *at once!* You know quite well how valuable it is and that it's enough to strike out the name of one of your fellow citizens for him to die on the spot.

[*Men and women crowd excitedly round the man who has the notebook. Cries of jubilation:* "We've got it!" "That's cooked their goose!" "We're saved!"

The JUDGE'S DAUGHTER *runs up, snatches away the notebook, and after retreating to a corner and skimming through the pages, strikes out an entry. A shrill cry in the Judge's house and the sound of a body falling heavily on the floor. Men and women rush at the girl.*]

A VOICE: You poisonous vixen! It's you who should be eliminated!

[*Someone takes the notebook from her; all gather round him and hunt until they find the name of the* JUDGE'S DAUGHTER. *A hand strikes it out. The girl drops without a cry.*]

NADA [*at the top of his voice*]:   Forward, let's all join in a general suppression. It's not enough suppressing others, let's suppress ourselves. Here we are gathered together, oppressors and oppressed, a happy band of victims waiting in the arena. Go to it, bull; now for the universal cleanup.

A BURLY MAN [*who now is holding the notebook*]:

That's so. There's plenty of cleaning up to do in this here city. We'll never have another chance like this of rubbing out some of those sons of bitches who's been living on the fat of the land while we were starving.

[*The* PLAGUE, *who has just come on the scene again, lets out an enormous guffaw, while the* SECRETARY *demurely steps back to her place beside him. Nobody moves while the Plague Guards roam the stage, replacing the scenery and symbols of the* PLAGUE.]

THE PLAGUE [*to* DIEGO]: You see! They're doing the work themselves. Do you really think they're worth all the trouble you are taking?

[*But meanwhile* DIEGO *and the* FISHERMAN *have leaped onto the raised platform where the man who holds the notebook is standing, and knocked him down.* DIEGO *takes the notebook and tears it up.*]

THE SECRETARY: That's no good. I have a duplicate.

[DIEGO *hustles the men toward the other side of the stage.*]

DIEGO: Get back to your work. You've been tricked.

THE PLAGUE: When they're frightened, their fear is for themselves. But their hatred is for others.

DIEGO [*coming back and facing him*]: Neither fear, nor hatred—therein lies our victory.

[*The Guards retreat before Diego's men.*]

THE PLAGUE: Silence! I am he who turns the wine bitter, and dries up the fruit. I nip the young vine when it is putting forth its grapes and rot it when it needs the fires of summer. I loathe your simple joys. I loathe this country in which men claim to be free without being rich. I have prisons and executioners on my side, power and blood are my ministers. This city will be wiped out, and upon its ruins history will expire at last in the august silence of all

perfect social orders. Silence then, or I destroy
everything.

[*A mimic hand-to-hand conflict ensues between
Diego's partisans and others, in the midst of an
appalling din—thuds of eliminations, buzzings in
the air, creakings of garottes, an avalanche of
slogans. Then, while the struggle gradually turns
in favor of Diego's men, the tumult dies down and
the voices of the* CHORUS, *indistinct as yet, drown
the noises of the* PLAGUE.]

THE PLAGUE [*with a furious gesture*]:   We still have
the hostages.

[*He makes a sign and the Plague Guards leave the
stage, while the others form up once more in
groups.*]

NADA [*standing on the summit of the palace*]:   Something always remains. Nothing goes on and everything goes on. And my offices, too, go on functioning. Even if the city falls in ruins and men forsake
the earth, these offices will continue opening at the
usual hour, to see to it that government goes on,
even if nothing is left to govern. I stand for eternity,
my paradise will have its records, office files, and
rubber stamps for ever.

[*Exit.*]

THE CHORUS: They are in flight. Summer is ending
with our victory. So, after all, man has won the day.
And for us victory takes the form of our women's
bodies quickened by the showers of love; of happy
flesh, warm and glistening like the clusters of September grapes round which the wood wasps buzz.
Harvests of the vine are heaped on the belly's wine
press and wine spurts red over the tips of drunken
breasts. Soon, O my love, you will see desire bursting like an overripe fruit and the glory of bodies
issuing at last in shining freedom. In every corner

of the sky mysterious hands are proffering flowers, from quenchless fountains the golden wine is flowing. Now is the festival of victory; let us make haste to join our women!

[*All fall silent as a stretcher, on which* VICTORIA *lies, is carried forward.* DIEGO *rushes toward it.*]

DIEGO: Ah, this makes one want to kill—to kill or to die!

[*He stands beside the body, which seems lifeless.*]

O Victoria, most glorious of women, fierce and unconquerable as love, turn your face toward me if only for a moment. Come back, Victoria! Do not let yourself be lured away to that dim place beyond the world where you will be lost to me forever. Do not leave me, the earth is cold. Struggle to keep your foothold on this narrow ledge of life where we are still together, and do not let yourself slip down into the abyss. For, if you die, it will be dark at noon on all the days that yet are given me to live.

CHORUS OF WOMEN: Now we are at grips with truth; till now it was but half in earnest. What we have before us is a human body, racked by agony. Thus, after the tumult and the shouting, the fine speeches, the cries of "long live death!," death comes in person and clutches the throat of the beloved. And then, at the very moment when it is too late for loving, love returns.

[VICTORIA *utters a low groan.*]

DIEGO: It's not too late. Look, she is trying to rise! Yes, Victoria, once again I shall see you standing before me, straight as a torch, with the black flames of your hair rippling in the wind, and that glory of love upon your face, whose radiance was ever with me in my darkest hour. For I had you with me in the thickest of the fight, and my heart saw me through.

VICTORIA: You will forget me, that's certain. Your heart will not see you through the years of absence. Did it not fail you in the hour of misfortune only a while ago? Ah, how cruel it is to die knowing one will be forgotten! [*Turns away.*]

DIEGO: I shall *not* forget you; my remembrance will outlast my life.

CHORUS OF WOMEN: O suffering body, once so desirable; O queenly beauty, once so radiant! A man cries for the impossible, a woman endures all that is possible. Bow your proud head, Diego, and accuse yourself—for the hour of repentance has struck. Deserter! That body was your homeland; without it you are nothing any more; do not count on your remembrance to save you.

[*The* PLAGUE, *who has come up quietly, is facing* DIEGO *across* VICTORIA'S *body.*]

THE PLAGUE: Well, do you throw in your hand? [DIEGO *gazes with despair at* VICTORIA'S *body.*] Your strength has turned to weakness, your eyes are wavering. But I have the steady gaze of power.

DIEGO [*after a short silence*]: Let her live, and kill me instead.

THE PLAGUE: What's that you say?

DIEGO: I propose an exchange.

THE PLAGUE: What exchange?

DIEGO: My life for hers.

THE PLAGUE: That's the sort of romantic notion one has when one is tired. Don't forget that dying is a far from pleasant process and she is through with the worst of it. So let's leave well alone.

DIEGO: It's the sort of notion one has when one's the stronger.

THE PLAGUE: Look at me! I am strength incarnate.

DIEGO: Take off your uniform.

THE PLAGUE: Are you crazy?

DIEGO: Strip, I tell you! When strong men take off their uniforms they are not pretty sights!

THE PLAGUE: Quite likely. Their strength lies in having invented uniforms.

DIEGO: Mine lies in rejecting them. Well, I stand by my offer.

THE PLAGUE: Don't be over-hasty in deciding. Life has its good points.

DIEGO: My life is nothing. What count for me are my reasons for living. I'm not a dog.

THE PLAGUE: The first cigarette of the day—will you tell me *that* is nothing? And the smell of dust at noon on the *rambla*, rain falling through the dusk, a woman unknown as yet, the second glass of wine —do these mean nothing to you?

DIEGO: They mean something, yes. But this girl will live better than I.

PLAGUE: No—provided you give up troubling yourself about others.

DIEGO: On the road I've chosen there is no turning back, even if one wants it. I shall not spare you!

THE PLAGUE [*changing his tone*]: Now, listen well. If you offer me your life in exchange for that girl's, I am bound to accept your offer, and she will live. But there's another arrangement we can make, if you agree to it. I'll give you that girl's life and let you *both* escape, provided you let me make my own terms with this city.

DIEGO: No. I know my power.

THE PLAGUE: In that case I will be frank with you. For me there can be no question of half measures; I must be master of all or I am master of nothing. So, if you escape me, this city escapes me. That's the law. An ancient law, whose origin I do not know.

DIEGO: But *I* do. It comes from the abyss of time, it

is greater than you, loftier than your gibbets; it is
the law of nature. We have won the day.

THE PLAGUE: Not yet. I have this girl's body as my
hostage. And this hostage is the last trump in my
hand. If any woman has life written on her face it's
she; she deserves to live, and you wish to have her
live. As for me, I am bound to give her back to
you—but only in exchange for your life, or for
the freedom of this city. Make your choice.

[DIEGO *gazes at* VICTORIA. *In the background a
murmuring of voices muted by the gags. He turns
toward the* CHORUS.]

DIEGO: It is hard to die.

THE PLAGUE: Yes, it's hard.

DIEGO: But it's hard for them as well.

THE PLAGUE: You fool! Don't you realize that ten
years of this girl's love are worth far more than a
century of freedom for those men?

DIEGO: This girl's love is my private property and I
can deal with it as I choose. But those men's freedom belongs to them; I have no rights over it.

THE PLAGUE: No one can be happy without causing
harm to others. That is the world's justice.

DIEGO: A justice that revolts me and to which I refuse to subscribe.

THE PLAGUE: Who asked you to subscribe to it?
The scheme of things will not be changed just because you'd like it to be otherwise. But if you really
want to change it, abandon idle dreams and face up
to reality.

DIEGO: No. I know those stale old arguments. To do
away with murder we must kill, and to prevent
injustice we must do violence. That's been dinned
into our ears till we took it for granted. For centuries fine gentlemen of your kind have been in-
fecting the world's wounds on the pretense of healing them, and none the less continuing to boast of

their treatment—because no one had the courage to laugh them out of court.

THE PLAGUE: No one laughs, because it's I who get things done; I am efficient.

DIEGO: Efficient, I don't deny. And practical. Like the headsman's ax.

THE PLAGUE: But isn't it enough to watch the way that men behave? You very soon realize that any kind of justice is good enough for them.

DIEGO: Since the gates of this city were closed I've had ample time for watching.

THE PLAGUE: In that case you certainly have learned that they will always fail you; you will always be alone. And the lonely man is doomed.

DIEGO: No, that's false. If I were alone, everything would be easy. But, whether they want it or not, they are with me.

THE PLAGUE: And what a fine herd they make! For one thing, they stink!

DIEGO: I know they are not pure. Nor am I, for that matter. After all I was born among them, and I live for my city and my age.

THE PLAGUE: An age of slaves.

DIEGO: No, the age of free men.

THE PLAGUE: Free men? You amaze me. I can't see any here. Where are they?

DIEGO: In your prisons and your charnel houses. The slaves are on the thrones.

THE PLAGUE: Only dress up your free men in my policemen's uniforms, and see what they become!

DIEGO: I don't deny that they can be cowardly and cruel at times. That is why they have no better right than you to hold the reins of power. No man is good enough to be entrusted with absolute power —that I grant you. But, by the same token, that is why these men are entitled to compassion, whereas you are not.

THE PLAGUE: The coward's way of living is to live as they do—mean, antlike lives, never rising above mediocrity.

DIEGO: On that level I can feel at one with them. And if I am not faithful to the humble truth I share with them, how could I keep faith with the greater, lonelier ideal that is mine?

THE PLAGUE: The only fidelity I know of is—scorn. [*Points to the* CHORUS *cowering in the background.*] Look! Isn't that enough?

DIEGO: I reserve my scorn for the oppressors. Whatever you do, these men will be greater than you. When one of them kills, he does it in a gust of passion. But you slaughter people logically, legally, cold-bloodedly. Why scoff at their bowed heads when for so many generations the comets of fear have been roaming the skies above them? Why laugh at their timid airs when for centuries death has been playing havoc with them, tearing their love like wastepaper? The worst of their crimes has always had an excuse. But I find no excuse for the wrong that has been done them since the dawn of time, and which you have legalized in your foul code. [*The* PLAGUE *approaches him.*] No, I will not lower my eyes.

THE PLAGUE: Yes, that's obvious; you will not lower them. So I may as well tell you that you have come through the last ordeal with success. If you had made over this city to me, you would have lost this girl, and you, too, would have been lost. As it is, this city has a good chance of being free. So, as you see, a madman like yourself suffices. . . . Naturally the madman dies. But, in the end, sooner or later, the rest are saved. [*Gloomily*] And they don't deserve to be saved.

DIEGO: The madman dies. . . .

THE PLAGUE: Ah, on second thought, you're not so

sure. But of course that's quite in order—a last-minute hesitation. Pride will triumph in the end.

DIEGO: I stood for honor. And today I shall regain my honor only among the dead.

THE PLAGUE: As I was saying, it's pride that kills them. But all this is very tiring for an old man like myself. [*Harshly*] Get ready!

DIEGO: I am ready.

THE PLAGUE: There are the marks. They hurt. [DIEGO *gazes horror-struck at the marks, which have reappeared on him.*] Good. Suffer a little before dying. That, anyhow, I can insist on. When hatred flames up in me, the suffering of others is a healing dew. Groan a little; that does me good. And let me watch your suffering before I leave this city. [*To the* SECRETARY] Now then, my dear, get to work.

THE SECRETARY: Yes, I suppose I must.

THE PLAGUE: Tired already, is that it? [*The* SECRETARY *nods, and as she does so her whole aspect changes and she becomes an old woman, with a death's-head face.*] I always knew your hatred did not strike deep enough. Whereas mine is insatiable; I must ever have new victims. Well, get things over quickly, and we'll begin again elsewhere.

THE SECRETARY: You are right; I haven't hatred to uphold me, because my duties do not call for it. But in a way it is your fault, too. When one has to drudge away at keeping up statistics, one loses the power of feeling emotion.

THE PLAGUE: Mere words! If you want something to uphold you, as you call it, you can find it [*Points to* DIEGO, *who sinks onto his knees*] in the pleasure of destruction. That, anyhow, falls within your duties.

THE SECRETARY: So be it, let's destroy. But I must say it goes against the grain.

THE PLAGUE: What authority have you to question
my orders?

THE SECRETARY: The authority of memory. For I
have not forgotten what I was before you came.
Then I was free, an ally of the accidental. No one
hated me, I was the visitant who checks the march
of time, shapes destinies, and stabilizes loves. I
stood for the permanent. But you have made me the
handmaid of logic, rules, and regulations. And I
have lost the knack I had of sometimes being helpful.

THE PLAGUE: Who wants your help?

THE SECRETARY: Those who are not big enough to
face a sea of troubles. Nearly everyone, that is to
say. Quite often I could work in a sort of harmony
with them; I existed, in my fashion. Today I do
violence to them, and one and all they curse me
with their last breath. Perhaps that's why I like this
man whom you are telling me to kill. He chose me
freely, and, in his way, he pitied me. Yes, I like
people who meet me halfway.

THE PLAGUE: You'd do better not to irritate me.
. . . We have no need for pity.

THE SECRETARY: Who could need pity more than
those who themselves have none? When I say I
like this man, what I mean is really that I envy
him. For, with conquerors like us, love takes the
ugly form of envy. You know this well and you
know, too, that for this reason we deserve a little
pity.

THE PLAGUE: That's enough! I order you to keep
silent!

THE SECRETARY: You know it well and you know,
too, that when one kills enough one comes to envy
the innocence of those one kills. Oh, if only for a
moment, let me call a halt to this ruthless logic,
and let me fancy that at last I am leaning on a

human body. I am so sick of shadows! And I envy all these wretched people—yes, even that girl [*Points to* VICTORIA] who when she returns to life will start howling like a wounded animal. But at least she will have her grief to lean on.

[DIEGO *is collapsing. The* PLAGUE *helps him to his feet.*]

THE PLAGUE: Stand up, man! The end cannot come until my charming companion takes the necessary steps. And, as you see, she is indulging in sentiment just now. But don't be afraid, she will do her duty; it's in the rules and she knows what is expected of her. The machine is creaking a bit, that's all. But, before it folds completely, you shall have your wish, young fool; I give you back this city. [*Shouts of joy from the* CHORUS. *The* PLAGUE *turns toward them.*] Yes, I am going, but do not overdo your glee. I am pleased with myself, here, too, we have made a success of it. I like my name to live upon men's lips, and I know you will not forget me. Look at me! Look for a last time at the only power in the world, acclaim your one true monarch, and learn to fear. [*Laughs.*] In the old days you professed to fear God and his caprices. But your God was an anarchist who played fast and loose with logic. He thought He could be both autocratic and kindhearted at the same time—but that was obviously wishful thinking, if I may put it so. *I,* anyhow, know better. I stand for power and power alone. Yes, I have chosen domination which, as you have learned, can be more formidable than Hell itself.

For thousands and thousands of years I have strewn your fields and cities with dead bodies. My victims have fertilized the sands of Libya and black Ethiopia, the soil of Persia still is fat with the sweat of

my corpses. I filled Athens with the fires of purifi-
cation, kindled on her beaches thousands of funeral
pyres, and spread the seas of Greece so thick with
ashes that their blue turned gray. The gods, yes,
even the poor gods were revolted by my doings.
Then, when the temples gave place to cathedrals,
my black horsemen filled them with howling mobs.
For years untold, on all five continents, I have been
killing without respite and without compunction.

As systems go, mine was not a bad one. There was
a sound idea behind it. Nevertheless, that idea was
somewhat narrow. If you want to know the way I
feel about it, I'll say a dead man is refreshing
enough, but he's not remunerative. Not nearly so
rewarding as a slave. So the great thing is to secure
a majority of slaves by means of a minority of well-
selected deaths. And, thanks to our improved tech-
nique, we now can bring this off. That's why, after
having killed or humiliated the requisite number of
persons, we shall have whole nations on their knees.
No form of beauty or grandeur will stand up to us,
and we shall triumph over everything. . . .

THE SECRETARY: We shall triumph over everything—
—except pride.

THE PLAGUE: Who can tell? Men are not so unintel-
ligent as you may think, and very likely pride itself
will peter out. [*Sounds of trumpet calls and people
moving in the distance.*] Listen! My star's in the
ascendant once again. Those are your former masters returning, and you will find them blind as ever
to the wounds of others, sodden with inertia and
forgetfulness of the lessons of the past. And when
you see stupidity getting the upper hand again
without a struggle, you will lose heart. Cruelty
provokes, but stupidity disheartens. All honor, then,
to the stupid, who prepare my ways! They are

my hope and strength. Perhaps there will come a day when self-sacrifice will seem quite futile, and the never-ending clamor of your rebels will at last fall silent. Then I shall reign supreme, in the dead silence of men's servitude. [*Laughs.*] It's just a question of sticking to it, isn't it? But, never fear, I have the low brow of the stubborn man. [*Begins to move away.*]

THE SECRETARY: I am older than you, and I know that their love, too, can be stubborn.

THE PLAGUE: Love? What's that? [*Exit.*]

THE SECRETARY: Rise, woman. I'm tired, and I want to get it over.

[VICTORIA *rises. But at the same moment* DIEGO *falls. The* SECRETARY *retreats a little, into a patch of shadow.* VICTORIA *runs toward* DIEGO.]

VICTORIA: Oh, Diego, what have you done to our happiness?

DIEGO: Good-by, Victoria. I am glad it's so.

VICTORIA: Don't talk like that, my love! That's one of those horrible things men say. [*Weeping.*] No one has the right to be glad to die.

DIEGO: But I *am* glad, Victoria. I did what I was called upon to do.

VICTORIA: No, you should have chosen me, though all the powers of heaven forbade you. You should have preferred me to the whole earth.

DIEGO: I have squared up accounts with death—there lies my strength. But it is an all-devouring strength; happiness has no place in it.

VICTORIA: What did your strength matter to me? It was you—the man you were—that I loved.

DIEGO: I have burned myself out in the struggle. I am no longer a man and it is right that I should die.

VICTORIA [*flinging herself on him*]: Then take me with you.

DIEGO: No this world needs you. It needs our women

to teach it how to live. We men have never been capable of anything but dying.

VICTORIA: Ah, it was too simple, wasn't it, to love each other in silence and to endure together whatever had to be endured? I preferred your fear, Diego.

DIEGO: [*gazing at* VICTORIA]:   I loved you with my whole soul.

VICTORIA [*passionately*]:   But that wasn't enough! No, even that was not enough! You loved me with your soul, perhaps, but I wanted more than that, far more.

[*The* SECRETARY *stretches her hand toward* DIEGO. *The death agony begins, while the women hasten toward* VICTORIA *and gather round her.*]

CHORUS OF WOMEN: Our curse on him! Our curse on all who forsake our bodies! And pity on us, most of all, who are forsaken and must endure year after year this world which men in their pride are ever aspiring to transform! Surely, since everything may not be saved, we should learn at least to safeguard the home where love is. Then, come war, come pestilence, we could bravely see them through with you beside us. Thus, instead of this solitary death, haunted by foolish dreams and nourished with words, your last end would be shared by us, we would die united in an all-consuming flame of love. But no! Men go whoring after ideas, a man runs away from his mother, forsakes his love, and starts rushing upon adventure, wounded without a scar, slain without a dagger, a hunter of shadows or a lonely singer who invokes some impossible reunion under a silent sky, and makes his way from solitude to solitude, toward the final isolation, a death in the desert.

[DIEGO *dies. The women keen while a rising wind sweeps the city.*]

THE SECRETARY: Do not weep. The bosom of the earth is soft for those who have loved her greatly. [*She goes away. Carrying* DIEGO, VICTORIA *and the women move to the side of the stage. Meanwhile the sounds in the background are becoming more distinct. There is a burst of music and* NADA *is heard shouting on the battlements.*]

NADA: Here they are, the old gang! They all are coming back: the men of the past, the fossils, the dead-enders, the triflers, smooth-tongued, comfortable—the army of tradition, robust and flourishing, spick and span as ever. So now we can start all over again, and what a relief for everyone! From zero naturally. Here they come, the tailors of nonentity, you'll have your new suits built to order. But there's no need to worry, their method is the best. Instead of shutting the mouths of those who air their grievances, they shut their own ears. We were dumb, we are going to be deaf. [*Trumpet calls.*] Look! The writers of history are coming back and we shall soon be reading all about our heroes of the plague. They will be kept nice and cool under the flagstones. But there's nothing to complain of; the company above the flagstones is really too, too mixed! [*In the background official ceremonies are taking place, in pantomime.*] Look! Do you see what they're up to? Conferring decorations on each other! The banquet halls of hatred are always open, and the soil is never so exhausted that the dead wood of the gallows fails to rise from it. The blood of those you call the just ones still glistens on the walls—and what are those fine fellows up to? Giving each other medals! Rejoice, my friends, you're going to have your prize-day speeches. But before the platform is brought forward, I'd like to give you mine—a few well-chosen words. That young man,

whom somehow I couldn't help liking, died cheated.
[*The* FISHERMAN *makes a rush at* NADA. *The Guards
arrest him.*] As you see, fishermen and governments may come and go, the police are always with
us. So, after all, justice *does* exist.

CHORUS: No, there is no justice—but there are limits.
And those who stand for no rules at all, no less than
those who want to impose a rule for everything,
overstep the limit. Open the gates and let the salt
wind scour the city.
[*The gates are opened, the wind is growing stronger
and stronger.*]

NADA: Justice exists—the justice done to my disgust.
Yes, you are going to start again; but henceforth
it's no concern of mine. And don't count on me to
supply you with the plaintive, perfect scapegoat;
plaintiveness is not my line. So now, old world, it's
time for me to leave you, your executioners are
tired, their hatred's gone too cold. I know too many
things; even scorn has had its day. So good-by,
my worthy fellow citizens, one day you'll find out
for yourselves that man is nothing and God's face is
hideous!
[NADA *rushes through the wind, which has now
reached storm pitch, to the jetty, and flings himself
into the sea. The* FISHERMAN, *who has run after
him, stands gazing down.*]

THE FISHERMAN: The sea has closed upon him. The
great sea-horses are ravaging him, choking his
breath out with their white manes. That lying
mouth is filling up with salt; at last it will keep
silent. See how the swirling waves are glowing,
like anemones! Their anger is our anger, they are
avenging us, calling on all the men of the sea to
meet together, all the outcasts to make common
cause. O mighty mother, whose bosom is the home-

land of all rebels, behold thy people who will never yield! Soon a great tidal wave, nourished in the bitter dark of underseas, will sweep away our loathsome cities.

CURTAIN

THE JUST ASSASSINS

A PLAY IN FIVE ACTS

O love! O life! not life, but love in death!
ROMEO AND JULIET   ACT IV, SCENE 5

CHARACTERS IN THE PLAY

DORA DULEBOV

THE GRAND DUCHESS

IVAN KALIAYEV

STEPAN FEDOROV

BORIS (BORIA) ANNENKOV

ALEXIS VOINOV

SKURATOV

FOKA

THE GUARD

LES JUSTES (THE JUST ASSASSINS) *was presented for the first time at the* THÉÂTRE-HÉBERTOT, *Paris, on December 15, 1949.*

ACT I

The terrorists' headquarters: a sparsely furnished apartment of an ordinary type. The morning sun is shining through a window overlooking a main street in Moscow. When the curtain rises DORA DULEBOV *and* BORIS ANNENKOV *are standing in the middle of the room. For some moments there is complete silence; then the front doorbell rings once.* DORA *seems about to say something, but* ANNENKOV *signals to her to keep quiet. Two more rings in quick succession.*

ANNENKOV: It's he. [*He goes out.* DORA *waits, still motionless; she has not moved at all since the curtain rose.* ANNENKOV *returns with* STEPAN, *whom he is grasping affectionately by the shoulders.*] Here he is! Stepan's back again!

DORA [*going toward* STEPAN *and clasping his hand*]: Welcome back, Stepan.

STEPAN: Good morning, Dora.

DORA [*gazing at him*]: Three years—just think!

STEPAN: Yes, three long, empty years. That day when they arrested me I was on my way to join you.

DORA: We were expecting you every moment. I'll never forget how my heart sank, deeper and deeper, as the minutes ticked away. We didn't dare to look each other in the face.

ANNENKOV: And of course we had to move at once to a new apartment.

STEPAN: I know.

DORA: And over there, Stepan, how was it?

STEPAN: Over there?

DORA: In the prison, I mean.

STEPAN: One escapes . . . with luck.

ANNENKOV: Yes. When we heard that you'd got through to Switzerland, well, you know how we felt.

STEPAN: Switzerland, too, is a prison.

ANNENKOV: Oh, come now! They're free there, anyhow.

STEPAN: Freedom can be a prison, so long as a single man on earth is kept in bondage. I myself was free, of course, but all the time I was thinking of Russia and her slaves.

[*A short silence.*]

ANNENKOV: I'm glad, Stepan, that the party sent you here.

STEPAN: They had to. That atmosphere of smug inertia was stifling me. Ah, to act, to *act* at last . . . ! [*Looks at* ANNENKOV.] We shall kill him, you're sure of that?

ANNENKOV: Quite sure.

STEPAN: We shall kill that bloodthirsty tyrant! Ah! You're the leader, Boria, and I shall obey you, never fear.

ANNENKOV: I don't need your promise, Stepan. We all are brothers.

STEPAN: But discipline's essential. That's something I learned in the convict prison. The Revolutionary Socialist Party cannot do without it. We must be disciplined if we're to kill the Grand Duke and put an end to tyranny.

DORA [*going up to him*]: Sit down, Stepan. You must be tired after that long journey.

STEPAN: I'm never tired. [*A short silence.* DORA *sits down.*] Is everything ready, Boria?

ANNENKOV [*in a different, brisker manner*]: For

a month now, two of our group have been watching
the Grand Duke's movements hour by hour. Dora
has compiled all the facts we need to know.

STEPAN: Has the proclamation been drawn up?

ANNENKOV: Yes. All Russia will know that the Revolutionary Socialist Party has executed the Grand
Duke Serge so as to bring nearer the day when the
Russian people are set free. And the Imperial Court
will learn that we are resolved to carry on the
reign of terror, of which this bomb is the beginning, until the land is given back to its rightful
owners, to the people. Yes, Stepan, everything's set,
and we won't have long to wait.

STEPAN: Where exactly do I come in on this?

ANNENKOV: To begin with, you will help Dora.
You'll replace Schweitzer, who used to work with
her.

STEPAN: Has he been killed?

ANNENKOV: Yes.

STEPAN: How?

ANNENKOV: In an accident.

[STEPAN *looks at* DORA. *She lowers her eyes.*]

STEPAN: And then?

ANNENKOV: Then . . . we'll see. You must be on
hand to replace me if the need arises, and to ensure
our liaison with the Central Committee.

STEPAN: And our comrades here—who are they?

ANNENKOV: You met Voinov in Switzerland. He's
only a youngster, but thoroughly dependable. Then
there's Yanek; you don't know him, do you?

STEPAN: Yanek?

ANNENKOV: His real name is Ivan Kaliayev. "The
Poet" is another name we have for him.

STEPAN: That's no name for a terrorist.

ANNENKOV [*laughing*]: Yanek wouldn't agree with
you. He says all poetry is revolutionary.

STEPAN: There's only one thing that is revolutionary:

the bomb. [*A short silence.*] Do you think, Dora, that I can be of help to you?

DORA: I'm sure you can. The great thing to be careful about is not to break the tube.

STEPAN: And if it breaks?

DORA: That's how Schweitzer died. [*Again, a short silence.*] Why are you smiling, Stepan?

STEPAN: Am I smiling?

DORA: Yes.

STEPAN: I sometimes do—not very often, though. [*Pauses. He seems to be reflecting.*] Tell me, Dora, would one bomb be enough to blow up this house?

DORA: To blow it up? Hardly that. But it would do quite a lot of damage.

STEPAN: How many bombs would be needed to blow up Moscow?

ANNENKOV: Have you gone crazy? . . . Or what do you mean?

STEPAN: Oh, nothing.

[*A ring at the front doorbell. They wait, listening. Two more rings.* ANNENKOV *goes out into the hall and comes back with* VOINOV.]

VOINOV: Stepan!

STEPAN: Good morning, Voinov.

[*They shake hands.* VOINOV *goes up to* DORA *and kisses her.*]

ANNENKOV: Everything go off all right, Alexis?

VOINOV: Yes.

ANNENKOV: Have you studied the route from the palace to the theater?

VOINOV: I can make a sketch of it right away. Look! [*He draws a plan.*] Turnings, narrow streets, crossings. . . . The carriage will go by under our windows.

ANNENKOV: What do those two crosses mean?

VOINOV: One's a little square where the horses will

have to slow down; the other's the theater where they will stop. Those are the best places in my opinion.

ANNENKOV: Right. Give it to me.

STEPAN: Many police spies around?

VOINOV [*uneasily*]:   I'm afraid so.

STEPAN: Ah! Do they rattle you?

VOINOV: Well, I can't say I feel at ease when they're around.

ANNENKOV: Nobody does. You needn't worry over that.

VOINOV: It's not that I'm afraid; only somehow I can't get used to lying.

STEPAN: Everybody lies. What's important is to lie well.

VOINOV: That's what I find so hard. When I was at the university the other students were always teasing me because I never could hide my feelings. I always blurted everything out. Finally, I was expelled.

STEPAN: Why?

VOINOV: In the history course my tutor asked me how Peter the Great founded Saint Petersburg.

STEPAN: That's a good question.

VOINOV: I answered: "With blood and the knout." I was promptly expelled.

STEPAN: Yes? And then?

VOINOV: Then I realized that just to denounce injustice wasn't enough. One must give one's life to fighting it. And now I'm happy.

STEPAN: And yet—you have to lie?

VOINOV: For the present, yes. But I'll be done with lying on the day I throw the bomb.

[*The bell purrs: two rings in quick succession, then a single ring.* DORA *runs out.*]

ANNENKOV: That's Yanek.

STEPAN: It wasn't the same signal.

ANNENKOV: Oh, that's one of Yanek's little jokes. He has his private signal.

[STEPAN *shrugs his shoulders.* DORA *is heard speaking in the hall.* DORA *and* IVAN KALIAYEV *enter arm in arm.* KALIAYEV *is laughing.*]

DORA: Yanek, this is Stepan, who's replacing Schweitzer.

KALIAYEV: Welcome, brother.

STEPAN: Thanks.

[DORA *and* KALIAYEV *sit down, facing the others.*]

ANNENKOV: Yanek, are you sure you'll recognize the carriage?

KALIAYEV: Yes, I've had two good long looks at it. I'd recognize it among a thousand, a hundred yards away. I have noted every detail—for instance, that one of the panes of the left-hand lamp is chipped.

VOINOV: And the police spies?

KALIAYEV: A host of them. But we're old friends; they buy cigarettes from me. [*Laughs.*]

ANNENKOV: Has Pavel confirmed our information?

KALIAYEV: The Grand Duke is due to go to the theater this week. In a few minutes Pavel will know the exact day and leave a message with the door porter. [*He turns to* DORA *with a laugh.*] We're in luck, Dora!

DORA [*Staring at him*]: I see you've discarded your peddler's outfit. You're quite the grand gentleman today, and I must say it suits you. But don't you miss your smock?

KALIAYEV [*laughing*]: I certainly do. You can't think how proud of it I was. [To STEPAN *and* ANNENKOV.] I began by spending two months watching peddlers on their job; then another month or so practicing in my little bedroom. My colleagues never suspected a thing. I heard one of them saying: "He's

a wonder! Why, he'd sell the Czar's horses and
get away with it!" In fact they tried to learn my
tricks.

DORA: And of course you laughed.

KALIAYEV: You know quite well I can't help laughing. Anyhow, it was all so entertaining—the plunge
into a brand-new life, wearing that fancy dress. . . .

DORA: I can't bear fancy dress. Look at what I'm
wearing now. Some actress's castoff frock. Really,
Boria might have chosen something else. There's
nothing of the actress about me. I've an incorrigibly
simple heart.

KALIAYEV [*laughing*]:   But you look so pretty in it.

DORA: Pretty! I'd like to be pretty . . . but that's
one of the things I mustn't think about.

KALIAYEV: Why not? Dora, there's always such a sad
look in your eyes. But you should be gay, you
should be proud. There's so much beauty in the
world, so much joy. "In those quiet places where
my heart once spoke to yours . . ."

DORA [*smiling*]:   ". . . I breathed eternal summer."

KALIAYEV: Oh, Dora, you remember those lines!
And you're smiling! How glad I am!

STEPAN [*brusquely*]:   We're wasting our time. Boria,
hadn't we better go down and see the porter?

[KALIAYEV *stares at him, puzzled.*]

ANNENKOV: Yes. Would you go down, Dora? Don't
forget the tip. Then Voinov will help you to get
the stuff together in the bedroom.

[*They go out by different doors.* STEPAN *moves
toward* ANNENKOV, *with an obstinate expression on
his face.*]

STEPAN [*fiercely*]:   I want to throw the bomb.

ANNENKOV: No, Stepan. That's already been decided.

STEPAN: Boria, I beg you to let me throw it—you
know how much that means to me.

ANNENKOV: No. Orders are orders. [*A short silence.*]

I'm in the same position; I have to stay here while others man the firing line. It's hard, but discipline must be maintained.

STEPAN: Who is to throw the first bomb?

KALIAYEV: I am. And Voinov the second.

STEPAN: You?

KALIAYEV: Why do you sound so surprised? Don't you feel I can be trusted?

STEPAN: Experience is needed.

KALIAYEV: Experience? But you know quite well that one throws a bomb just once—and then . . . No one has ever had a second chance.

STEPAN: A steady hand is needed.

KALIAYEV [*stretching out his hand*]: Look! Do you think that hand will tremble? [*Stepan looks away.*] It'll be steady as a rock, I assure you, when the time comes. Or do you suppose I'd hesitate when I have that tyrant in front of me? No, you can't seriously imagine that. And even if for some reason my arm started shaking, I know a certain way of killing the Grand Duke.

ANNENKOV: What way?

KALIAYEV: I'd throw myself under the horses' feet. [*With a petulant heave of his shoulders,* STEPAN *goes to the back of the room and sits down.*]

ANNENKOV: No, that's not on the program. Your orders are to try to get away. The group needs you, and you must save your life, if you can.

KALIAYEV: Then—so be it! I realize the honor that's being done me, and I promise to be worthy of it.

ANNENKOV: You, Stepan, will be in the street while Yanek and Alexis are waiting for the carriage. I want you to stroll up and down in front of our windows; we'll settle on the signal you're to give. I and Dora will wait here, ready to launch our manifesto when the moment comes. With any reasonable luck we'll lay the Grand Duke low.

KALIAYEV [*excitedly*]:   Yes, I'll lay him low. And how glorious if it comes off! Though, of course, the Grand Duke's nothing. We must strike higher.

ANNENKOV: The Grand Duke to begin with.

KALIAYEV: And suppose we fail? Then, Boria, we must act like the Japanese.

ANNENKOV: What do you mean?

KALIAYEV: During the war the Japanese never surrendered. They killed themselves.

ANNENKOV: No, Yanek, don't think of suicide.

KALIAYEV: Of what, then?

ANNENKOV: Of carrying on our work, of terrorism.

STEPAN [*speaking from the back of the room*]:   To commit suicide a man must have a great love for himself. A true revolutionary cannot love himself.

KALIAYEV [*swinging round on him*]:   A true revolutionary? Why are you behaving to me like this? What have you got against me?

STEPAN: I don't like people who dabble with revolution simply because they're bored.

ANNENKOV: Stepan!

STEPAN [*rising to his feet and coming toward them*]:   Yes, I'm brutal. But for me hatred is not just a game. We haven't joined together to admire each other. We have joined together *to get something done.*

KALIAYEV [*gently*]:   Why are you being rude to me? Who told you I was bored?

STEPAN: There was no need to tell me. You change the signals, you enjoy dressing up as a peddler, you recite poems, you want to throw yourself under horses' feet, and now you're talking about suicide. [*Looks him in the eyes.*] No, I can't say you inspire me with confidence.

KALIAYEV [*mastering his anger*]:   You don't know me, brother. I'm never bored, and I love life. I joined the revolution because I love life.

STEPAN: I do not love life; I love something higher —and that is justice.

KALIAYEV [*with a visible effort to control himself*]: Each of us serves the cause of justice in his own manner; you in yours and I in mine. Why not agree to differ? And let's love each other if we can.

STEPAN: We cannot.

KALIAYEV [*losing control*]: What then are you doing among us?

STEPAN: I have come to kill a man, not to love him, or to agree to differ from him.

KALIAYEV [*passionately*]: You will not kill him single-handed, or on behalf of nothing. You will kill him with us, on behalf of the Russian people. That is what justifies your act.

STEPAN [*fiercely*]: Don't prate of justification! I got all the justification I need three years ago, one night in the convict prison. And I refuse to tolerate . . .

ANNENKOV: That's enough. Have you both gone off your heads? Have you forgotten what binds us together? That we all are brothers, working hand in hand, to punish the tyrants and set our people free? Together we shall kill, and nothing can divide us. [*They are silent. He gazes at them for a moment.*] Come along, Stepan, we'll have to settle on the signal. [STEPAN *leaves the room. To* KALIAYEV.] Don't take it to heart, Yanek. Stepan has suffered terribly. I'll talk to him.

KALIAYEV [*who is very pale*]: He insulted me, Boria. [DORA *enters.*]

DORA [*after a glance at* KALIAYEV]: What's wrong?

ANNENKOV: Nothing. [*Goes out.*]

DORA [*to* KALIAYEV]: What's wrong?

KALIAYEV: We've come to words already. He doesn't like me.

[DORA *sits down. For some moments neither speaks.*]

DORA: Stepan doesn't like anybody; that's how he is.

But he will be happier when everything is over. Don't be sad, Yanek.

KALIAYEV: I *am* sad. I want you all to love me. When I joined the group I cut adrift from everything, and if my brothers turn against me, how can I bear it? Time and again I feel they do not understand me. Perhaps it's my fault. I know I'm often clumsy, I don't say the right things, I . . .

DORA: They love you and they understand you. Only, Stepan's different.

KALIAYEV: No. I can guess what he thinks; I heard Schweitzer say much the same thing: "Yanek's too flighty, too eccentric for a revolutionary." I'd have them know that I'm not the least bit flighty. I imagine I strike them as being impulsive, crackbrained very likely. Yet I believe in our ideal quite as firmly as they do. Like them, I'm ready to give my life up for it. I, too, can be cunning, silent, resourceful, when it's called for. Only, I'm still convinced that life is a glorious thing, I'm in love with beauty, happiness. That's why I hate despotism. The trouble is to make them understand this. Revolution, by all means. But revolution for the sake of life—to give life a chance, if you see what I mean.

DORA [*impulsively*]: Yes, I do! [*After a short silence, in a lower voice.*] Only—what we're going to give isn't life, but death.

KALIAYEV: We? Oh, I see what you mean. But that's not the same thing at all. When we kill, we're killing so as to build up a world in which there will be no more killing. We consent to being criminals so that at last the innocent, and only they, will inherit the earth.

DORA: And suppose it didn't work out like that?

KALIAYEV: How can you say such a thing? It's unthinkable. Then Stepan would be right—and we'd have to spit in the face of beauty.

DORA: I've had more experience than you in this work, and I know that nothing's so simple as you imagine. But you have faith, and faith is what we need, all of us.

KALIAYEV: Faith? No. Only one man had faith in that sense.

DORA: Well, let's say then that you have an indomitable soul, and you will see it through, no matter at what cost. Why did you ask to throw the first bomb?

KALIAYEV: When one's a terrorist can one talk of direct action without taking part in it?

DORA: No.

KALIAYEV: And one must be in the forefront, of course. . . .

DORA [*musingly*]:   Yes, there's the forefront—and there's also the last moment. We all should think of that. That's where courage lies, and the selfless ardor we all need . . . you, too, need.

KALIAYEV: For a year now that has never left my thoughts; I've been living for that moment day by day, hour by hour. And I know now that I'd like to die on the spot, beside the Grand Duke. To shed my blood to the last drop, or blaze up like tinder in the flare of the explosion and leave not a shred of me behind. Do you understand why I asked to throw the bomb? To die for an ideal—that's the only way of proving oneself worthy of it. It's our only justification.

DORA: That's the death I, too, desire.

KALIAYEV: Yes, the happiest end of all. Sometimes at night when I'm lying awake on the thin straw mattress that's all a peddler can afford, I'm worried by the thought that they have forced us into being murderers. But then I remind myself that I'm going to die, too, and everything's all right. I smile to myself like a child and go happily to sleep.

DORA: That's how it should be, Yanek. To kill, and to die on the spot. But, to my mind, there's a still greater happiness. [*She falls silent.* KALIAYEV *gazes at her. She lowers her eyes.*] The scaffold!

KALIAYEV [*with feverish excitement*]: Yes, I, too, have thought of that. There's something incomplete in dying on the spot. While between the moment the bomb is thrown and the scaffold, there is an eternity, perhaps the only eternity a man can know.

DORA [*clasping his hands; earnestly*]: And that's the thought which must help you through. We are paying more than we owe.

KALIAYEV: What do you mean?

DORA: We're forced to kill, aren't we? We deliberately immolate a life, a single life?

KALIAYEV: Yes.

DORA: But throwing the bomb and then climbing the scaffold—that's giving one's life *twice*. Thus we pay more than we owe.

KALIAYEV: Yes, it's dying twice over. Thank you, Dora. There's nothing with which anyone can reproach us. Now, I'm sure of myself. [*A short silence.*] What is it, Dora? Why are you silent?

DORA: I'd like to help you in another way as well. Only . . .

KALIAYEV: Only . . . what?

DORA: No, I'd better not. . . .

KALIAYEV: Don't you trust me?

DORA: It's not that I don't trust *you*, darling; I don't trust myself. Ever since Schweitzer's death, I've been having . . . queer ideas. And anyhow it's not for me to tell you what will be so difficult.

KALIAYEV: But I like things that are difficult. Unless you have a very low opinion of me, say what you have in mind.

DORA [*gazing at him*]: I know. You're brave. That, in fact, is what makes me anxious. You laugh, you work yourself up, you go forward to the sacrifice in a sort of rapture. But in a few hours' time you'll have to come out of your dream and face reality, the dreadful thing you are to do. Perhaps it's best to speak of this beforehand—so that you won't be taken by surprise, and flinch.

KALIAYEV: That's nonsense! I shall *not* flinch. But please explain . . .

DORA: Throwing the bomb, the scaffold, dying twice over—that's the easier part. Your heart will see you through. But standing in the front line. . . . [*She pauses, scans him again, and seems to hesitate.*] You'll be standing in front, you'll see him. . . .

KALIAYEV: See whom?

DORA: The Grand Duke.

KALIAYEV: Oh, only for a moment at most.

DORA: A moment during which you'll look at him. Oh, Yanek, it's best for you to know, to be fore-warned! A man is a man. Perhaps the Grand Duke has gentle eyes, perhaps you'll see him smiling to himself, scratching his ear. Perhaps—who knows? —you'll see a little scar on his cheek where he cut himself shaving. And, if he looks at you, at that moment. . . .

KALIAYEV: It's not he I'm killing. I'm killing despot-ism.

DORA: That's quite true. And despotism must be killed. I'll get the bomb ready and when I'm screw-ing in the tube—that's the moment when it's touch and go, and one's nerves are taut—I'll feel a queer little thrill . . . of joy. But, then, I don't know the Grand Duke; it wouldn't be anything so easy if while I was screwing in the tube he were sitting in front of me, looking at me. But you'll see him quite near, from only a yard or two away.

KALIAYEV [*vehemently*]: I shall *not* see him.

DORA: Why? Will you shut your eyes?

KALIAYEV: No. But, with God's help, my hatred will
surge up just in time, and blind me.
   [*A single ring at the bell. They keep very still.*
   STEPAN *and* VOINOV *enter. Voices in the hall. Then*
   ANNENKOV, *too, comes in.*]

ANNENKOV: It's the porter. The Grand Duke's going
to the theater tomorrow. [*Looks at them.*] Please
see that everything is ready, Dora.

DORA [*in a low, toneless voice*]:   Yes. [*She walks
   slowly out.*]

KALIAYEV [*after watching her receding form, turns to*
   STEPAN *and says with quiet assurance.*] I shall kill
him. With joy!

C U R T A I N

ACT II

Scene as before. Night has fallen. BORIS *is at the window,* DORA *beside the table.*

ANNENKOV: They're at their posts. Stepan has just lit his cigarette.

DORA: When is the Grand Duke expected to drive by?

ANNENKOV: Any moment now. Listen! Isn't that a carriage? . . . No.

DORA: Don't fidget like that! Do sit down.

ANNENKOV: What about the bombs?

DORA: Do sit down. . . . There's nothing more we can do.

ANNENKOV: Yes, there is. We can envy them.

DORA: Your place is here. You are the leader.

ANNENKOV: I'm the leader, yes. But Yanek's a better man than I, and perhaps he is the one who . . .

DORA: The risk's the same for all. For the man who throws and for the man who doesn't throw.

ANNENKOV: In the long run, yes, the risk's the same. But at this moment Yanek and Alexis are in the firing line. Oh, I know I haven't the right to be with them. Still, I can't help fearing sometimes that I'm a little too ready to play my part; after all it . . . it makes things easier, not having to throw the bomb oneself.

DORA: What if it does? The only thing that matters is for you to do your duty, to the end.

ANNENKOV: How calm you are, Dora!

DORA: I am not calm; I'm frightened. . . . Let me tell you something. I've been with the group for

three years, haven't I? And for two years I've been
making the bombs. I have done all I was told to do,
and I don't think I ever let you down. That's so,
isn't it?

ANNENKOV: Of course it is, Dora.

DORA: Well, all those three years I have been afraid;
I have been haunted by that creeping fear that leaves
you only when you go to sleep, and are lucky
enough not to dream; but when you wake up, there
it is, waiting at your bedside. . . . So the only thing
was to get used to it. I've trained myself to keep
calm just when I'm most afraid. But it's nothing to
be proud of.

ANNENKOV: On the contrary, you *should* feel proud.
Look at me! I've never mastered anything. Do you
know, I often catch myself regretting the bad old
days—a gay life, pretty women, and all the rest of
it! Yes, I was fond of women, wine, dancing through
the night. . . .

DORA: I'd guessed as much, Boria, and that's why I
am so fond of you. Your heart is not dried up. Even
if it's still hankering after pleasure, surely that's better than the hideous silence that often settles in at
the very place where voices used to rise—authenti-
cally human voices.

ANNENKOV: Dora! I can't believe my ears! *You*, of
all people, feel like that?

DORA: Ssh! Listen. [*She puts a finger to her lips,
listening intently. A distant rumble of wheels; then
silence.*] No. It's not he, not yet. My heart's thumping. You see! I've still a lot to learn.

ANNENKOV [*going to the window*]:   Ah! Stepan's
made a sign. He's coming. [*Again there is a rumble
of wheels; it comes nearer and nearer, passes below
the windows, then gradually recedes. A long silence.*] In a few seconds . . . [*They listen.*] How
long it seems! [DORA *makes a fretful gesture.*

A long silence. Suddenly, a peal of bells in the distance.] What *can* have happened? Yanek should have thrown his bomb by now. The carriage must have reached the theater. And what about Alexis? Look! Stepan's turned, now he's running toward the theater.

DORA [*clinging to him*]: Yanek's been arrested. I'm sure it's that. Oh, Boria, we must do something, we . . .

ANNENKOV: Wait. [*Listens.*] No, nothing. That settles it.

DORA: I don't understand. How can Yanek have been arrested when he hasn't done anything? Oh, I know he was quite ready for it. In fact, prison, the trial, were what he wanted. But after he'd killed the Grand Duke. Not like this, not like this!

ANNENKOV [*looking out*]: Here's Voinov. Open, quick! [DORA *opens the door.* VOINOV *enters; he is greatly agitated.*] What's happened, Alexis?

VOINOV: I've no idea. I was waiting for the first bomb. Then I saw the carriage rounding the corner, and nothing'd happened. I was completely baffled. I thought a bit, then I concluded you had called it off at the last minute. So I ran back here.

ANNENKOV: What about Yanek?

VOINOV: I haven't seen him.

DORA: He's been arrested.

ANNENKOV [*who is still looking out of the window*]: No. There he is. He's coming back.

[*Dora opens the door.* KALIAYEV *enters, his face streaming with tears.*]

KALIAYEV: Brothers . . . forgive me . . . I couldn't bring myself . . .

[DORA *goes to him and clasps his hand.*]

DORA [*soothingly*]: That's all right. Don't worry. . . .

ANNENKOV: What happened?

DORA [*to* KALIAYEV]: Don't take it so hard, Yanek.

Sometimes it's like that, you know; at the last minute
everything goes wrong.

ANNENKOV: No, I can't believe my ears.

DORA: Let him be. You're not the only one, Yanek.
Schweitzer, too, couldn't bring it off the first time.

ANNENKOV: Yanek, were you . . . afraid?

KALIAYEV [*indignantly*]: Afraid? Certainly not—
and you haven't the right . . .

[*A knocking at the door in the agreed code.
At a sign from* ANNENKOV, VOINOV *goes out.* KALI-
AYEV *seems completely prostrated. A short silence.*
STEPAN *enters.*]

ANNENKOV: Well?

STEPAN: There were children in the Grand Duke's
carriage.

ANNENKOV: Children?

STEPAN: Yes. The Grand Duke's niece and nephew.

ANNENKOV: But Orlov told us the Grand Duke would
be by himself.

STEPAN: There was the Grand Duchess as well. Too
many people, I suppose, for our young poet. Luckily, the police spies didn't notice anything.

[ANNENKOV *speaks in a low tone to* STEPAN. *All are
gazing at* KALIAYEV, *who now looks up and fixes
his eyes on* STEPAN.]

KALIAYEV [*wildly*]: I'd never dreamed of anything
like that. Children, children especially. Have you
ever noticed children's eyes—that grave, intent
look they often have? Somehow I never can
face it. I have to look away. . . . And, to think,
only a moment before I was so gloriously happy,
standing at the corner of that little side street, in a
patch of shadow. The moment I saw the carriage
lamps twinkling in the distance, my heart began to
race. With joy, I can assure you. And as the rumble
of wheels came nearer, it beat faster and faster.
Thumping inside me like a drum. I wanted to leap

into the air. I'm almost sure that I was laughing, laughing for joy. And I kept on saying: "Yes . . . Yes . . ." Do you understand? [*Averting his gaze from* STEPAN, *he relapses into his dejected attitude.*] I ran forward. It was then I saw the children. They weren't laughing, not they! Just staring into emptiness, and holding themselves very straight. How sad they looked! Dressed up in their best clothes, with their hands resting on their thighs, like two little statues framed in the windows on each side of the door. I didn't see the Grand Duchess. I saw only them. If they had turned my way, I think I might have thrown the bomb—if only to extinguish that sad look of theirs. But they kept staring straight ahead. [*Raising his head, he looks at the others. Silence. Then, in a still lower voice*] I can't explain what happened to me then. My arms went limp. My legs seemed to be giving way beneath me. And, a moment afterwards, it was too late. [*Another silence; he is staring at the floor.*] Dora, did I dream it, or was there a peal of bells just then?

DORA: No, Yanek, you did not dream it.

[*She lays her hand on his arm.* KALIAYEV *looks up and sees their eyes intent on him. He rises to his feet.*]

KALIAYEV: Yes, look at me, brothers, look at me. . . . But I'm no coward, Boria, I did not flinch. Only I wasn't expecting them. And everything went with such a rush. Those two serious little faces, and in my hand that hideous weight. I'd have had to throw it at *them*. Like that! Straight at them. No, I just couldn't bring myself . . . [*He scans their faces.*] In the old days when I used to go out driving on our estate in the Ukraine, I always drove hell-for-leather. I wasn't afraid of anything, except of running down a child—that was my one fear. I pictured a sort of brittle thud as the small head hit the roadway, and the mere thought of it

made me shudder. [*He is silent for some moments.*]
Help me . . . [*Another silence.*] I meant to kill
myself just now. I came back only because I thought
I owed it to you; you were the only people who
could judge me, could say if I was wrong or right,
and I'd abide by your decision. But here I am—and
you don't say anything. [DORA *comes beside him, her
hand brushing his shoulder. He looks round, then
continues in a toneless voice*] This is what I propose.
If you decide that those children must be killed, I
will go to the theater and wait till they are coming
out. Then I shall handle the situation by myself,
unaided; I shall throw the bomb and I can promise
not to miss. So make your decision; I'll do whatever
the group decides.

STEPAN: The group had given you orders to kill the
Grand Duke.

KALIAYEV: That's so. But I wasn't asked to murder
children.

ANNENKOV: Yanek's right. That wasn't on the program.

STEPAN: It was his duty to obey.

ANNENKOV: I was in charge of operations and I'm to
blame. Every possibility should have been foreseen,
so that no one could feel the least hesitation about
what to do. Well, now we have to settle whether
we let this chance go by, or tell Yanek to wait outside the theater for them to come out. You, Alexis,
what do you advise?

VOINOV: I don't know what to say. I suspect I'd have
done as Yanek did. But I'm not sure of myself. [*In
an undertone*] My hands—I can't trust them not
to tremble.

ANNENKOV: And you, Dora?

DORA [*emphatically*]:   I'd have behaved like Yanek.
So how can I ask of others what I couldn't bring
myself to do?

STEPAN: I wonder if you people realize what this decision means? Two solid months of shadowing, of hairbreadth escapes—two wasted months! Egor arrested to no purpose. Rikov hanged to no purpose. Must we start that all over again? Weeks and weeks of harrowing suspense without a break; of sleepless nights, of plotting and scheming, before another opportunity like this comes our way. Have you all gone crazy?

ANNENKOV: In two days' time, as you know quite well, the Grand Duke will be going to the theater again.

STEPAN: Two days during which we run the risk of being caught at any moment; why, you've said so yourself!

KALIAYEV: I'm off!

DORA: No, wait. [*To* STEPAN] You, Stepan, could you fire point blank on a child, with your eyes open?

STEPAN: I could, if the group ordered it.

DORA: Why did you shut your eyes then?

STEPAN: What? Did I shut my eyes?

DORA: Yes.

STEPAN: Then it must have been because I wanted to picture . . . what you describe, more vividly, and to make sure my answer was the true one.

DORA: Open your eyes, Stepan, and try to realize that the group would lose all its driving force, were it to tolerate, even for a moment, the idea of children's being blown to pieces by our bombs.

STEPAN: Sorry, but I don't suffer from a tender heart; that sort of nonsense cuts no ice with *me*. . . . Not until the day comes when we stop sentimentalizing about children will the revolution triumph, and we be masters of the world.

DORA: When that day comes, the revolution will be loathed by the whole human race.

STEPAN: What matter, if we love it enough to force

our revolution on it; to rescue humanity from itself
and from its bondage?

DORA: And suppose mankind at large doesn't want
the revolution? Suppose the masses for whom you
are fighting won't stand for the killing of their children? What then? Would you strike at the masses,
too?

STEPAN: Yes, if it were necessary, and I would go on
striking at them until they understood. . . . No,
don't misunderstand me; I, too, love the people.

DORA: Love, you call it. That's not how love shows
itself.

STEPAN: Who says so?

DORA: *I* say it.

STEPAN: You're a woman, and your idea of love is
. . . well, let's say, unsound.

DORA [*passionately*]: Anyhow, I've a very sound idea
of what shame means.

STEPAN: Once, and once only, in my life I felt
ashamed of myself. It was when I was flogged. Yes,
I was flogged. The knout—you know what that is,
don't you? Vera was there beside me and she killed
herself, as a protest. But I . . . I went on living. So
why should I be ashamed of anything, now?

ANNENKOV: Stepan, all of us love you and respect you.
But whatever private reasons you may have for
feeling as you do, I can't allow you to say that everything's permissible. Thousands of our brothers have
died to make it known that everything is *not* allowed.

STEPAN: Nothing that can serve our cause should be
ruled out.

ANNENKOV [*angrily*]: Is it permissible for one of us
to join the police and play a double game, as Evno
proposed to do? Would *you* do it?

STEPAN: Yes, if I felt it necessary.

ANNENKOV [*rising to his feet*]: Stepan, we will forget

what you've just said, for the sake of all that you have done for us and with us. . . . Now, let's keep to the matter in hand. The question is whether, presently, we are to throw bombs at those two children.

STEPAN: Children! There you go, always talking about children! Cannot you realize what is at stake? Just because Yanek couldn't bring himself to kill those two, thousands of Russian children will go on dying of starvation for years to come. Have you ever seen children dying of starvation? I have. And to be killed by a bomb is a pleasant death compared with that. But Yanek never saw children starving to death. He saw only the Grand Duke's pair of darling little lapdogs. Aren't you sentient human beings? Or are you living like animals for the moment only? In that case by all means indulge in charity and cure each petty suffering that meets your eye; but don't meddle with the revolution, for its task is to cure all sufferings present and to come.

DORA: Yanek's ready to kill the Grand Duke because his death may help to bring nearer the time when Russian children will no longer die of hunger. That in itself is none too easy for him. But the death of the Grand Duke's niece and nephew won't prevent any child from dying of hunger. Even in destruction there's a right way and a wrong way—and there are limits.

STEPAN [*vehemently*]: There are no limits! The truth is that you don't believe in the revolution, any of you. [*All, except* KALIAYEV, *rise to their feet.*] No, you don't believe in it. If you did believe in it sincerely, with all your hearts; if you felt sure that, by dint of our struggles and sacrifices, some day we shall build up a new Russia, redeemed from despotism, a land of freedom that will gradually spread out over the whole earth; and if you felt convinced that then and only then, freed from his masters and his superstitions, man will at last look up toward the sky, a god in his own right—how, I ask you, could the deaths of two children be weighed in the balance against such a faith? Surely you would claim for yourselves the right to do anything and everything that might bring that great day nearer! So now, if you draw the line at killing these two children, well, it simply means you are not sure you have that right. So, I repeat, you do *not* believe in the revolution. [*There is a short silence.* KALIAYEV, *too, rises to his feet.*]

KALIAYEV: Stepan, I am ashamed of myself—yet I cannot let you continue. I am ready to shed blood, so as to overthrow the present despotism. But, behind your words, I see the threat of another despotism which, if ever it comes into power, will make of me a murderer—and what I want to be is a doer of justice, not a man of blood.

STEPAN: Provided justice is done—even if it's done by assassins—what does it matter which you are? You and I are negligible quantities.

KALIAYEV: We are not, and you know it as well as anyone; in fact it's pride, just pride, that makes you talk as you are doing now.

STEPAN: My pride is my concern alone. But men's pride, their rebellion, the injustice that is done them —these are the concern of all of us.

KALIAYEV: Men do not live by justice alone.

STEPAN: When their bread is stolen, what else have they to live by?

KALIAYEV: By justice, and, don't forget, by innocence.

STEPAN: Innocence? Yes, maybe I know what that means. But I prefer to shut my eyes to it—and to shut others' eyes to it, for the time being—so that one day it may have a world-wide meaning.

KALIAYEV: Well, you must feel very sure that day is coming if you repudiate everything that makes life worth living today, on its account.

STEPAN: I am certain that that day is coming.

KALIAYEV: No, you can't be as sure as that. . . . Before it can be known which of us, you or I, is right, perhaps three generations will have to be sacrificed; there will have been bloody wars, and no less bloody revolutions. And by the time that all this blood has dried off the earth, you and I will long since have turned to dust.

STEPAN: Then others will come—and I hail them as my brothers.

KALIAYEV [*excitedly, raising his voice*]: Others, you say! Quite likely you are right. But those *I* love are the men who are alive today, and walk this same earth. It's they whom I hail, it is for them I am fighting, for them I am ready to lay down my life. But I shall not strike my brothers in the face for the sake of some far-off city, which, for all I know, may not exist. I refuse to add to the living injustice all around me for the sake of a dead justice. [*In a lower voice, but firmly*] Brothers, I want to speak to you quite frankly and to tell you something that even the simplest peasant in our backwoods would say if you asked him his opinion. Killing children is a crime against a man's honor. And if one day the revolution thinks fit to break with honor, well, I'm through with the revolution. If you decide that I must do it, well and good; I will go to the theater when they're due to come out—but I'll fling myself under the horses' feet.

STEPAN: Honor is a luxury reserved for people who have carriages-and-pairs.

KALIAYEV: No. It's the one wealth left to a poor man. You know it, and you also know that the revolution has its code of honor. It's what we all are ready to

die for. It's what made you hold your head up,
Stepan, when they flogged you, and it's behind what
you have been saying to us today.

STEPAN [*shrilly*]:   Keep quiet! I forbid you to speak
of that!

KALIAYEV [*angrily*]:   Why must I keep quiet? I took
it lying down when you said I didn't believe in the
revolution. Which was as good as telling me that I
was ready to kill the Grand Duke for nothing; that
I was a common murderer. I let you say that—and
somehow I kept my hands off you!

ANNENKOV: Yanek!

STEPAN: It's killing for nothing, sometimes, not to kill
enough.

ANNENKOV: Stepan, none of us here agrees with you.
And we have made our decision.

STEPAN: Then I bow to it. Only, let me tell you once
again that squeamishness is out of place in work like
ours. We're murderers, and we have chosen to be
murderers.

KALIAYEV [*losing all self-control*]:   That's a lie! I
have chosen death so as to prevent murder from
triumphing in the world. I've chosen to be innocent.

ANNENKOV: Yanek! Stepan! That's enough of it. The
group has decided that the slaughter of these children would serve no purpose. We must start again
from the beginning, and be ready for another try
at it in two days' time.

STEPAN: And supposing the children are there again?

KALIAYEV: Then we shall await another opportunity.

STEPAN: And supposing the Grand Duchess is with
the Duke?

KALIAYEV: *Her* I shall not spare.

ANNENKOV: Listen!

[*A rumble of carriage wheels.* KALIAYEV *is drawn
irresistibly to the window. The carriage approaches,
rattles past, recedes.*]

VOINOV [*looking at* DORA, *who has come toward him*]:
Well, Dora, that settles it; we'll have to make another
try . . .

STEPAN [*disdainfully*]: Yes, Alexis, another try! . . .
But of course we must do something for our precious honor!

CURTAIN

ACT III

Two days later; the same place, at the same hour.

STEPAN: What's Voinov up to? He should be here.

ANNENKOV: He needs some sleep, and we've still a good half hour before us.

STEPAN: Suppose I went down to see if there's any news?

ANNENKOV: No. We must take no unnecessary risks. [*A short silence.*] Yanek, why are you so silent?

KALIAYEV: I've nothing to say. But you needn't feel any anxiety about me. [*A ring at the bell.*] Ah, here he is. [VOINOV *enters.*] Did you sleep?

VOINOV: Yes, a bit.

ANNENKOV: Did you sleep all night?

VOINOV: No, not quite all the night.

ANNENKOV: Well, you should have. There are ways of making oneself sleep.

VOINOV: I tried them. But I must have been over-tired.

ANNENKOV: Your hands are shaking.

VOINOV: No. [*All gaze at him.*] Why are you eying me like that? Surely there's nothing so terrible about one's feeling tired?

ANNENKOV: That's not the point. It's about *you* we're troubled.

VOINOV [*with sudden vehemence*]:   You should have thought about all that two days ago. If the bomb had been thrown then, we wouldn't be feeling tired to-day.

KALIAYEV: I'm sorry, Alexis; it's all my fault. I've made things harder for everybody.

VOINOV [*in a quieter tone*]: What do you mean? Why harder? I'm tired, and that's all there is to it!

DORA: Well, it won't be long now. In an hour's time all will be over.

VOINOV: Yes, all will be over. In an hour's time. [*He glances uneasily round the room.* DORA *goes up to him and clasps his hand. He leaves his hand in hers for a moment, then snatches it away.*] Boria, I want to talk to you.

ANNENKOV: In private?

VOINOV: Yes, in private.

[*They exchange glances; then* KALIAYEV, DORA, *and* STEPAN *leave the room.*]

ANNENKOV: Yes? What is it? [VOINOV *keeps silent.*] Out with it, Alexis!

VOINOV: I'm ashamed, Boria. [*Silence.*] Bitterly ashamed. But I must tell you the truth.

ANNENKOV: You don't want to throw the bomb, is that it?

VOINOV: I . . . I can't bring myself to do it.

ANNENKOV: Do you mean you've panicked at the last moment? Is that all? There's nothing shameful in that.

VOINOV: I'm afraid, and I'm ashamed of my fear.

ANNENKOV: I can't understand. The day before yesterday you were so gay—and brave. Your eyes were sparkling when you went out.

VOINOV: I've always been afraid. Only somehow, the day before yesterday, I'd screwed up my courage. When I heard the carriage in the distance I said to myself: "Good! Only a minute more!" I gritted my teeth, every muscle in my body was taut as steel, and if I'd flung the bomb at that moment I really believe its mere impact would have killed the Grand Duke. I waited, waited, for the first explosion, which was going to release that pent-up energy. But it never came. The carriage rumbled

by. How fast it went! It was past me in a flash. And
then I realized that Yanek hadn't thrown his bomb.
I went cold all over, icy cold. And suddenly all the
strength went out of me and I felt weak as a child.

ANNENKOV: Don't take it to heart, Alexis. That was
just a passing lapse; life and strength come back.

VOINOV: Two days have gone by but they haven't
come back to me. Just now I lied to you; I couldn't
sleep a wink last night. My heart was racing,
racing. . . . Oh, Boria, I'm so miserable, so sick of
everything!

ANNENKOV: Don't let what's happened get you down,
Alexis. We've all had the same experience at some
time or another. You won't be asked to throw the
bomb. You must take a month's rest in Finland, and
then come back to us.

VOINOV: No, it's not so simple as all that. If I don't
throw the bomb today I shall *never* throw one.

ANNENKOV: Oh, come now! You're exaggerating.

VOINOV: No, Boria, it's the simple truth. I'm not made
for terrorism; I realize that now. The best thing is
for me to leave you. I'll do my bit in propaganda,
on committees, and so forth.

ANNENKOV: The risk's the same.

VOINOV: Yes. But you can keep your eyes shut; you
don't *know*—and that makes all the difference.

ANNENKOV: I don't follow.

VOINOV: One doesn't see what happens. It's easy to
attend meetings, work out plans, and then pass
orders for their carrying out. You risk your life of
course, but there's a sort of veil between you and
the—the real thing. It's a very different matter
going down into the street when night is falling on
the city, taking your stand among the crowds of
people hurrying home to their evening meal, their
children, the wife who's watching on the doorstep
—and having to stand there, grim and silent, with

the weight of the bomb tugging at your arm—
and knowing that in three minutes, in two minutes,
in a few seconds, you will dash out toward a carriage, bomb in hand. That's what terrorist action
means and I know now that I couldn't start it all
over again without feeling all the blood drained
from my veins. Yes, I'm bitterly ashamed. I aimed
too high. I must be given the place I am fit for.
Quite a humble place, in the rank and file. The only
one of which I am worthy.

ANNENKOV: There's no such place for any of us. All
our paths lead to the same end: jail, the gallows.

VOINOV: Yes, but you don't see them as you see the
man you have to kill. You have to imagine them.
And, luckily for me, I have no imagination. [*With
a brief, nervous laugh*] Do you know, I've never
really believed in the secret police! Absurd, isn't
it, for a terrorist? I'll believe they exist only when
I get my first kick in the belly. Not before.

ANNENKOV: And when you are in prison? In prison
you can't help knowing, and seeing. There's no
more shutting your eyes to the facts.

VOINOV: In prison you have no more decisions to
make. What a relief to feel that everything's decided
for you! You haven't got to tell yourself: "Now
it's up to you, you must decide on the moment
when to strike." One thing I'm sure of now is that
I shall not try to escape; for escaping, too, you
need to make decisions, you have to take the initiative. If you don't try to escape, the others keep
the initiative—they do all the work!

ANNENKOV: Sometimes the work they do is—hanging
you!

VOINOV: I know that. But dying won't be so hard as
carrying my life and another man's in the hollow of
my hand and having to decide on the moment when
I fling them both into a fiery death. No, Boria, the

only way I have of making good is to accept myself as—what I am. [ANNENKOV *keeps silent.*] Even
cowards can help the revolution. It's up to them to
find out in just what way they can be useful.

ANNENKOV: Then, in the last analysis, we all are
cowards. Only, we don't always have opportunities
of showing ourselves up. . . . That's settled then,
Alexis; you'll do as you prefer.

VOINOV: I prefer to leave at once. I don't think I
could bring myself to face them. But you'll tell
them, won't you?

ANNENKOV: I'll tell them. [*Moves toward* VOINOV.]

VOINOV: Tell Yanek it's not his fault. And that I love
him, as I love you all.

[*A short silence.* ANNENKOV *embraces him.*]

ANNENKOV: Good-by, brother. All things have an
end. One day Russia will be a happy land.

VOINOV [*as he hurries out of the room*]: Yes, yes!
May she be happy! May she be happy!

ANNENKOV [*going to the door*]: Come.

[*All enter.*]

STEPAN: What's happened?

ANNENKOV: Voinov will not throw the bomb. He's
exhausted and he might muff it.

KALIAYEV: It's my fault, isn't it?

ANNENKOV: He asked me to tell you that he loves
you.

KALIAYEV: Shall we see him again?

ANNENKOV: Perhaps. For the present, he's leaving us.

STEPAN: Why?

ANNENKOV: He'll be more useful on the committees.

STEPAN: Did he ask for this? Has he lost his nerve?

ANNENKOV: No. The decision was mine and mine
only.

STEPAN: So at the eleventh hour you are changing
all our plans?

ANNENKOV: At the eleventh hour, I've had to come

to a decision, by myself. It was too late to talk it over with you. I shall take Voinov's place.

STEPAN: No. I have first claim to it.

KALIAYEV [*to* ANNENKOV]: You are our leader. Your duty is to stay here.

ANNENKOV: Sometimes a leader's duty is to act the coward. But on condition that he proves his courage when the need arises. I've made my decision. You, Stepan, will replace me for as long as is needed. Now, you must hear the program I've fixed up for each of you. Come!

[*They go out.* KALIAYEV *sits down.* DORA *goes up to him, stretches out her hand; then thinks better of it.*]

DORA: It's not your fault.

KALIAYEV: I've hurt him, hurt him cruelly. Do you know what he said to me the other day?

DORA: He was always saying how happy he was.

KALIAYEV: Yes. But he told me there was no happiness for him outside our comradeship. This is what he said: "We—the organization—stand for all that matters in the world today. It's like an order of chivalry come back to earth." Oh, Dora, what a shame this has happened!

DORA: He'll come back.

KALIAYEV: No. I can picture how I'd feel if I were in his position. I'd be heartbroken.

DORA: And now? Aren't you heartbroken?

KALIAYEV: Now? But I'm with you all, and I am happy—as he was happy.

DORA [*musingly*]: Yes, it's a great happiness.

KALIAYEV: None greater. Don't you feel as I do?

DORA: Yes . . . But why then are you so depressed? Two days ago you looked so cheerful. Like a schoolboy going on vacation. But today . . .

KALIAYEV: [*rising to his feet; with a rush of bitterness*]: Today I know something I did *not* know then. You were right, Dora; it's not so simple as it seems. I thought it was quite easy to kill, provided one has courage and is buoyed up by an ideal. But now I've lost my wings. I have realized that hatred brings no happiness. I can see the vileness in myself, and in the others, too. Murderous instincts, cowardice, injustice. I've got to kill—there are no two ways about it. But I shall see it through to the end. I shall go beyond hatred.

DORA: Beyond? There's nothing beyond.

KALIAYEV: Yes. There is love.

DORA: Love? No, that's not what is needed.

KALIAYEV: Oh, Dora, how can you say that? You of all people, you whose heart I know so well!

DORA: Too much blood, too much brutal violence—there's no escape for us. Those whose hearts are set on justice have no right to love. They're on their toes, as I am, holding their heads up, their eyes fixed on the heights. What room for love is there in such proud hearts? Love bows heads, gently, compassionately. We, Yanek, are stiff-necked.

KALIAYEV: But we love our fellow men.

DORA: Yes, we love them—in our fashion. With a vast love that has nothing to shore it up; that brings only sadness. The masses? We live so far away from them, shut up in our thoughts. And do they love us? Do they even guess we love them? No, they hold their peace. Ah, that silence, that unresponsive silence!

KALIAYEV: But surely that's precisely what love means—sacrificing everything without expecting anything in return?

DORA: Perhaps. Yes, I know that love, an absolute, ideal love, a pure and solitary joy—and I feel it burning in my heart. Yet there are times when I wonder if love isn't something else; something more than a lonely voice, a monologue, and if there isn't sometimes a response. And then I see a picture floating up before my eyes. The sun is shining, pride dies from the heart, one bows one's head gently, almost shyly, and every barrier is down! Oh, Yanek, if only we could forget, even for an hour, the ugliness and misery of this world we live in, and let ourselves go—at last! One little hour or so of thinking of ourselves, just you and me, for a change. Can you see what I mean?

KALIAYEV: Yes, Dora, I can; it's what is called love —in the simple, human sense.

DORA: Yes, darling, you've guessed what I mean— but does that kind of love mean anything to you, really? Do you love justice with that kind of love? [KALIAYEV *is silent.*] Do you love our Russian people with that love—all tenderness and gentleness and self-forgetting? [KALIAYEV *still says nothing.*] You see. [*She goes toward him. Her voice is very low.*] And how about *me*, Yanek? Do you love me —as a lover?

KALIAYEV [*after gazing at her in silence for some moments*]: No one will ever love you as I love you.

DORA: I know. But wouldn't it be better to love— like an ordinary person?

KALIAYEV: I'm not an ordinary person. Such as I am, I love you.

DORA: Do you love me more than justice, more than the organization?

KALIAYEV: For me, you, justice, the organization are inseparable. I don't distinguish between you.

DORA: Yes. But do, please, answer me. Do you love me all for yourself . . . selfishly . . . possessively? —oh, you know what I mean! Would you love me if I were unjust?

KALIAYEV: If you were unjust and I could love you. it wouldn't be you I loved.

DORA: That's no answer. Tell me only this; would
    you love me if I didn't belong to the organization?

KALIAYEV: Then what would you belong to?

DORA: I remember the time when I was a student. I
    was pretty then. I used to spend hours walking
    about the town, dreaming all sorts of silly day-
    dreams. I was always laughing. Would you love me
    if I were like that now—carefree, gay, like a young
    girl?

KALIAYEV [*hesitantly, in a very low voice*]:   I'm
    longing, oh, how I'm longing to say Yes.

DORA [*eagerly*]:   Then say Yes, darling—if you
    mean it, if it's true. In spite of everything: of
    justice, of our suffering fellow men, of human
    bondage. Do try to forget for a moment all those
    horrors—the scaffold, the agony of little children, of
    men who are flogged to death.

KALIAYEV: Dora! Please!

DORA: No, surely for once we can let our hearts take
    charge. I'm waiting for you to say the word, to
    tell me you want me—Dora, the living woman—
    and I mean more to you than this world, this foully
    unjust world around us.

KALIAYEV [*brutally*]:   Keep quiet! My heart yearns
    for you, and you alone. . . . But, a few minutes
    hence I'll need a clear head and a steady hand.

DORA [*wildly*]:   A few minutes hence? Ah, yes, I
    was forgetting. [*Laughing and sobbing at once*] No,
    darling, I'll do as you want. Don't be angry with
    me—I was talking nonsense. I promise to be sen-
    sible. I'm overtired, that's all. I, too, I couldn't have
    said—what I wanted you to say. I love you with
    the same love as yours: a love that's half frozen,
    because it's rooted in justice and reared in prison
    cells. . . . Summer, Yanek, can you remember
    what that's like, a real summer's day? But—no, it's

never-ending winter here. We don't belong to the world of men. We are the just ones. And outside there is warmth and light; but not for us, never for us! [*Averting her eyes.*] Ah, pity on the just!

KALIAYEV [*gazing at her with despair in his eyes*]: Yes, that's our lot on earth; love is . . . impossible. But I shall kill the Grand Duke, and then at last there will be peace for you and me.

DORA: Peace? When shall we find peace?

KALIAYEV [*violently*]: The next day.

[ANNENKOV *and* STEPAN *enter.* DORA *and* KALIAYEV *move away from each other.*]

ANNENKOV: Yanek!

KALIAYEV: I'm ready. [*Draws a deep breath.*] At last! At last!

STEPAN [*going up to him*]: Brother, I'm with you.

KALIAYEV: Good-by, Stepan. [*Turning to* DORA] Good-by, Dora.

[DORA *comes toward him. They are standing very close, but neither touches the other.*]

DORA: No, not good-by. *Au revoir. Au revoir, mon chéri.* We shall meet again.

[*They gaze at each other in silence for some moments.*]

KALIAYEV: *Au revoir,* Dora. I . . . I . . . Russia will be free.

DORA [*weeping*]: Russia will be free.

[KALIAYEV *crosses himself as he passes the icon; then walks out of the room with* ANNENKOV. STEPAN *goes to the window.* DORA *remains statue-still, staring at the door.*]

STEPAN: How straight he's walking! Yes, I was wrong not to feel confidence in Yanek. But his enthusiasm was too . . . too romantic for my liking. Did you notice how he crossed himself just now? Is he religious?

DORA: Well, he's not a churchgoer.

STEPAN: Still, he has leanings toward religion. That's why we didn't hit it off. I'm more bitter than he. For people like me, who don't believe in a God, there is no alternative between total justice and utter despair.

DORA: To Yanek's mind there's an element of despair in justice itself.

STEPAN: Yes, he has a weak soul. But happily he's better than his soul, his arm won't falter. Yanek will kill the Grand Duke, I'd swear to it. And it will be a good day's work, a very good day's work. Destruction, that's what's wanted. But you're not saying anything. [*Scans her face attentively.*] Are you in love with him?

DORA: Love calls for time, and we have hardly time enough for—justice.

STEPAN: You are right. There's so much still to do; we must smash this world we live in, blast it to smithereens! And after that . . . [*Looks down into the street.*] They're out of sight. They must have reached their posts by now.

DORA: Yes? "After that," you said. What will happen after that?

STEPAN: After that we shall love each other.

DORA: If we are still alive.

STEPAN: Then others will love each other. Which comes to the same thing.

DORA: Stepan, say *hatred*.

STEPAN: What?

DORA: I just want you to utter that word: *hatred*.

STEPAN: Hatred.

DORA: Yes, that's right. Yanek could never say it well.

[*A short silence. Then* STEPAN *comes toward her.*]

STEPAN: I understand; you despise me. Still, are you quite sure you're right to despise me? [*Pauses. Then goes on speaking, with rising passion.*] You're all alike. Counting the cost of what you do in terms of your despicable love! I'm different, I love nothing, and I hate, yes I *hate* my fellow men. Why should I want their precious love? I learned all about it three years ago, in the convict prison. For three years I've borne its marks on me. And you want me to turn sentimental, and carry the bomb as if it were a cross. But I'm damned if I will! [*He tears his shirt open.* DORA *makes a gesture of horror and shrinks away when she sees the marks of the lash.*] There you are! There are the marks of their love! Now, do you still despise me?

[*She goes up to him, and kisses him hastily.*]

DORA: Who could despise suffering? I love you, too.

STEPAN [*gazing at her, murmurs*]: Sorry, Dora. [*After a short silence he turns away.*] Perhaps it's only weariness, the burden of all those years of struggle and suspense, of police spies, hard labor in the prison and—to crown everything!—this. [*Points to the scars.*] How could I have the energy to love? But, anyhow, I still have the energy to hate. And that's better than feeling nothing at all.

DORA: Yes, you're right, it's better.

[*He looks at her. A clock strikes seven.*]

STEPAN [*swinging round*]: The Grand Duke will be going by. [DORA *goes to the window, pressing her forehead against a pane. A long silence. Then, in the distance, a rumble of carriage wheels. It grows louder, then recedes.*] Let's hope he is by himself. . . . [*The rumble of wheels dies into the distance. A violent explosion rattles the windows.* DORA *gives a start and buries her head in her hands. A long silence.*] Boria hasn't thrown his bomb. That means Yanek has brought it off! The people have triumphed!

DORA [*bursting into tears and flinging herself against*

him]:   And it's we who have killed him. It's we
who have killed him. It's I!

STEPAN [*shrilly*]:   What do you mean? Killed whom?
Yanek?

DORA: The Grand Duke.

C U R T A I N

ACT IV

A cell in the Pugatchev Tower of the Butirki Prison. Morning light is filtering through a barred window. When the curtain rises Kaliayev is looking toward the door. A GUARD *enters, followed by a prisoner carrying a mop and bucket.*

THE GUARD: Now then! Get down to it!
  [*The* GUARD *takes his stand at the window.* FOKA, *the prisoner, begins to wash the floor; he takes no notice of* KALIAYEV. *A short silence.*]

KALIAYEV: What's your name, brother?

FOKA: Foka.

KALIAYEV: Are you a convict?

FOKA: What else should I be?

KALIAYEV: What did you do?

FOKA: I killed.

KALIAYEV: You were hungry, no doubt?

THE GUARD: Ssh! Not so loud!

KALIAYEV: What?

THE GUARD: Don't speak so loud. It's really against the rules for you to talk. So I'd advise you to talk quietly, like the old man.

KALIAYEV: Is that why you killed—because you were hungry?

FOKA: No. I was thirsty.

KALIAYEV: Yes? And then?

FOKA: There was a hatchet lying around and I laid about with it good and proper. I killed three people, so they tell me. [KALIAYEV *gazes at him.*] Ah, my

young gentleman, I see you don't call me brother
any more. Cooled off, have you?

KALIAYEV: No. I, too, have killed.

FOKA: How many?

KALIAYEV: I'll tell you, brother, if you want me to.
But tell me first; you're sorry for . . . for what
happened, aren't you?

FOKA: Sure, I'm sorry. Twenty years' hard, that's a
long stretch. Enough to make anyone feel sorry.

KALIAYEV: Twenty years. I come here when I'm
twenty-three—and when I go out, my hair is gray.

FOKA: Oh, cheer up! There's no knowing with a
judge; depends on whether he's married, and what
his wife is like. Maybe he'll be in a good humor and
let you off easy. And then you're a fine gentleman.
It ain't the same for a gentleman and people like
me. You'll get off lightly.

KALIAYEV: I doubt it. And anyhow I don't want to.
Feeling shame for twenty years—how horrible that
would be!

FOKA: Shame? Where does the shame come in?
That's just one of those crackbrained notions you
gentlemen have. . . . How many people did you
kill?

KALIAYEV: One man.

FOKA: One man? Why, that's nothing!

KALIAYEV: I killed the Grand Duke Serge.

FOKA: The Grand Duke? Well, I'll be damned! You
fine gentlemen never know where to draw the line.
Yes, it looks black for you.

KALIAYEV: Very black. But I had to do it.

FOKA: Why? What business does a man like you have
getting himself into trouble like that? Ah, I see.
Over a woman, wasn't it? A good-looking young
lad like you . . . *I* see!

KALIAYEV: I am a socialist.

THE GUARD: Not so loud.

KALIAYEV [*deliberately raising his voice*]: I am a revolutionary socialist.

FOKA: What a story! And why the hell did you have to be . . . what you said just now? You had only to stay put, and you were on velvet. The world is made for bright young noblemen like you.

KALIAYEV: No. It is made for *you*, my friend. There are too many crimes, there's too much poverty in the world today. When some day there is less poverty, there will be fewer crimes. If Russia were free you would not be here.

FOKA: That's as it may be. One thing's sure: whether one's free or not, it doesn't pay to take a drop too much.

KALIAYEV: That's so. Only a man usually takes to drink because he is oppressed. A day will come when there's no more point in drinking, when nobody will feel ashamed, neither the fine gentleman, nor the poor devil who is down and out. We shall all be brothers and justice will make our hearts transparent. Do you know what I'm talking about?

FOKA: Yes. The Kingdom of God, they call it.

THE GUARD: Not so loud.

KALIAYEV: No, you're wrong there, brother. God can't do anything to help; justice is *our* concern. [*A short silence.*] Don't you understand? Do you know that old tale about Saint Dimitri?

FOKA: No.

KALIAYEV: He had made a date with God, far out in the steppes. When he was on his way to keep the appointment he came on a peasant whose cart was stuck in the mud. And Saint Dimitri stopped to help him. The mud was thick and the wheels were so deeply sunk that it took him the best part of an hour, helping to pull the cart out. When this was done Dimitri made haste to the appointed place. But he was too late. God had left.

FOKA: And then?

KALIAYEV: Then—there are some who always arrive too late, because there are too many bogged carts on the way, too many brothers to help out. [FOKA *is fidgeting uneasily.*] What's the matter?

THE GUARD: Not so loud. And you, my man, don't dawdle!

FOKA: I don't feel easy! It ain't natural, all this stuff you're telling me about saints and carts and whatnot. Sounds to me crazy, getting oneself put in prison for ideas like that. And then, there's something else.

KALIAYEV [*looking at him*]:   Something else? What do you mean?

FOKA: What's done to people who kill Grand Dukes?

KALIAYEV: They're hanged.

FOKA: You've said it!
[*He begins to move away. The* GUARD, *who has been grinning, gives a loud guffaw.*]

KALIAYEV: Stop! What have you got against me?

FOKA: Nothing. Only, fine gentleman as you are, I wouldn't like to make a fool of you. It's all right talking like we've been doing just to pass the time —but if you're going to be hanged, no, it ain't playing fair, like.

KALIAYEV: Why not?

THE GUARD [*laughing*]:   Come on, old man! Spit it out!

FOKA: Because all this talk about you and me being brothers just won't wash. I'm the hangman.

KALIAYEV: Oh! I thought you were a prisoner, like me.

FOKA: So I am. But they've given me that job, and I get a year knocked off my sentence for every man I hang. It's gravy for nothing!

KALIAYEV: So, to atone for your crimes, they make you commit new ones?

FOKA: Oh, come now, you can't call them crimes;
I'm only carrying out orders. And anyhow, crimes
or not, they don't care. If you want to know what
I think, they ain't Christians.

KALIAYEV: And how many times have you officiated
since you came here?

FOKA: Twice. That's two years to the good.

[KALIAYEV *shrinks away from him. The* GUARD
shepherds FOKA *toward the door.*]

KALIAYEV: So you're an executioner?

FOKA [*from the doorway*]:   And you, sir—what
about you?

[FOKA *goes out. A sound of footsteps, words of
command, in the corridor. Followed by the* GUARD,
SKURATOV *enters; he is very spick and span.*]

SKURATOV [*to the* GUARD]:   You can go. [*To* KA-
LIAYEV] Good morning. You don't know who I
am, do you? But *I* know *you.* [*Laughs.*] Quite
a celebrity, aren't you? May I introduce myself?
[KALIAYEV *keeps silent.*] Ah, you don't feel like
talking—I understand. That's the effect of solitary
confinement: seven days and nights. It wears a man
down. Well, we've put a stop to that; from now on
you may have visitors. Indeed, you've had one already—that old fellow, Foka. A queer customer,
isn't he? I thought he'd interest you. . . . You must
be pleased at the change; it's good to see a human
face again after a week's solitary confinement, isn't
it?

KALIAYEV: That depends on the face.

SKURATOV: Ah, a neat retort! I see you know your
own mind, my young friend. [*A short silence.*]
So, unless I am much mistaken, my face displeases
you?

KALIAYEV: Yes.

SKURATOV: That's a great pity. Still, I have hopes
that you may change your mind. For one thing,

the lighting here is bad; these basement cells make everyone look ghastly. And then, of course, you don't know me. Sometimes a man's face puts one off at first, later, when one gets to know the man himself . . .

KALIAYEV: That's enough. Who are you?

SKURATOV: Skuratov, Chief of Police.

KALIAYEV: In other words, a flunky.

SKURATOV: Have it your own way. Still, if I were in your position, I wouldn't throw my weight around. But perhaps you will find that out for yourself, by and by. One begins by wanting justice—and one ends by setting up a police force. Anyhow, I'm not afraid of the truth, and I shall talk to you quite frankly. You interest me. I'd like to help you to get off.

KALIAYEV: What do you mean?

SKURATOV: Surely it's obvious. I can get you a free pardon. I am bringing you a chance for your life.

KALIAYEV: Who asked you for it?

SKURATOV: One doesn't ask for life, my friend. One's given it. Have *you* never let anybody off? [*A short silence.*] Think hard.

KALIAYEV: Well, I don't want your pardon, and that's an end of it.

SKURATOV: Anyhow, please hear what I have to say. Appearances notwithstanding, I am not your enemy. I won't even say that your ideas are wrong. Except when they lead to murder.

KALIAYEV: I forbid you to use that word.

SKURATOV: Ah, your nerves are out of order, that's the trouble? [*Pauses.*] Quite honestly, I want to help you.

KALIAYEV: To help me? I am ready to pay the price of what I've done. But I refuse to tolerate this familiarity on your part. Leave me in peace.

SKURATOV: The accusation you have to face. . . .

KALIAYEV: That's incorrect.

SKURATOV: I beg your pardon?

KALIAYEV: Accusation is not the word. I am a prisoner of war, not an accused person.

SKURATOV: Put it that way, if you prefer. Still, there's been damage done, you must admit. Let's leave politics out of it and look at the human side. A man has been killed—and killed in a particularly horrible manner.

KALIAYEV: I threw the bomb at your tyranny, not at a man.

SKURATOV: Perhaps. But it was a living human being whom it blew to bits. It wasn't a pretty sight, let me tell you, my young friend. When they had pieced the body together, the head was missing. Completely disappeared! And as for the rest, an arm and a bit of a leg were all that had escaped undamaged.

KALIAYEV: I carried out a verdict.

SKURATOV: That's as it may be. Nobody blames you for the verdict. What's a verdict? Just a word about which one might wrangle endlessly. What you're accused of—sorry, I know you don't like that word—is, let's say, a sort of amateurishness, doing a messy job in fact. The results, anyhow, were plain enough to see; there's no disputing *them*. Ask the Grand Duchess. There was blood, you know, a lot of blood.

KALIAYEV: Keep quiet, damn you!

SKURATOV: Very well. All I want to say is that if you persist in talking about a "verdict" and asserting that it was the party, and the party alone, that tried and executed the victim—that, in short, the Grand Duke was killed not by a bomb but by an idea—well, in that case, you don't need a pardon. Suppose, however, we get down to brass tacks;

suppose we say that it was you, Ivan Kaliayev, who
blew the Grand Duke's head to pieces—that puts a
rather different complexion on the matter, doesn't
it? Then undoubtedly you stand in need of pardon.
And that's where I can be of aid, out of pure fellow
feeling, I assure you. [*Smiles.*] That's how I'm
built; I am not interested in ideas, I'm interested in
human beings.

KALIAYEV [*furiously*]: But, damn it, I don't recognize your right or the right of your employers to
sit in judgment on me. You can kill me if you
think fit, and that is the only right you have over
my person. Oh, I can see what you're leading up to.
You are trying to find a chink in my armor, you are
hoping to make me feel ashamed of myself, burst
into tears, repent of what you call my crime. Well,
you won't get anywhere; what I am is no concern
of yours. What concerns me is our hatred, mine
and my brothers'. And you are welcome to it.

SKURATOV: That, too, is an idea, or rather, an obses-
sion. But murder isn't just an idea; it is something
that takes place. And, obviously, so do its consequences. Which are repentance for the crime, and
punishment. There we get down to the heart of
the matter, and that in fact is why I joined the
police. I like being at the heart of things. But you
don't want to hear me talking about myself. . . .
[*Pauses. Then moves slowly toward* KALIAYEV.] All I
wish to say is that you should not forget, or profess
to forget, the Grand Duke's head. If you took it
into account, you would find that mere ideas lead
nowhere. For instance, instead of feeling pleased
with yourself, you'd be ashamed of what you did.
And, when once you felt ashamed, you would want
to live, in order to atone. So the great thing is that
you decide to live.

KALIAYEV: And suppose I decided to live, what then?

SKURATOV: A pardon for you and for your comrades.

KALIAYEV: Have you arrested them?

SKURATOV: No. As a matter of fact we haven't. But
if you decide to live, we shall arrest them.

KALIAYEV: I wonder if I've really understood. . . .

SKURATOV: Certainly you have. Don't lose your tem-
per—that would be premature. Think it over first.
Obviously from the standpoint of the idea—the
ideal, if you prefer the word—you cannot hand
them over to us. But from a practical point of view
you'd be doing them a service. You would be pre-
venting them from getting into further trouble, and
by the same token, you'd be saving them from the
gallows. And, best of all, you would regain your
peace of mind. So, from whatever angle you look
at it, you'd be doing the best thing. [KALIAYEV *is
silent.*] Well?

KALIAYEV: My friends will give you the answer before long.

SKURATOV: Another crime! Decidedly, it's a vocation! Very well, I have had my say. And I confess
I'm disappointed. It's all too obvious that you cling
to your ideas like a lamprey; there's no detaching
you.

KALIAYEV: You cannot detach me from my brothers.

SKURATOV: *Au revoir.* [*He starts to go out, then
turns back.*] Why then did you spare the Grand
Duchess and her nephews?

KALIAYEV: Who told you about that?

SKURATOV: Your informer. He was informing us as
well—up to a point. But, I ask you, why did you
spare them?

KALIAYEV: That's no concern of yours.

SKURATOV [*laughing*]: Oh, come now! . . . Well,
I'll tell you why. An ideal can murder a Grand
Duke, but it balks at murdering children. That was

the discovery you made that day. But let's carry it
a stage further. If an ideal balks at murdering children, is one justified in murdering a Grand Duke
on its behalf? [KALIAYEV *makes a fretful gesture.*]
No, don't answer *me*. It's not I who am concerned
in this. You will give your answer to the Grand
Duchess.

KALIAYEV: The Grand Duchess?

SKURATOV: Yes, she wants to see you. And my chief
reason for coming here was to make sure that this
was feasible. It is. It may even make you change
your mind. The Grand Duchess is a very Christian
lady. Indeed one might say she makes a hobby of
the soul. [*Laughs.*]

KALIAYEV: I refuse to see her.

SKURATOV: I'm sorry, but she will not take No for
an answer. And, after all, you owe her some con-
sideration. What's more, it seems that since her
husband's death she has become—how shall I put
it?—mentally unbalanced. So we thought it better
not to oppose her wishes. [*Standing in the doorway.*] If you change your mind, don't forget my
proposal. I shall be seeing you again. [*A short silence. He is listening.*] Here she comes. You certainly can't complain of being neglected! But it all
hangs together. Imagine God without prisons! One
would be lost without the other.

[*He goes out. Voices and words of command in the
corridor. The* GRAND DUCHESS *enters. She stands
silent, unmoving, for some moments. The door remains open.*]

KALIAYEV: What do you want?

THE GRAND DUCHESS [*lifting her veil*]:   Look! [KA-
LIAYEV *says nothing.*] Many things die with a man.

KALIAYEV: I knew it.

THE GRAND DUCHESS [*in a faint, weary, but quite natural voice*]:   No, murderers do not know that. If

they did, how could they bring themselves to kill?
[*A short silence.*]

KALIAYEV: I have seen you. Now I wish to be alone.

THE GRAND DUCHESS: No. I, too, must look at you.
[KALIAYEV *shrinks away. The* GRAND DUCHESS *sits down; she seems exhausted.*] I can't remain alone any longer. In the old days when I was sad, he used to share my sorrow—and I did not mind suffering . . . then. But now . . . No, I cannot bear being alone and keeping silent any longer. But to whom am I to speak? The others do not *know*. They pretend to be distressed. And perhaps they really are, for an hour or two. Then they go off to eat—or to sleep. To sleep especially. Somehow, I felt you must be like me. You, too, don't sleep, I am sure. And to whom could I speak of the crime, except to the murderer?

KALIAYEV: What crime? All I remember is an act of justice.

THE GRAND DUCHESS: The same voice! You have exactly the same voice as his. But, I suppose, all men use the same tone when they speak of justice. He used to say "That is just," and nobody had a right to question it. And yet perhaps he was mistaken; perhaps you, too, are mistaken.

KALIAYEV: He was an incarnation of that supreme injustice under which Russia has been groaning for centuries untold. And in return for this he was given privileges, rewards, and honors. But, as for me, even if I am mistaken, my wages are imprisonment and death.

THE GRAND DUCHESS: Yes, you are suffering. But he is dead, you killed him.

KALIAYEV: He died suddenly, unaware. A death like that is nothing.

THE GRAND DUCHESS: Nothing? [*In a lower voice*] That's true. They took you away immediately. I'm told that you made speeches while the police officers were surrounding you. I understand. That must have helped you. But it was different for me. I came some minutes later, and I *saw*! I put on a bier all that I could collect. What quantities of blood! [*Pauses.*] I was wearing a white dress.

KALIAYEV: Keep silent.

THE GRAND DUCHESS: Why? I am telling the truth, only the truth. Do you know what he was doing two hours before he died? He was sleeping. In an armchair with his feet propped up on another chair —as he often did. He was sleeping, and you—you were waiting for him in the cruel twilight. [*She is weeping.*] Oh, help me now, please help me! [*He stiffens up, and moves away.*] You are young, surely you can't be wicked.

KALIAYEV: I have never had time to be young.

THE GRAND DUCHESS: Oh, why are you so hard, so callous? Do you never feel pity for yourself?

KALIAYEV: No.

THE GRAND DUCHESS: You're wrong. It consoles. Yes, that's my last, miserable consolation—pity for my-self. But it doesn't stop my suffering. Ah, you should have killed me with him, instead of sparing me.

KALIAYEV: It was not you I spared, but the children you had with you.

THE GRAND DUCHESS: I know . . . I didn't like them much. [*Pauses.*] They were the Grand Duke's niece and nephew. Weren't they guilty, like their uncle?

KALIAYEV: No.

THE GRAND DUCHESS: How can you be so sure? My niece is a heartless little girl. When she's told to give something to poor people, she refuses. She won't go near them. Is not she unjust? Of course she is. But my poor husband was very fond of the peasants. He used to drink with them. And now you've killed him! Surely you, too, are unjust. The world is empty, cruel as the desert. . . .

KALIAYEV: You are wasting your time. You want to sap my strength and drive me to despair. But you will not succeed. So let me be.

THE GRAND DUCHESS: Won't you join with me in prayer, and repent? Then we should be less lonely.

KALIAYEV: Let me prepare myself to die. If I did not die—it's then I'd be a murderer.

THE GRAND DUCHESS [*rising to her feet*]: To die? You want to die? No. [*Going toward* KALIAYEV, *with rising emotion.*] It is your duty to accept being a murderer. Did you not kill him? God alone will justify you. . . .

KALIAYEV: What God? Yours or mine?

THE GRAND DUCHESS: The God of our Holy Church.

KALIAYEV: What has the Church to do with it?

THE GRAND DUCHESS: It serves a Master who, like you, had experience of prison.

KALIAYEV: The times have changed. Don't forget the Church has chosen what it wanted from its Master's legacy.

THE GRAND DUCHESS: I don't follow.

KALIAYEV: The Church has kept to itself the exercise of grace, and left to us the exercise of charity.

THE GRAND DUCHESS: Whom do you mean by *us?*

KALIAYEV [*with shrill exasperation*]: Why, those you hang!

[*A short silence.*]

THE GRAND DUCHESS [*gently*]: I am not your enemy.

KALIAYEV [*passionately*]: You are! You are! And so are all your kind. There is something even fouler than being a criminal; it's forcing into crime a man who is not made for it. Look at me! I swear to you I wasn't made to be a murderer.

THE GRAND DUCHESS: Please do not talk to me as if I

were an enemy. Look! [*She goes to the door and shuts it.*] Now I am in your hands. I trust you. [*Weeping*] There is a man's blood between us. But, even though we are parted in this world of sin and suffering, we can meet in God. . . . Will you pray with me?

KALIAYEV: No, I will not. [*Goes toward her.*] The only feeling I have toward you is pity; you have touched my heart. And now I will speak quite frankly, for I would like you to understand. I have given up counting on the agreement that I once made with God. But, in dying, I shall keep the agreement I made with those I love, my brothers, who are thinking of me at this moment. And it would be betraying them to pray.

THE GRAND DUCHESS: What do you mean?

KALIAYEV [*excitedly*]: Nothing—except that I shall soon be happy, gloriously happy! An ordeal lies before me, but I shall see it through. Then, when sentence has been pronounced and all is ready for the execution—ah, then, at the foot of the scaffold, I shall turn my back on you and on this loathsome world forever, and at last my heart will flood with joy, the joy of love fulfilled. . . . Can you understand?

THE GRAND DUCHESS: There is no love where God is not.

KALIAYEV: Yes, there is. Love for His creatures.

THE GRAND DUCHESS: His creatures are . . . abject! One can forgive them or destroy them—what else is there to do?

KALIAYEV: To die with them.

THE GRAND DUCHESS: One always dies alone. *He* died alone.

KALIAYEV [*desperately*]: No, no! One can die with them. Those who love each other today must die together if they wish to be reunited. In life they are parted—by injustice, sorrow, shame; by the evil that men do to others . . . by crimes. Living is agony, because life separates.

THE GRAND DUCHESS: God reunites.

KALIAYEV: Not on this earth. And the only meetings that mean anything to me take place on earth.

THE GRAND DUCHESS: This earth is the meeting place of dogs, who keep their noses to the ground, sniffing here and there, and never finding what they want.

KALIAYEV [*looking away, toward the window*]: Soon I shall know the truth. [*He is silent for some moments.*] And yet—cannot one picture a love existing here and now on this sad earth between two people, people who have abandoned any hope of joy and love each other in sorrow; people whose only meeting place, whose only link is sorrow? [*Looks at her.*] Cannot we picture them being bound together thus, in life no less than in death?

THE GRAND DUCHESS: A love whose only link is sorrow! What sort of love is that?

KALIAYEV: The only sort of love that you and your kind have ever allowed us.

THE GRAND DUCHESS: I, too, loved—the man you killed.

KALIAYEV: I know. That is why I forgive you for the wrongs that you and your kind have done me. [*Pauses.*] Now leave me, please.

[*A long silence.*]

THE GRAND DUCHESS [*rising*]: Yes, I will leave you. I came here to lead you back to God, but now I realize that you wish to be your own judge; to save yourself, unaided. That is beyond your power. But God can do it, if you live. I will ask that you be given a pardon.

KALIAYEV: Oh, I beg you, don't do that! Let me die —or else I shall hate you, hate you!

THE GRAND DUCHESS [*on the threshold*]: I shall ask for your pardon—from man and from God.

KALIAYEV: No, no! I forbid you! [*He runs to the door.* SKURATOV *confronts him.* KALIAYEV *shrinks away, closing his eyes. A short silence. Then he opens his eyes and looks at* SKURATOV.] I am glad you have come.

SKURATOV: Delighted to hear it. May I know why?

KALIAYEV: Because I needed to despise again.

SKURATOV: A pity! . . . Well, I've come for your answer.

KALIAYEV: You have it.

SKURATOV [*in a different tone*]: No, you're wrong there. Now, listen well. I authorized this meeting between you and the Grand Duchess so as to be able to publish an account of it in the papers. The report will be correct, except on one point. It will contain a statement that you repented of your crime. Your friends will think you have betrayed them.

KALIAYEV [*quietly*]: They will not believe it.

SKURATOV: I will stop publication of this report on one condition: that you make a full confession. You have the night in which to decide. [*Goes back to the doorway.*]

KALIAYEV [*louder*]: They will not believe it.

SKURATOV [*turning round*]: Why not? Have *they* never had their lapses?

KALIAYEV: You do not know their love.

SKURATOV: No. But I know that a man cannot believe in brotherhood a whole night through without faltering for a moment. So I shall wait for you to falter. [*Shuts the door and plants himself with his back to it.*] Take your time, my friend. I am patient. [*They remain face to face.*]

CURTAIN

ACT V

A week later. The terrorists' apartment: not the same as in the first act, but furnished in much the same style. The time is night, a little before daybreak. DORA *is walking to and fro, her nerves on edge. For some moments no one speaks.*

ANNENKOV: Do try to rest, Dora.

DORA: I'm cold.

ANNENKOV: Come here and lie down for a while. Put the rug over you.

DORA [*still pacing to and fro*]: The night is long. Oh, Boria, I'm so dreadfully cold. [*A knocking at the door: one knock, then two.* STEPAN *enters, followed by* VOINOV, *who goes up to* DORA *and kisses her. She hugs him to her breast.*] Oh, Alexis!

STEPAN: Orlov thinks it's for tonight. All the junior officers who are not on duty have been told to report to the prison. That's how he'll be present.

ANNENKOV: Where are you to meet him?

STEPAN: At the restaurant in Sophiskaya Street. He'll wait for us—Voinov and myself—there.

DORA [*who has at last sat down, utterly exhausted*]: So it's for tonight, Boria.

ANNENKOV: There's still a chance. It depends on the Czar's decision.

STEPAN: It depends on the Czar, if Yanek has asked for clemency.

DORA: He hasn't.

STEPAN: Why should he have seen the Grand Duchess if it wasn't about a pardon? She's been telling

everybody that he repented. How is one to know
the truth?

DORA: We know what Yanek said at the trial, and we
have his letter. Didn't he say that his one regret was
that he had not another life, so as to hurl it, too, in
the face of the autocrats? Could the man who said
that plead for a pardon, or repent? No, he wanted,
and he still wants, to die. There can be no going
back on what he's done.

STEPAN: All the same he should have refused to see
the Grand Duchess.

DORA: He is the sole judge of that.

STEPAN: No. According to our principles it was his
duty not to see her.

DORA: Our duty is to kill, and that's the end of it.
So now he is free; free at last.

STEPAN: Not yet.

DORA: He's free, I tell you. Now that he is on the
brink of death, he has the right to do exactly as
he chooses. For he is going to die, my friends—
you won't be disappointed.

ANNENKOV: Really, Dora!

DORA: Why shirk the issue? If he were pardoned that
would be another matter. It would prove that the
Grand Duchess had told the truth, that he has repented and betrayed. But if he dies all will be well.
You will believe in him and you'll be able to love
him still. [*Gazes at them.*] Ah, your love costs
dear!

VOINOV [*going toward her*]:   You're wrong, Dora.
We never doubted him.

DORA [*pacing the room again*]:   Didn't you? Well,
perhaps not. I'm sorry. Still what does it matter
after all? We shall know the truth tonight, in a
few hours' time. . . . But Alexis, my poor dear,
why have you come back like this?

VOINOV: To replace him. When I read what he'd

said at the trial I shed tears—how proud I was! You remember his words? "Death will be my supreme protest against a world of tears and blood." When I read that my hands shook, I could hardly hold the paper. . . .

DORA: "A world of tears and blood." Yes, he said that.

VOINOV: He said it. Oh, Dora, what glorious courage! And at the end of his speech, those words that rang out like a trumpet call: "If I have proved equal to the task assigned, of protesting with all the manhood in me against violence, may death consummate my task with the purity of the ideal that inspired it!" It was then I decided to return to you.

DORA [*burying her face in her hands*]: Yes, it was purity he longed for. But oh the cruelty of that consummation!

VOINOV: Don't cry, Dora. Remember what he asked —that none of us was to weep for him. How well I understand him—now! All my doubts are swept away. . . . I was miserable because I'd played the coward. And then I threw the bomb at Tiflis. So now I am like Yanek. When I learned he had been sentenced to death, I had only one idea: to take his place, since I had been unable to take my stand beside him.

DORA: Who can take his place tonight? Tonight he stands alone, Alexis.

VOINOV: We must uphold him with our pride, as he upholds us with his example. Don't cry, dear.

DORA: Look! My eyes are dry. But proud—ah, no, never again can I be proud.

STEPAN: Dora, don't misjudge me. I want Yanek to live. We need men like him.

DORA: But Yanek does *not* want to live. So it's our duty to wish that he may die.

ANNENKOV: You're crazy, Dora.

DORA: I tell you, it's our duty. I know his heart. Only in death will he find peace. So—let him die! [*In a lower voice*] But quickly . . . oh, let him die quickly!

STEPAN: Well, Boria, I'm off. Come, Alexis. Orlov's expecting us.

ANNENKOV: Yes, you'd better be off now. But come back as soon as you can.

[STEPAN *and* VOINOV *walk to the door. On the way* STEPAN *casts a glance at* DORA.]

STEPAN: In a few minutes we shall know everything. . . . Look after her, Boria.

[DORA *is standing at the window.* ANNENKOV *keeps his eyes fixed on her.*]

DORA: Death! The gallows! Always, death! Oh, Boria . . . !

ANNENKOV: Yes, little sister. But there's no other solution.

DORA: Don't say that. If death is the only solution, then we have chosen the wrong path. The right path leads to life, to sunlight. . . . One can't bear feeling cold all the time.

ANNENKOV: The path we have chosen, also, leads to life. To life for others. Russia will live, our children's children will live. Do you remember what Yanek used to say? "Russia will become the land of our dream."

DORA: Our children's children, others—yes. But Yanek is in prison and the rope is cold. He is facing death. Perhaps he is already dead—so that others, after him, may live. And, Boria, suppose . . . suppose that, after all, the others *did not live?* Suppose he is dying for nothing?

ANNENKOV: Keep silent!

[*A short silence.*]

DORA: Oh, how cold it is! And yet spring has come.

There are trees in the prison yard, aren't there? I expect he's looking at them.

ANNENKOV: Don't give way to your imagination, Dora. And do please try to stop shivering.

DORA: I'm so cold that I've the impression of being dead already. [*Pauses.*] All this ages one so quickly; never, never again shall we feel young again. With the first murder youth ends forever. One throws a bomb and in the next second a whole lifetime flashes by, and all that remains is death.

ANNENKOV: Thus we die like brave men, fighting to the end.

DORA: You have gone about it too fast. You are no longer men.

ANNENKOV: Don't forget that human misery and injustice go fast as well. In the world of today there's no scope for patience and quiet progress. Russia is in a hurry.

DORA: I know. We have taken on our shoulders the sorrows of the world. He, too, took them on his shoulders, and went forth alone. That called for courage. Yet I sometimes can't help thinking such pride will be punished.

ANNENKOV: It's a pride we pay for with our lives. No one can go farther. It's a pride to which we are justly entitled.

DORA: Are you so sure that no one can go farther? Sometimes when I hear what Stepan says, I fear for the future. Others, perhaps, will come who'll quote our authority for killing; and will *not* pay with their lives.

ANNENKOV: That would be shameful.

DORA: Who knows? Perhaps that is what justice means—in the long run. And then nobody will want to look justice in the face again.

ANNENKOV: Dora! [*She is silent.*] Are you losing faith? I've never known you like this before.

DORA: I'm cold, oh, so cold! And I'm thinking of
him—how he's trying to keep himself from shivering, so as not to seem afraid.

ANNENKOV: Are you no longer with us, Dora?

DORA [*flinging herself against him*]:   Oh, no, Boria,
don't imagine *that*! I am with you. With you to the
end. I loathe tyranny and I know we can't act otherwise than as we do. Only—it was with a happy
heart that I embarked on our great adventure, and
it's with a sad heart that I keep to it. That's where
the difference lies; we are prisoners.

ANNENKOV: All Russia is in prison. But we shall
shatter her prison walls.

DORA: Only give me the bomb to throw, and then
you'll see! I shall walk among the flames and I
swear I shall not flinch. It's easy, ever so much
easier, to die of one's inner conflicts than to live with
them. Tell me, Boria, have you ever loved anyone
—*really* loved?

ANNENKOV: Yes. But so long ago that I've forgotten
all about it.

DORA: How long ago?

ANNENKOV: Four years.

DORA: And how long have you been head of the
organization?

ANNENKOV: Four years. [*Pauses.*] Now it's the organization that I love.

DORA [*walking to the window*]:   Loving, that's
very well . . . but to be loved, that's another matter. . . . No! We must go on and on and on. How
good it would be to rest a bit! But that's impossible.
On and on! Sometimes one wants to let oneself relax and take things easy. But that foul thing injustice
sticks to us like a leech. Onward! So, you see, we're
doomed to being greater than ourselves. Human
beings, human faces—that's what we'd like to love.
To be in love with love, instead of justice. But no!

There's no respite for us. Forward, Dora! Forward, Yanek! [*She bursts into tears.*] But, for him, the end is near.

ANNENKOV [*taking her in his arms*]: He'll be pardoned.

DORA: You know quite well he won't be. You know quite well that's . . . unthinkable. [ANNENKOV *averts his eyes.*] Perhaps at this very moment he is going out into the prison yard. And all the people there are falling silent as he approaches. Let's only hope he isn't feeling cold, like me. . . . Boria, do you know how men are hanged?

ANNENKOV: With a rope. . . . Dora, that's enough.

DORA [*wildly*]: And the hangman leaps onto their shoulders, doesn't he? The neck cracks, like a broken twig. Ghastly, isn't it?

ANNENKOV: Yes . . . in one sense. In another sense it's happiness.

DORA: Happiness?

ANNENKOV: To feel a man's hand on you just before you die. [DORA *flings herself into a chair.*] When it's over, you must go away, and take a short rest.

DORA: Go away? With whom?

ANNENKOV: With me, Dora.

DORA [*gazing at him intently*]: To go away? Ah! [*Turns to the window.*] The day is breaking. Yanek is dead by now—I'm certain of it.

ANNENKOV: I am your brother.

DORA: Yes, you're my brother; all of you are my brothers, my brothers whom I love. [*There is a patter of rain outside. The light is growing. In a low voice, hardly more than a whisper*] But what a foul taste brotherhood has, sometimes!

[*A knock at the door.* VOINOV *and* STEPAN *enter. Both stand quite still.* DORA *sways, then with an effort steadies herself.*]

STEPAN [*In a low voice*]: Yanek was faithful to the end.

ANNENKOV: Could Orlov see?

STEPAN: Yes.

DORA [*coming forward with firm steps*]: Sit down. Now tell us. . . .

STEPAN: What's the use?

DORA: Tell everything. I have the right to know, and I insist on hearing all. Down to the last detail.

STEPAN: I couldn't do it. And, anyhow, we must leave at once.

DORA: No. You must tell me first. When was he notified?

STEPAN: At ten last night.

DORA: When was he hanged?

STEPAN: At two in the morning.

DORA: So he remained waiting in his cell for four hours?

STEPAN: Yes, without a word. After that, everything went with a rush. . . . It's all over now.

DORA: Four hours without speaking, you say? Wait a moment. How was he dressed? Had he his fur-lined coat?

STEPAN: No. He was in a black suit, without an overcoat. And he was wearing a black felt hat.

DORA: What was the weather like?

STEPAN: A pitch-black night. The snow was dirty. Then a shower came and turned it into slush.

DORA: Was he shivering?

STEPAN: No.

DORA: Could Orlov catch his eye?

STEPAN: No.

DORA: Whom was he looking at?

STEPAN: At everyone, and no one in particular—so Orlov told me.

DORA: And then? What happened next?

STEPAN: That's enough, Dora.

DORA: No, I have to know. If nothing else, his death belongs to me.

STEPAN: The judgment of the court was read out to him.

DORA: What did he do while it was being read?

STEPAN: Nothing. Except that at one moment he moved his leg, so as to shake off a fleck of mud that had settled on his shoe.

DORA [*burying her face in her hands*]: A fleck of mud! . . .

ANNENKOV [*sharply*]: How do you know all this? [STEPAN *keeps silent.*] So you asked Orlov to tell you every detail. Why was that?

STEPAN [*looking away*]: There was something between Yanek and myself.

ANNENKOV: What do you mean?

STEPAN: I was jealous of him.

DORA: Go on, Stepan. What happened next?

STEPAN: Father Florenski held the crucifix to him. He refused to kiss it. This is what he said: "I have already told you that I am through with life, and have squared up accounts with death."

DORA: In what sort of voice did he say it?

STEPAN: In his usual voice. Except that the note of fretfulness we used to hear in it was gone.

DORA: Did he look happy?

ANNENKOV: Are you crazy, Dora?

DORA: No, but I'm sure he looked happy. Really it would be too unfair if, after rejecting happiness in his life so as to prepare himself the better for the sacrifice, he did not win through to happiness in the hour of his death. He was happy, and he walked quite calmly to the scaffold, didn't he?

STEPAN: He walked straight ahead. Someone was singing to an accordion on the river down below. And just then some dogs barked.

DORA: Then he climbed the steps. . . .

STEPAN: He climbed, and was swallowed up by the
darkness. One had vague glimpses of the shroud
with which the hangman covered him from head
to foot.

DORA: And then? . . .

STEPAN: Queer muffled sounds.

DORA: Muffled sounds! Oh, Yanek! And then? . . .
[STEPAN *keeps silent.*] Tell me what happened
next. [STEPAN *is still silent.*] I insist. What came
next?

ANNENKOV: A hideous crash!

DORA: Ah! [*Flings herself against the wall.* STEPAN
looks away uneasily. ANNENKOV *is silently weeping.*
DORA *swings round and gazes at them, her back to
the wall. Her voice is changed, tense with emotion
as she continues speaking.*] No, do not cry. There
is no need for tears. Don't you realize this is
the day of our justification? Something has come
to pass which testifies for us; a sign for all the
revolutionaries of the world. Yanek is a murderer
no longer. A hideous crash! That was enough to
plunge him back into the carefree joy of childhood.
Do you remember his laugh? Often he'd laugh for
no reason at all. How young he was! Well, I am
sure he's laughing now, his face pressed to the
earth. [*Goes toward* ANNENKOV.] Boria, you are my
brother, aren't you, and you promised to help me?

ANNENKOV: Yes.

DORA: Then do something for me. Give me the
bomb. [ANNENKOV *stares at her.*] Yes, give me
the bomb . . . next time. I want to throw it. I want
to be the first to throw.

ANNENKOV: You know quite well it's against our
rules for women to be in the firing line.

DORA [*shrilly*]: Am I a woman . . . now?
[*They gaze at her. A short silence.*]

VOINOV [*softly*]: Let her have her way, Boria.

STEPAN: Yes, agree.

ANNENKOV: It was your turn, Stepan.

STEPAN [*looking at* DORA]: Give your consent, Boria. She is as I am, now.

DORA: You *will* give it to me, won't you? Then I shall throw it. And, after that, one cold night . . .

ANNENKOV: Yes, Dora.

DORA [*weeping*]: Yanek! A cold night . . . and the same rope. Everything will be easier now.

CURTAIN

A NOTE ABOUT THE AUTHOR

ALBERT CAMUS was born in Mondovi, Algeria, in 1913 of peasant stock and was brought up in a poor suburb of Algiers. He worked his way through school and university, writing a thesis in philosophy while dividing his spare time between rugby and a theatrical stock company he organized. He had overcome a serious threat of tuberculosis and before he was twenty had begun writing essays and stories. Then journalism took him to the French mainland.

In occupied France of 1942 he published *The Myth of Sisyphus* and *The Stranger,* a philosophical essay and a novel that first brought him to the attention of intellectual circles. But after the Liberation the public learned that the young author of these books had meanwhile been fighting in the underground and it was he who was responsible for the celebrated editorials that appeared in the clandestine paper *Combat.*

Camus continued to distinguish himself with three widely praised works of fiction—*The Plague, The Fall,* and *Exile and the Kingdom,* with his essay *The Rebel* and three published volumes of *Actuelles,* and with his writing for the theater, which included *Caligula and Three Other Plays* and his adaptation of Dostoevsky's *The Possessed.* The official citation accompanying the 1957 Nobel Prize for Literature said that Camus was awarded this highest international honor because of "his important literary production, which with clearsighted earnestness illuminates the problems of the human conscience in our times."

On January 4, 1960, Albert Camus was killed in an automobile accident.

December 1960

A NOTE ON THE TYPE

The text of this book was set on the Linotype in JANSON, *a recutting made direct from the type cast from matrices made by Anton Janson. Whether or not Janson was of Dutch ancestry is not known, but it is known that he purchased a foundry and was a practicing type-founder in Leipzig during the years 1600 to 1687. Janson's first specimen sheet was issued in 1675. His successor issued a specimen sheet showing all of the Janson types in 1689.*

His type is an excellent example of the influential and sturdy Dutch types that prevailed in England prior to the development by William Caslon of his own incomparable designs, which he evolved from these Dutch faces. The Dutch in their turn had been influenced by Garamond in France. The general tone of Janson, however, is darker than Garamond and has a sturdiness and substance quite different from its predecessors.

This book was composed by KINGSPORT PRESS, INC., *Kingsport, Tennessee, and printed and bound by* H. WOLFF, *New York. Designed by* HARRY FORD.